DATE DUE

MR 25 '94			
AP 22 '94			
MY 19 '95			
NO 3'98			

DEMCO 38-296

THE
NORIEGA
YEARS

THE NORIEGA YEARS

U.S.-Panamanian Relations, 1981-1990

Margaret E. Scranton

Lynne Rienner Publishers • Boulder & London

For Alfred and Hildegarde George

Published in the United States of America in 1991 by
Lynne Rienner Publishers, Inc.
1800 30th Street, Boulder, Colorado 80301

and in the United Kingdom by
Lynne Rienner Publishers, Inc.
3 Henrietta Street, Covent Garden, London WC2E 8LU

Library of Congress Cataloging-in-Publication Data
Scranton, Margaret E.
    The Noriega years: U.S.-Panamanian relations, 1981–1990/
Margaret E. Scranton.
    Includes bibliographical references and index.
    ISBN 1-55587-204-2 (alk. paper)
    1. United States—Foreign relations—Panama. 2. Panama—Foreign
relations—United States. 3. United States—Foreign
relations—1981–1989. 4. United States—Foreign relations—1989–
5. Noriega, Manuel Antonio, 1934–   . I. Title.
E183.8.P2S37   1991   91-3256
327.7307287—dc20   CIP

British Cataloguing in Publication Data
A Cataloguing in Publication record for this book
is available from the British Library.

Printed and bound in the United States of America

The paper used in this publication meets the requirements
of the American National Standard for Permanence of
Paper for Printed Library Materials Z39.48-1984

Contents

Preface

In this book I have tried to explain U.S. policy toward Panama during the 1980s, the Noriega years. In the process, this has also become a book about Panama. This is not the same book a Panamanian would write; it cannot be. I have tried to do justice to the Panamanian context and to various Panamanian perspectives, without which one simply cannot decipher the interactions that U.S.-Panamanian relations entail. My primary concern, however, is to account for the objectives and actions of U.S. policy.

The first part of the book presents my analysis and explanations. An overview and summary explanation are presented in the Introduction. Chapters 1 through 3 contain detailed explanations at three levels of analysis: international system, nation-state, and decisionmaking. The arguments presented in these explanatory chapters are based on a narrative case study of events in Panama and Washington, which is contained in Chapters 4 through 8.

Chapter 1 uses the international system level of analysis to explain U.S. Panama policy as a security concern for the United States and to explain how international dynamics, in the long term and during the 1980s, have affected U.S. national interests and shaped Panama's identity. Chapter 2 presents a state level analysis of developments in Panama, focusing primarily on the Spadafora crisis as a watershed. This crisis was Noriega's "Watergate," in which the survival tactics used eventually undermined the regime. The Spadafora crisis is also considered as a developmental event for the opposition and its ability to successfully contest the 1989 election. This chapter also considers an important internal development in the United States: changes in the foreign policy consensus and the impact of foreign policy beliefs on U.S. Panama policy. Chapter 3 uses the decisionmaking level of analysis to explain U.S. attempts to strike a deal with Noriega and the crisis dynamics that shaped U.S. policy and the decision to invade Panama.

I begin the narrative portion of the book with a discussion of three men

who shaped Panamanian politics and relations with the United States during
the 1980s: Arnulfo Arias, Omar Torrijos, and Manuel Noriega. Chapter 4
introduces these central figures, their legacies, and some of the formative
events that must be known before the 1980s can be explored.

The next four chapters comprise the case study and relate the story of
U.S.-Panamanian relations and events in both countries during the Noriega
years. I have divided the decade according to three U.S. foreign policy
objectives: "Play Ball with Noriega," "Noriega Must Go, But How?" and
finally "Civilians In, Military Out" and "Civilians In, But for How Long?"
This division reflects noticeable shifts in the intent and strategies of U.S.
foreign policy. Chapter 8, which considers U.S. Panama policy and
developments since the invasion, concludes with an assessment of
Panamanian politics today and the challenges that face U.S.-Panamanian
relations in the 1990s.

As with any study of contemporary events, this work is bound by the
sources and evidence available. Given the salience of U.S. Panama policy and
the significance of the U.S. invasion, additional information will bring errors
to light and provide new insights on the decade.

Margaret E. Scranton

Acknowledgments

The idea for this book grew out of my long-standing interest in U.S. policy toward Panama. Two years ago, long before the invasion, I wrote a paper for the annual meeting of the American Political Science Association in which I tried to explain why it was so difficult for the United States to remove Noriega. That paper attracted the attention of Lynne Rienner; the result of her interest is this book. I gratefully acknowledge her assistance and the considerable talents of Martha Peacock and Steve Barr of her staff, and of Sandra Rush, the copyeditor.

Unlike many issues, where writing about foreign policy is often hampered by lack of information and inaccessible sources, Panama policy has been a bonanza. High-level policymakers, whose precious time is seldom spent on scholars, have given detailed television interviews that can be taped for review and analysis. During the invasion, Cable News Network (CNN) televised daily briefings from the White House, Pentagon, and Department of State. Advisers talked eagerly with reporters. I am deeply indebted to all who, having no intention of aiding my research, provided evidence and insight for my work.

I found another serendipitously available source to be equally valuable. When John Dinges finished his book on Noriega, *Our Man in Panama*, he donated all of the government documents he obtained through freedom of information requests to the National Security Archive, a nonprofit research institute in Washington, D.C. I was fortunate to have access to that collection. I am deeply grateful to Tom Blanton and Linda Davis, who shepherded me through hundreds of pages of cables, memos, reports, and other files.

I also found very useful a smaller collection of declassified documents at the Department of State's Freedom of Information Office. I am grateful to Olga Luck for guiding me through the files in the reading room.

I owe debts of gratitude to colleagues, U.S. officials, Panamanian citizens, and others who have shared their time, expertise, and insights with me: William Furlong, Steve Ropp, Max Manwaring, Berta Thayer, John Fishel, Lee Colwell, Hoyt Purvis, Jennie K. Lincoln, Miguel Bernal, Ed Corr, Fred Woerner, Gabriel Marcella, Jack Pryor, and Tomás Herrera. Their help and encouragement have been invaluable to my understanding and to the accuracy of the book. Some of the people I used as sources must remain anonymous due to their personal preference, possible repercussions in Panama, or pending legal actions against Noriega. Although I cannot name them, I extend to them my thanks. Special thanks are due to Bill Furlong for his helpful critique, and to his students at Utah State University, on whom I tried out some of my ideas. I am also extremely grateful to Steve Ropp for his constructive comments on an earlier draft of the manuscript. Any mistakes that remain are, of course, my own.

I continue to be indebted to the scholars who have shaped my approach to understanding foreign policy and my research agenda: Charles O. Jones, Richard Cottam, Robert Walters, and Ernest Duff. I see their influence in my work more clearly than ever; I hope they do, too.

I also gratefully acknowledge my university, which provided financial support for my research and the computer that became my constant companion.

A final word of thanks is due to my family, especially for having to spend the 1989 Christmas and New Year holidays with CNN's coverage of the invasion and Noriega's surrender. For help and understanding, thank you, Robert, Jessica, and Grandma. This book is dedicated to my grandparents, Hildegarde and Alfred George.

M. E. S.

Introduction:
Explaining U.S.-Panamanian Relations
During the Noriega Years

During the 1980s, U.S. interests in Panama were defined differently as the decade progressed. The United States pursued three objectives: first, to work with the military regime in order to further other U.S. goals; second, to remove General Manuel Antonio Noriega from power and reform the military regime; and third, to destroy Noriega's regime and install civilian government. This introduction summarizes U.S. objectives and presents an integrated explanation of U.S. Panama policy during the Noriega years.

Panamanian politics and relations with the United States have been shaped in recent decades by three leaders: Dr. Arnulfo Arias, Gen. Omar Torrijos, and Gen. Manuel Noriega. An analysis of the Noriega years must begin with an assessment of the legacies of Arias and Torrijos. Noriega emerged as Panama's strongman after Torrijos died in 1981, and his tenure was shaped by the military's revolution of 1968 and its opposition to President Arias and Panama's oligarchy.

From 1981 until 1987, the United States was content, if not willing, to let Noriega be Noriega; it adopted a "play ball" strategy of working with Panama's military regime. Until mid-1987, other U.S. priorities in Central America justified close relations with Panama's government.

In 1987, however, as those priorities changed and criticism of Noriega mounted, U.S. objectives changed. The United States decided that Noriega must go and implemented various strategies to remove him from power. None of these worked. Noriega refused to step back, negotiate a transition and exit, or to be pressured out of office. In Panama, the opposition grew stronger, initiating public protests and economic strikes and effectively contesting the 1989 presidential election. The regime withstood and countered these internal challenges, however, and became increasingly repressive.

Finally, after a military coup failed to dislodge Noriega in October 1989, U.S. objectives changed again. The United States decided that Noriega and his regime must go and also that the Defense Forces of the Republic of Panama (PDF) must be transformed. The United States launched a massive military invasion to remove Noriega, paralyze his forces, and install a civilian government. Thereafter, U.S. objectives focused on supporting that government, aiding Panama's economic recovery, and managing tensions between civilians and the military.

At the beginning of the 1980s, having previously reached an accommodation with the military regime, the United States was willing to live with the militarization of Panama. The administrations of three presidents—Richard Nixon, Gerald Ford, and Jimmy Carter—were willing to work with the military regime to negotiate a new Panama Canal treaty. After new treaties were ratified in 1978, U.S. relations with the military regime grew even closer. During the 1980s cooperative relations contributed to several U.S. priories: intelligence collection, the Contra war in Central America, and drug enforcement.

During Noriega's rise to power and early tenure as commander of the National Guard, the United States adopted a live-and-let-live posture toward the Panamanian military. Why did the United States play ball with Noriega? System-level analysis, focused on U.S. national interests, provides the best answer to this question, as discussed in Chapter 1. The United States had several important security interests in Panama: continued implementation of the Panama Canal treaties; access to U.S. bases in Panama plus facilities for intelligence gathering; support for the Contras; and hopes to obtain a post-treaty military base agreement. To promote these interests, the United States looked the other way while Noriega steadily consolidated his power and expanded the reach and scope of corrupt and illegal activities and the power of the military.

During the Carter years, U.S. interests in concluding new canal treaties skewed officials' perceptions of the military; as a result, they minimized the problem of growing militarization, repression, and involvement in drug trafficking. Concurrently, Torrijos's plans to restore civilian rule following a six-year process of demilitarization allowed the Carter administration to hope that Torrijos's regime would reform itself. During Ronald Reagan's administration, strongly anti-Communist beliefs had a similar effect, distorting officials' perceptions and skewing U.S. priorities in Panama. Perceptions of severe threats caused U.S. security interests in Panama to be valued so far above democratization that the latter retained rhetorical support but little else. In 1984, when the military's commitment to return to the barracks was put to the test, it became clear that if democratization were to be achieved, the United States would have to oppose the military. Rather than force the demilitarization issue, and possibly lose access to security assets and cooperation, the United States let the democratization objective slip to the bottom of the agenda. Faced with this value trade-off, the United States preferred canal security and good working relations with the military.

During 1987, various officials and agencies of the U.S. government concluded that Noriega must go. Up to this point, Noriega had done everything that the United States had asked. Moreover, he had done well. In 1986, however, some of his favors, particularly aid for the Contras and involvement in narcotics trafficking, had begun to attract negative press coverage and congressional attention. In mid-1987, U.S. evaluations of the balance of perceived assets and liabilities shifted against Noriega. The Department of State took this position earliest; as others moved toward opposition, the administration appeared to be sending mixed signals to Noriega. By the end of the year, only the Drug Enforcement Administration (DEA) still considered working with Noriega to be more valuable than removing him.

Why, then, did the Reagan administration experience such difficulty in ousting Noriega? Two other levels of analysis are required to account for the second U.S. objective to remove Noriega and for the failure of repeated U.S. attempts to do so. A state-level analysis addresses the question from the perspective of Noriega's bargaining strength and ability to evade U.S. pressure, as seen in Chapter 2. The state level explains the long-term deterioration of Noriega's power base despite his short-term successes in bargaining with the United States and repressing the opposition. The decisionmaking level answers the question from the U.S. perspective and explains why the administrations of Ronald Reagan and George Bush failed to remove Noriega from power (see Chapter 3). Agreement that Noriega must go did not produce a consensus on a plan to remove him or a concerted strategy supporting the attempts that were made. Instead, U.S. Panama policy was managed as a prolonged crisis without the benefits of presidential attention and interagency consensus.

Perceptions of a crisis during the October 1989 coup and a policy review by senior advisers to President George Bush after the coup failed were responsible for the shift to the U.S. objective to remove the military regime and install a civilian government. Two levels of analysis account for this objective and the U.S. decision to invade Panama in December 1989. The system level asserts that concerns about U.S. security and stability in Panama made Noriega's regime appear, as perceived and considered at the decisionmaking level, incompatible with immediate and long-term U.S. interests. During 1989, the worse Noriega was revealed to be, the easier it was for the United States to redefine a stable Panamanian future in terms of civilian politicians and a different military force. The objective of working with the military regime without Noriega was replaced with a new objective: to destroy the old regime and establish a civilian government along with changes, nebulously defined at the time, in civilian-military relations. The decisionmaking level, particularly crisis dynamics, accounts for the choice of a massive military invasion as the means for achieving that objective.

Thus the objectives of U.S. policy toward Panama appear, superficially, to have come full circle during the 1980s. The United States had begun the decade considering Torrijos's plans for democratization and demilitarization as contributing to U.S. security interests in Panama. During the early 1980s, however, these objectives were displaced by higher regional priorities associated with security threats in Central America. As time passed, the Noriega regime not only resisted democratization but actually further militarized the regime. The United States placed a higher value on the cooperation and services Noriega could provide; security took priority over democratization in Panama. After October 1989, these two objectives were rejoined; U.S. security and stability in Panama were defined in terms of democratization. The United States ended the decade by forcibly installing a civilian government and attempting to restructure the military and civilian-military relations in Panama. Whether these means can truly promote democratization in Panama remains to be seen.

Recent U.S. policy toward Panama may reflect a fundamental regional policy shift away from viewing military institutions in terms of a national security doctrine. Instead, stability during the 1990s may be defined in terms of government by *tecnicos* (experts from the civilian sector) and party politicians rather than military strongmen. In Panama, as elsewhere, the military has been discredited; it is therefore the civilians' turn to try to govern once again.

The system level of analysis predicts that as U.S. perceptions of threats in the hemisphere diminish, especially in Nicaragua but also from decreasing Soviet support for Cuba, the United States may be willing to tolerate less predictable, more disorderly politics in Panama and elsewhere. Panamanians, in contrast, may have a different time perspective and less tolerance for deferred results. The state level cautions that developments in Panama can operate independently of U.S. concerns and objectives, creating conditions that limit U.S. choices.

U.S. interests in the Panama Canal continue to shape its priorities regarding Panama. The United States is scheduled to turn the canal and all other assets over to Panama on December 31, 1999. Three years in advance, in 1997 or even earlier, the United States will begin to negotiate a new agreement to allow it to maintain at least two bases in Panama. The degree of U.S. commitment to maintaining those bases will strongly affect U.S. policy toward Panama. System level, and previous conceptions of U.S. security, would predict two alternatives for U.S. policy. The United States may conclude that its security interests, defined in terms of continued bases in Panama, will again require a trade-off with democratization. Alternatively, the United States may return to the 1974 concept of Panamanian consent as the best guarantor of the canal's security, and conclude that Panamanian opposition to a new bases agreement may threaten the canal. Conditions in the hemisphere during the late 1990s, particularly the emergence of new security threats, will continue to structure U.S.-Panamanian relations.

1

For Reasons of State: System Level of Analysis

The premise of system level of analysis is that the behavior of the United States and Panama is a function of the global and regional system structures in which these countries exist.[1] This level bases explanations on the two states' power positions and alignments and their resulting national interests and security concerns. National security is typically conceived in terms of threats to interests and opportunities to increase security. Unlike the decisionmaking level, which deals with policymakers as individuals with motives and perceptions, the system level conceptualizes a state's national interests. National interests exist as symbols, images, and ideas that shape the real-life deliberations that are analyzed from a decisionmaking perspective. Access to the canal or stability in Panama can be measured, concretely, at the state level of analysis; at the system level, however, these interests constitute objectives or values that motivate behavior.

System structures and conceptions of national security have historical attributes that influence current policy. In the case of Latin and Central America generally, and Panama in particular, cycles of attention and neglect are associated with emerging and receding security threats. When global and regional power structures change, new tension lines emerge and national interests are redefined. Structural changes usually yield a reconsideration of objectives and options and changes in states' actions.

What emerges from a system level of analysis of U.S. Panama policy is the priority of security concerns, among competing U.S. objectives, that pulled the United States first toward working with Noriega and then toward moderate and finally extreme antagonism to his regime. To the question "Why did the United States support Noriega so long?" this level answers that Noriega provided services deemed valuable to U.S. security at the time. As Noriega's value as a security asset declined, and as the drug war and democratization emerged as regional priorities, U.S. policy toward Panama changed.

This level also sheds light on the relationship between security concerns, on the one hand, and democratization in Panama, on the other. Both were affected by policies for Central America that were designed to counter regional security threats. Regional policies to prevent the spread of revolution beyond Nicaragua and to promote democratization through elections were applied to Panama as well.

System level provides the following explanation for a "play ball" strategy with Noriega (see Chapter 5). The Reagan administration identified severe security threats emerging from Nicaragua and implemented an anti-Sandinista offensive in Central America. At this point, Panama was bound to be drawn into that effort, whether or not General Noriega had been there, ready and willing to cooperate. Similarly, when regional policies for managing the Sandinista threat shifted from the Contra war to the Contadora peace process invigorated by the Arias plan, the U.S. definition of its interests in Panama also changed. Noriega, who had been an active ally in the covert Contra war, shifted from asset to liability for the United States. Moreover, when demilitarization and democratization became regional policy lines, and the United States worked for military reform in El Salvador and Guatemala, Panama policy was also pulled in these directions. Support for elections took on greater significance as 1989–1990 approached, when national elections were scheduled in almost a dozen nations in the region. Events in Panama during the late 1980s were considered in light of a U.S. regional initiative to restore democratic rule.[2]

The system level also provides a major explanation for the question, "Why did the United States invade Panama?" by stating that national interests and national security were at stake. System level would rank U.S. priorities differently than their order in the official U.S. government rationale. First, and most important, were long-term U.S. interests in a stable Panamanian government—an objective not on President George Bush's list, particularly during the decade culminating in 2000 when the Panama Canal is scheduled for transfer to Panamanian control. Related to this, as a second priority, were long-term interests in U.S. bases in Panama. Current base rights will expire on December 31, 1999, unless a new agreement is negotiated, and a new agreement will be possible only if the Panamanian government concurs. Thus, the closer the year 2000 appeared, the more concerned the United States became with Panama's prospects for stability. Events occurring in the mid-1980s were evaluated in terms of Panama's domestic stability in the year 2000.

More generally, the system level explains why the United States behaved as if it had a right to intervene in Panama's internal affairs. This level provides an answer to the question "What makes Panama's government and politics and the nature of its military the business of the United States?" The answer has strong historical roots in the Monroe Doctrine and, more importantly, the Roosevelt Corollary. The 1989 invasion and President George Bush's rationale are direct descendants of President Theodore Roosevelt's claim of a U.S. right to exercise an "international police power" to redress "chronic wrongdoing" by unfit governments. Its traditional hegemonic role, based on the regional power position of the United States and a presumed right to intervene in this hemisphere, motivated repeated U.S. attempts to remove Noriega and invade Panama.

The most important short-term U.S. security concerns were immediate threats to U.S. personnel and to canal security, both of which were cited by President Bush. Impending chaos in Panama in mid-December 1989, reinforced by two incidents involving U.S. personnel, triggered the invasion. The United States invaded Panama because events spiraling out of control presented an imminent threat to U.S. citizens, a traditional reason for intervention. This motive was reinforced by a concurrent perception that U.S. rights under the 1978 treaties—in the form of danger to facilities and personnel needed for canal defense, operation, and maintenance—were at greater risk. This crisis dynamic is explored in greater detail in Chapter 3.

Far behind these three priorities, system level would consider two factors as supporting, but not significant, influences on the U.S. decision to invade Panama. One concerns the installation of a civilian government, an objective cited by President Bush. Restoration of civilian rule in Panama was consistent with global and regional patterns of resurgence of democracy and demise of dictatorship. However, U.S. support for those trends was not a sufficient cause for the United States to invade Panama. President Bush listed installing civilian government as one of his four reasons, but this analysis strongly diminishes that motive. The civilians had been waiting to take power for more than seven months. Without increased threats from Noriega and the December crisis spiral, the United States never would have invaded to install them in power.

Bush cited apprehending Noriega and bringing him to trial in the United States as another objective, but this, too, played a minor role in motivating the invasion. Removing Noriega and reforming the PDF were steps that contributed to the regional priority of fighting international narcotics trafficking. However, drug traffickers elsewhere in the region were far more significant players in the drug war than Noreiga; capturing him and cracking down on Panama's money-laundering centers were minor motives in the decision to invade.

The main explanation that a system level of analysis suggests for U.S. behavior is raison d'état, the traditional motive on which large powers act when they are able: to protect their interests for reasons of state. The United States worked with Noriega when it was to the U.S. advantage to do so, and the United States took drastic measures to remove him from power when his actions ignited a crisis spiral that threatened immediate U.S. interests and longer-term prospects for stability in Panama.

A system level of analysis sheds some light on Noriega's ability to withstand U.S. pressure, primarily through alliance networks that provided resources he needed. A system level also explains the content of the national values and symbols Noriega tried to use to maintain power at home and allies abroad—values of independence and national dignity and symbols of interventionism, aggression, small powers as victims, and imperialism.

Enduring U.S. Security Interests in Panama

Panama, because of its location astride major sea lanes and because of the canal, constitutes an important, and some would say vital, national security interest for the United States. Beyond Panama's long-standing strategic significance, during the 1980s Noriega's regime provided additional security and intelligence assets. Partly as a result of Noriega's deliberate cultivation of U.S. favor and partly at U.S. initiative, 1981–1987 witnessed the growth of an increasingly varied and more intimate security relationship. This growth created a net dependency in Panama's favor that Noriega used quite effectively in bargaining with the United States.

The Panama Canal and U.S. Security

Whether one considers the viewpoint of Panama or the United States, U.S.-Panamanian relations are conditioned by the Panama Canal and each country's interest in the canal. The United States is interested in Panama's internal and external affairs because of the canal; likewise, Panama has had an unusually close relationship with the United States because of the canal. The level of attention the United States pays to the relationship and the degree of its closeness have varied since 1903. Historically, whenever the United States perceived threats to security or stability, its canal interests have drawn it into intervening in Panama's internal affairs. When these threats receded, so did U.S. attention and the likelihood of intervention.

Prior to 1978, when new canal treaties were ratified, the United States and Panama had conflicting objectives. The United States wanted to maintain its control over canal administration and defense for as long as possible, preferably well into the twenty-first century. Panama wanted to recover its sovereignty over the canal and end U.S. control over the waterway. These conflicting objectives were reconciled in the 1978 Panama Canal treaty, which provided for transfer of the canal to Panama on December 31, 1999. The treaty established a schedule of progressive increases in Panamanian participation in canal administration, management, and defense. A second

Treaty Concerning the Permanent Neutrality of the Panama Canal specified security guarantees and defense rights for the United States and Panama that continue after the year 2000.

To understand U.S.-Panamanian relations during the Noriega years, one must comprehend the significance of the 1978 treaties in the context of bilateral conflict over the 1903 treaty and the way the 1978 treaties resolved the canal issue. The treaties embodied certain assumptions about U.S. security interests, about how these were related to domestic developments in Panama, and about the nature of international reality (see Chapter 2). The treaties marked a turning point in Panama's national destiny, its achievement of an objective sought since 1903, and its expectation of prosperity for the future. Although both the United States and Panama implemented the treaties with only minor complaints against each other, Panama experienced a decade of disappointed hopes and dashed expectations in the 1980s.

U.S. Bases in Panama

A time perspective bounded by the year 2000 exerted a subtle but significant influence on U.S. considerations of its security and Panamanian politics. The closer the year 2000 grew, the worse Noriega and his increasingly militarized regime looked as partners. As the ouster crisis proceeded, General Noriega repeatedly charged that the United States opposed him in order to renege on the treaties. His aim was to marshall support at home, but he also reminded U.S. leaders of the significance of the year 2000 for U.S. security interests. As the ouster crisis worsened, congressional critics urged the executive to scrap or renegotiate the 1978 treaties; several flatly stated that the United States could not turn over the canal if Noriega were still in charge. Such statements confirmed Noriega's beliefs; they also reflected the security motives that affected U.S. choices.

Noriega claimed that the real reason the United States opposed him and planned to abrogate the treaties was its desire to control bases in Panama. From the U.S. perspective, bases in Panama are convenient and desirable, but the official position is that the United States will withdraw unless a new bases agreement is concluded. Speaking anonymously in one of the very few public statements on the bases issue, a U.S. official in Panama said, "The U.S. considers access to military bases here vital to American combat readiness in the region. For that reason, U.S. officials hope Panama may be persuaded to extend permission to operate bases here beyond the year 2000 deadline agreed upon."[3] The Bush administration's position is that the base issue is something for both governments to address beginning about 1997. When that time arrives, U.S. objectives will be a function of its global bases policy, federal budget constraints, similar agreements negotiated with the Philippines and Greece, and the situation in Panama. The system level of analysis would predict that U.S. concern with stability in Panama and the bases policy of its government will increase as 2000 draws near. Perceived threats or opportunities could trigger U.S. intervention.

Panama's Interests in the Canal

Recovery of the Panama Canal has been an objective of Panamanian leaders since 1904, if not 1903 when the Hay–Bunau-Varilla treaty was negotiated by a Frenchman on Panama's behalf and to its detriment. From Panama's perspective, its relations with the United States focused, decade after decade, on one overriding issue: a quest for sovereignty over its territory and control over the canal. For many years the quest was a futile one; the United States adamantly refused, at treaty negotiations in 1936 and 1954, to consider the sovereignty question; that issue was entirely off limits. But for Panamanians, sovereignty was *the* issue. Burns' characterization in 1974 remains true today: the canal divides Panama, but it unites Panamanians.[4] Noriega shared this quest, writing in 1975 that

> To exercise sovereignty you need the capacity for independence. . . .
> That means that within Panamanian territory only the competence of the
> Panamanian State should be exerted. With this conviction and under this
> doctrine, the Panamanian Revolution [of 1968] began the battle for
> sovereignty, which will end when territory under American jurisdiction
> is returned to Panamanian jurisdiction under a just and equitable
> treaty.[5]

Panama's longing for sovereign independence is only one of several national values that have been affected by its position in the international system. Despite its small size, Panama's major distinguishing feature has been its global role as a transit site. Panama's destiny and prosperity have always been linked to the trade, transit, and related services it can provide international commerce. Panama's transit role has involved contraband as well as legal goods and services; involvement in international narcotics trafficking fit this traditional pattern.

The fact that the United States built and controlled a canal bisecting Panama's territory has strongly affected Panama's national identity. This history has fostered canal-related meanings for Panamanian values of independence, sovereignty, prosperity, nationalism, and national dignity. These values are manifest and shaped at the state level of analysis, but the system level accounts for much of their meaning. For many years Panamanians believed that to truly be a nation, the country must erase the blot on its history created by the 1903 treaty. To Panama—whether it was governed by oligarchs, Arnulfo Arias, or the military—gaining control over the canal symbolized the nation's destiny. That dream was pursued by many and finally achieved, in the form of the 1978 treaties, by Gen. Omar Torrijos.

Recent U.S. Security Interests

Votes in the U.S. Senate on the canal treaties were taken in March and April 1978, just as changes in the regional context were making their rationale less tenable. Just one year later, in late 1979, the Carter administration's differences with the Sandinistas had intensified into open conflict with the new Nicaraguan government. Carter initiated covert operations to support an opposition movement and promote pluralist tendencies in Nicaragua. Perceptions of regional security threats were heightened by a rapid deterioration in U.S.-Soviet relations after the Soviet invasion of Afghanistan in December 1979. Within two years after the canal treaties were ratified, in 1980, U.S. security was defined as preventing "another Nicaragua" in the form of a leftist revolution in neighboring El Salvador.

The Reagan administration's threat perceptions were even more intense. Halting the spread of communism and leftist revolution in Central America was a high priority during the early Reagan years. The administration's stated regional policies, covert operations, and "off the shelf" unauthorized covert activities pulled Panama into new alliance networks and informal connections. At the same time, Noriega was eager to initiate and sustain such linkages. These regional developments created opportunities that Noriega was eager to pursue.

Regional Conflicts and U.S. Security

After the 1978 Panama Canal treaties were concluded, significant, unanticipated developments occurred in the region that constituted fundamental changes in the context in which the treaties were implemented. The first half of the 1980s witnessed the Nicaraguan revolution and subsequent conflict between the Sandinista government and Contra rebels, which escalated into a full-scale covert war. Related to this was a rebellion by the Farabundo Martí National Liberation Front (FMLN) against the repressive military government of El Salvador. A second development, in the latter half of the decade, involved international drug trafficking by cartels based in Colombia. These developments enhanced Panama's importance to the United States and pulled the United States toward a "play ball" strategy with the military regime in Panama.

The fact that Nicaragua and El Salvador rose to the top of the foreign policy agenda during 1979–1981 had a direct effect on U.S.-Panamanian relations. Conflict involving these Central American neighbors caused the Reagan administration to seek the active support of allies nearby, most noticeably in Honduras, but also, even if less visibly, in Panama.

The main priorities of the United States were to overthrow the Nicaraguan government and prevent the creation of "another Nicaragua" in El Salvador.[6] Initially, Panama was on the "enemy" side of U.S. policy. Panama, like many neighboring states, had actively supported the revolution against Anastasio Somoza Debayle, providing arms and transmitting materiel to the Sandinistas. Both General Torrijos and Colonel Noriega, who then headed the National Guard intelligence division, strongly endorsed the Nicaraguan revolution and the new Sandinista government. Both Panamanians later changed sides, and Panama became a major asset in the U.S. covert war against the Sandinistas. Whereas Torrijos and the Panamanian revolutionary activist, Hugo Spadafora, supported Edén Pastora's Contras in Costa Rica, Noriega switched Panama's support to Contra leaders based in Honduras.

From 1982 to 1985, arms for the Contras were provided covertly through Operation Black Eagle. Materiel for the Contras in Honduras was first flown to airfields at Ilopango, El Salvador; supplies for Edén Pastora's Contras were ferried from airfields in Panama. Noriega allowed Operation Black Eagle to use front companies "to conceal payrolls and other transactions."[7] Later, Noriega permitted General Richard Secord to establish front companies in Panama for Iran-Contra sales and supply networks.

Black Eagle brought Noriega and his inner circle into close contact with Mossad, the Israeli intelligence agency, which was covertly assisting the U.S. arms supply operation. The main Israeli agent for this operation was Michael Harari, the man who led the attack on Black September terrorists who had massacred the Israeli Olympic team in Munich. Harari became a close personal adviser to Noriega and supervised the training of his personal security team.[8] Harari retired in the mid-1980s, having established businesses in Panama while he worked with Noriega; whether he maintained an official relationship with Mossad is debatable.[9] Much about this relationship remains unclear, but the connection to Harari seems to have strengthened Noriega's relations with the U.S. Central Intelligence Agency (CIA) and his ability to deflect opposition from the Department of State.[10] Harari disappeared from public view during the U.S. invasion.

In exchange for Panama's participation in Black Eagle, U.S. officials ignored Noriega's use of the arms transportation system for shipments of marijuana and cocaine into the southern United States. Thus, Noriega's involvement in drug trafficking began during his covert work with the United States, prior to his involvement with the Medellín cartel.

During 1980–1981, Panama also provided arms for the FMLN in its struggle to overthrow the U.S.-backed civilian government of El Salvador. After the United States pressured Panama to stop supporting the FMLN, General Noriega began supporting the Contras, shifting his arms trade from rebels opposed to a U.S.-backed government in El Salvador to rebels opposed to a U.S.-opposed government in Nicaragua. In the process, the United States changed Panama's role from enemy asset to U.S. ally. This process had direct consequences for Noriega to manipulate conflicting alliances within the Reagan administration, an aspect of his bargaining power (see Chapter 3).

As the war against the Contras disintegrated, as the Central American peace process proceeded, and as the Iran-Contra scandal became a major issue Noriega's value as an asset for covert operations declined concomitantly. By 1987, as the objectives of U.S. policy toward the Contras changed, Congress (and most of the executive branch) was simply unwilling to continue the covert war. And, from a bargaining perspective, once the Iran-Contra investigation exposed much of Noriega's role, his ability to use evidence of those activities to pressure (or blackmail) the United States also declined.

Thus, Noriega's value in providing security services peaked at the same time that his regime was beginning to look less and less capable of maintaining domestic stability as the year 2000 approached. Even though Noriega still held power in Panama, two mainstays of his power base—his intelligence services and his role as a strongman—were collapsing. The strongman image, which intensified in the 1980s, worked to his detriment when regional trends toward demilitarization progressed elsewhere but were reversed in Panama. By 1986–1990, globally and regionally, Noriega looked more and more like a problem and less and less capable of delivering the domestic stability U.S. security concerns required.

U.S. Defense and Intelligence Assets in Panama

Aside from the Contra war, Panama had acquired the status of a major intelligence asset for the United States during the 1980s. Due initially to the Reagan administration's need for intelligence about Nicaragua and Cuba, the National Security Agency (NSA) established major listening posts in Panama. The scope of these facilities extended well beyond tiny Panama or even Central America. From Panama, NSA could monitor "all of Central America and most of South America."[11] Such assets are not easily replaced, and by providing ready access Noriega enhanced his value to the United States. Later, when the Reagan administration debated whether to oust Noriega, the general's willingness to allow intelligence facilities and operations on Panamanian soil factored into arguments made in his favor.

General Noriega was also involved in more mundane intelligence activities for the United States, especially concerning Cuba. Some reports cite Noriega's first employment by the CIA as 1967; others go back to his high school years and early contacts with defense intelligence agencies. On January 18, 1991, the U.S. government admitted that Noriega's first payment from the U.S. Army was made in 1955. Monthly payments from the CIA began in 1971, were discontinued during the Carter administration, and were restored by Reagan administration, which later cut him off again.[12]

Noriega's government also ignored the U.S. use of bases and facilities in Panama for training Central American personnel, which violated a strict interpretation of canal treaty provisions that restricted use to canal defense. During these years, the regional defense mission of the U.S. Southern Command (SOUTHCOM), which was headquartered in Panama, assumed greater significance. Concomitantly, the U.S. stake in maintaining military bases and NSA facilities in Panama also increased. However, once serious opposition to Noriega emerged, the significance of his willingness to aid NSA and other intelligence services diminished.

Panama and the Medellín Cartel

The secret transportation network that Noriega established to move arms and materiel northward, first to the FMLN and then to the Contras, constituted a convenient resource that could be used for other commodities as well. A covert transportation system—including pilots, planes, airport security, staging and storage areas, and strategic drop sites—was already in place when the opportunity arose to use it for drug trafficking. Given the considerable effort entailed in putting so many assets in place, it seemed almost inevitable that an alternative commodity would be found to keep the system in business after Black Eagle and Contra aid ended. By coincidence, the Medellín cartel, due to an enforcement crackdown in Colombia, was looking for foreign partners at this same time. The fact that Panama already had a large, well-established international banking center conducive to large-scale money laundering, made it an even more attractive partner for the cartel.

Most analysts cite the years 1982 and 1983 as the time when Panama's involvement in international drug trafficking significantly increased; 1984 was a peak year. Throughout the 1980s, General Noriega was personally involved in overseeing, participating in, and profiting from the drug trade. Noriega became deeply connected to the Medellín cartel, involving himself and his close associates in drug transport and money laundering, and gaining large sums from bribes, "cuts" on loads delivered, and protection money. In the process he involved others, in Panama and along the northbound route, in this growing network of economic dependency.

Thus, the two significant hemispheric developments of the 1980s— revolutionary conflict in Central America and international narcotics trafficking—had reinforcing, interrelated effects in Panama. Unfortunately and unexpectedly for the Reagan administration, its efforts to help the Salvadoran government and the Contras stimulated Panama's involvement in drug trafficking. Several years later, U.S. officials would regret overlooking the drug trade, as Noriega's reputation as a "drug thug" made his regime less and less compatible with U.S. security interests.

Availability of Allies for Panama

Two alliance dynamics affected U.S.-Panamanian relations during the 1980s: (1) the continued erosion of the cold war bloc system and the growing reluctance of states, especially in Latin America, to follow superpower leadership; and (2) the willingness of midlevel powers, including allies as well as enemies, to oppose the United States.

As east-west conflict patterns eroded during the late 1980s, Panama's alliance networks assumed unusual, even bizarre, combinations. Panama remained a close U.S. ally until 1988, but it simultaneously maintained close ties with Cuba, Nicaragua, and Libya—three of the Reagan administration's most egregious foes. Cuba used Panamanian front companies to acquire high technology and other goods prohibited by the long-standing U.S. embargo. The Noriega regime worked simultaneously with the U.S. Drug Enforcement Administration (DEA) and the Medellín cartel. Panama armed the Contras fighting the Sandinista government and hosted the Contadora peace process; when he needed regional support, Noriega appealed to President Daniel Ortega of Nicaragua.

Several states provided tangible help for Noriega during the "ouster crisis," the years when the United States tried various means to remove him from office. Mexico offered crude oil on easy credit terms in a deliberate attempt to ease the burden of U.S. sanctions during 1988–1989. Cuba furnished from thirty to fifty advisers to help organize a paramilitary force, the Dignity Battalions, during early 1988, and provided some sixteen tons of weapons in early 1988. Cuba also provided media technicians and advisers, who assisted in Noriega's information and psychological warfare campaigns. As he had for Torrijos, Fidel Castro provided advice to Noriega on how to deal with the United States. Libya provided infusions of cash that helped Noriega meet payrolls for his key constituents while the United States was using financial pressure to squeeze him out of power. So did U.S. allies Taiwan and Japan. Libya's enemy, Israel, had an even closer relationship with Noriega, in part because Israeli intelligence operations in Central America were directed against the Palestine Liberation Organization, which Libya was supporting.

Steve Ropp summarized this aspect of Panama's foreign policy: "As Torrijos did before him, General Noriega also played his 'leftist card' in the international arena."[13] This was evident in Noriega's early support for the Sandinistas, his continued close relations with Cuba, and his personal contacts with Fidel Castro. In playing his leftist card, Noriega deliberately signaled his willingness and ability to shift alliance patterns. Such connections constituted short-term bargaining advantages for Noriega, as long as the United States was willing to play a nonmilitary bargaining game.

But once the United States invaded Panama and Noriega took refuge in the Papal Nunciature, none of these allies offered him safe conduct out of Panama or exile. Cuba was the only state to make an offer, and it did so reluctantly, indicating that it would accept him in order to "tweak Uncle Sam's nose." Panama's complex alliances during the Noriega years were largely based on convenience; when Noriega lost power, most of these connections were broken.

Panamanian National Dignity

Panama has always considered respect for its national dignity to be an important element in its international relations, particularly with the United States. Prior to 1978, dignity was associated with regaining sovereignty over the canal. Once new treaties were accomplished, the dignity value lost some of its canal-relatedness, although it continues to be associated with correct implementation of treaty provisions. During the 1980s, the dignity value was increasingly monopolized by Noriega and the PDF, and it came to stand for resistance to the United States. The best known example is the name of Noriega's paramilitary force, the Dignity Battalions, which he claimed were necessary to resist a U.S. invasion. Their avowed mission was to defend Panama's national dignity, but their purpose soon shifted to defending Noriega. During the ouster crisis, other dignity symbols were used. In his famous "machete speech," Noriega brandished what he called the machete of Panamanian dignity. Grocery sacks distributed by the government to unpaid workers were called "dignity bags."[14] A popular horse race, traditionally held on the Fourth of July weekend and called the United States Classic, was renamed the National Dignity Classic.[15]

Noriega tried to use values and symbols, whose content was derived from regional power patterns and legacies, to try to mobilize support for his cause. In an open letter published in Nicaragua's *Barricada*, Noriega wrote, "The final battle for Latin American dignity against imperialism is being waged here in Panama."[16] Some observers, notably Gen. Frederick Woerner, argued that Noriega's attempts were a miserable failure. Woerner asserted that Noriega's use of dignity appeals and ideology to generate opposition to the United States did not succeed.[17] The dignity value was so salient in Panamanian politics, however, that Noriega's opponents also tried to use dignity symbols. When Col. Díaz Herrera broke with the regime in 1987 and his home became a center for opposition activity, opposition leaders referred to the site as "the headquarters of national dignity."[18]

Notes

1. My approach to system level has been influenced most strongly by the work of Richard W. Cottam, particularly his *Foreign Policy Motivation*, and *Iran and the United States: A Cold War Case Study*. My thinking about hemispheric structures and dynamics has been influenced by Cole Blasier, Abraham Lowenthal, Walter LaFeber, and Robert Pastor.

2. For an assessment of the 1984 and 1989 Panamanian elections in the context of these trends, see Scranton, "Elections as a U.S. Policy Option."

3. *U.S. News and World Report*, October 21, 1985, p. 46.

4. Burns, "Panama's Struggle for Independence," p. 19.

5. Noriega, "Psychological Operations."

6. The Reagan administration did not state its objectives this bluntly; instead, spokesmen referred to interdiction of arms from Nicaragua to El Salvador, and later, to pressuring the Sandinistas to negotiate with the Contras. However, most analysts—and the Contras themselves—asserted that the objective was to overthrow the Sandinistas, especially during 1981–1984, while the administration still believed that this could be achieved.

7. Kohn and Monks, "The Dirty Secrets of George Bush," p. 48. This article is one of the most complete investigative reports about Black Eagle.

8. After the invasion, a reporter visited the island of Coiba, where a commando training school was located. There, according to Panamanian officials, Israeli mercenaries had instructed the "special anti-terrorism unit" that Noriega used against his political opponents; David E. Pitt, "For Panama's Inmates, A Prison Like Devil's Island," *The New York Times*, January 7, 1990, p. 7.

9. Harari has denied it, and Israel has officially denied it; however, a leftist member of the Knesset told William Safire, "There is no doubt that Harari was Noriega's right-hand man, and we have to check if Noriega laundered drug money also with his right hand"; "The Lethal Fist," *The New York Times*, January 8, 1990, p. 21B.

10. Most of the evidence about these matters remains classified, so details simply cannot be verified. These activities are also politically sensitive because then Vice-President George Bush and his national security adviser Donald Gregg were involved.

11. Seymour M. Hersh, "Panama Strongman Said to Trade in Drugs, Arms, and Illicit Money," *The New York Times*, June 12, 1986, A14.

12. Bernal, "Panamanian Election," p. 1; Hersh, "Creation of a Thug," p. 88. For purposes of Noriega's trial, the U.S. government acknowledged that the CIA paid Noriega $300,000 in money and gifts over thirty-one years; the U.S. Army admitted to paying him $162,108 (Associated Press [AP] report, "Noriega Paid $300,000, Papers Show," *Arkansas Democrat*, January 19, 1991, p. A4).

13. Ropp, "Panama's Struggle for Democracy," p. 424.

14. AP report, *Arkansas Democrat*, March 15, 1989.

15. Steven Kinzer, "Panama's Government Unleashes Drive to Blame US for Troubles," *The New York Times*, July 5, 1987, p. 8.

16. Open Letter by M. A. Noriega, "Appeals for Regional Solidarity," FBIS-LAT 89-098, May 23, 1989, p. 23.

17. Interview, Washington, D.C., April 1990.

18. Kempe, *Divorcing the Dictator*, p. 213.

2

Internal Developments: State Level of Analysis

The state level of analysis considers influences on relations between the United States and Panama that originate in the domestic environment. Each nation's behavior results, in part, from internal influences and developments. Domestic factors mediate the effects of system level trends and conditions; they may also exert independent pressures on foreign policy.

For the United States, the system level stressed a national security perspective, focused on the year 2000, as a strong motive for intervention in Panama. The state level of analysis supplements that explanation with an analysis of the events and actors in Panama that presented opportunities and targets for U.S. intervention. Because most domestic influences on U.S. Panama policy are mediated through the policy process, this analysis considers them at the decisionmaking level. In explaining U.S. interests in Panama, the state level identifies one major domestic factor that interacted with system level trends—changes in the foreign policy consensus.

For Panama, the state level answers questions about Noriega's regime, its support structure (particularly the PDF), and challenges to the regime.[1] Explanations at this level concern Noriega's domestic power base, the development of opposition to the Noriega regime, and how the options available to the opposition were shaped by the nation's political culture and traditions.

Developments in the United States

The U.S. foreign policy, in general and toward Panama, has been shaped by the beliefs and axioms that analysts refer to as the foreign policy consensus. The willingness of the United States to negotiate new Panama Canal treaties was strongly influenced by the breakdown of the cold war consensus and the emergence of alternative beliefs characterized as post–cold war or liberal internationalism.[2] Similarly, changes in the Carter administration's approach

19

to Nicaragua during 1980 reflected changes in foreign policy beliefs held by officials, elites, and the general public. The Reagan administration's Central America policies represented a resurgence of the cold war belief system. Finally, once global and regional trends changed—specifically, improved U.S.-Soviet relations after 1986 and U.S. disenchantment with the Contra war—cold war views receded and the foreign policy consensus shifted toward liberal internationalism again. In each instance, U.S. Panama policy was associated with beliefs represented in the prevailing foreign policy consensus. Those beliefs provided guides for officials considering how to respond to situations in Panama and rationales for the choices they made.

Liberal Internationalism and
New Panama Canal Treaties

The Panama Canal treaties were concluded in 1977, and the liberal internationalism embodied by the treaties was accepted by Carter administration officials, significant U.S. economic interests, a fair-sized but not unduly large segment of the attentive public, and a bare majority of the U.S. Senate.[3] Those assumptions and that logic—the post–cold war beliefs— made sense in an international and regional context that was time-bound, and that period was about to end. The very ideas that made new canal treaties feasible were brought into question by events in Afghanistan, Nicaragua, and Iran during 1978 and 1979.

The logic on which the Carter administration justified the treaties made sense to many, but not a majority of the American people when Carter signed Presidential Review Memorandum 1, which made negotiation of a new canal treaty a high priority. That logic contained six interrelated ideas:

1. U.S. security interests in the canal consist in having the canal open, efficiently operating, and freely accessible, not in operation or control over the facility by U.S. personnel.
2. The canal cannot be defended from internal threats of sabotage; the best alternative is to remove the motive for sabotage and to create incentives to keep the canal open.
3. The most likely threat to canal security is sabotage instigated by Panamanians or from Panama, not from the Soviet Union or any other third party.
4. Panamanian consent, rather than U.S. military force, is the surest guarantor of the security of the canal.
5. Panama has just aspirations and legitimate grievances; satisfying these by giving Panama a greater economic stake in the canal's efficient operation will contribute to canal security.
6. Perpetuity is obsolete in the modern world; U.S. treaty rights and

base agreements with Panama should be no different from those with other nations.

These ideas were not created by the Carter administration, although its officials strongly endorsed them. Rather, this logic rested on an Agreement on Principles for new treaty negotiations that was signed in 1974 by Secretary of State Henry Kissinger and Foreign Minister Juan Antonio Tack. That agreement, in turn, closely paralleled a Statement of Principles issued by President Lyndon Johnson and President Marcos Robles in 1965. Thus, for almost fifteen years the United States had been developing canal policy objectives consistent with these ideas[4]—ideas, however, that would soon be challenged as obsolete.

The terms of the 1978 treaties are compatible with the six component ideas of this logic, particularly the plans to progressively increase Panamanian participation in canal management and defense and to grant Panama a share of canal tolls. This logic and the 1978 treaties fit a region free from significant conflicts and a time of relatively moderate U.S.-Soviet relations. The treaties were strongly endorsed by a unified Carter administration and former U.S. presidents, but they passed the Senate with only one vote to spare. Opinion polls yielded a mixture of public support and opposition for the treaties; the U.S. public did not wholeheartedly endorse a new relationship with Panama or giving up the canal.

These ideas, particularly the concept of Panamanian consent, also had implications for developments in Panama. A U.S. deal with one man, Omar Torrijos, could not constitute consent, nor could relationships with the National Guard, even new joint canal defense relationships, particularly because threats were defined as sabotage. Instead, consent had to come from the Panamanian people, initially through a popular plebiscite, a direct vote on the treaties, in March 1978. Throughout the treaty period, and projected to beyond the year 2000, the meaning of consent was nebulous, vaguely associated with traditional conceptions of stability and order. In 1977 and 1978, Torrijos talked about "civilianization" and a return to the barracks for the National Guard. The United States articulated these objectives as democratization and demilitarization. Thus, the security of the canal was expected to rest on concrete developments in Panama.

In late 1977, Torrijos's democratization schedule appeared to provide plenty of time, before the year 2000, for a transition from military to civilian rule and for building the institutions that democratization would require. First, Panama would hold its national ratification debate and plebiscite. This would mark the resumption of political rights and opposition press; in fact, many oppositionists, such as Miguel Bernal, first became involved in politics during the ratification campaign. Then, from 1980 to 1984, local and national legislative institutions would be built, election procedures and laws would be established, and, finally, national elections would be held.

However, the events that actually occurred (see Chapters 4 and 5) did not meet these expectations, and the 1984 election failed as a mechanism for registering Panamanian consent.

During 1977, however, Carter and Torrijos had hoped otherwise—1984 was six years away, and the United States and Panama seemed to have plenty of time for a domestic transition to occur. Absent from these calculations were two developments that disrupted the expected process: threats emerging in the region, in Nicaragua and El Salvador, and threats at home, where Torrijos died and Noriega assumed control.

Renewed Cold War and U.S.-Panamanian Relations

Recent criticisms of U.S. policy toward Panama during the Torrijos and Noriega years have asserted that the United States covered up evidence of wrongdoing in Panama. The state level of analysis would respond by asserting that the foreign policy consensus predisposed the Carter and Reagan administrations to overlook mounting evidence of abuses of power and drug trafficking by Panama's military regime. Instead, after 1980, renewed cold war beliefs pulled both administrations toward security objectives that so overshadowed negative developments in Panama that these simply did not figure in decisions on U.S. Panama policy. Panama, after all, was the one country on which President Carter could rely to provide a haven for the deposed shah of Iran. Moreover, Panama played a crucial role in the Reagan administration's various Central America policies. Later, as system level analysis suggests, receding threats, globally and in the region, diminished Noriega's value to the United States. Changes in threat perceptions were registered and reinforced by changes in the foreign policy consensus. When renewed cold war gave way to a return to post–cold war beliefs during the late 1980s, the rationale for the U.S. "play ball" strategy was undermined.

Developments in Panama

From a state level perspective, a primary characteristic of Panama's domestic environment in the 1980s was the transformation of the regime established by Gen. Omar Torrijos into a more authoritarian and corrupt system increasingly driven by Gen. Manuel Noriega's determination to gain and hold power. For Panama, the 1980s were the Noriega years.

Concurrently, each of the institutions the regime used to maintain control was weakened by manipulation and internal strife. Each element in the support structure—the presidency; the military's political party, the Democratic Revolutionary party (PRD); the National Assembly; the government-controlled media; and, finally, the PDF itself—lost legitimacy, credibility, and capacity to function. The first major challenge to the regime that damaged this support structure was the Spadafora crisis.

The Spadafora Crisis: Noriega's Watergate

The Spadafora crisis consisted of two events and their aftermath. First was the torture and murder of an opposition activist, Dr. Hugo Spadafora, in September 1985; three PDF officers were charged with committing the offense and Noriega was charged with ordering the death. Second was the PDF's ouster of President Nicolás Barletta after he failed to stifle opposition calls for an investigation of these charges (see Chapter 5). Spadafora's death and Barletta's ouster sparked a crisis for the regime that lasted six months, during which Noriega and his loyalists attempted to cover up their actions and diffuse the opposition.

The way in which these events were handled portrayed a regime that was not likely to survive. Its responses—manipulation of institutions, repression, disinformation, and a clumsy cover-up—caused a crisis from which Noriega and the PDF never recovered.

When top officers in the PDF decided to oust President Barletta, they reversed the modest step toward democracy the 1984 election represented. Once the precedent was set of ousting the first president elected in sixteen years, it was easier for the PDF to pressure and eventually fire his successor, President Arturo Delvalle. Concomitantly, Barletta's ouster made it harder for subsequent civilian presidents to assert their authority.

The removal of Barletta by the PDF demonstrated the military's conception of who governed Panama. Officers demanded his premature return from New York, held him in the Comandancía for fourteen hours, threatened him and his family, and used questionable procedures to steamroll his resignation and replacement by the National Assembly. This peremptory treatment returned the presidential office to the low level of legitimacy it had occupied before the 1984 election.

Divisions over how to manage the Spadafora crisis split the PRD, fragmenting the main institutional link between the PDF and its constituents. This split among party leaders spilled over into the legislature, where rival factions enervated the PRD's ability to act as a majority party. The National Assembly became more and more of a rubber stamp for Noriega's decisions. Ultimately, in December 1989, the Assembly expedited Noriega's fate by passing resolutions, including one referring to a state of war, that the United States would cite as provoking its invasion (see Chapter 7).

Reports in the government-controlled press became more and more divorced from reality. Deliberate disinformation had been used prior to the Spadafora affair, but the crisis solidified public perceptions of a credibility gap. This resulted, in part, from a two-month long duel with the opposition press, in which rival scenarios of Spadafora's death and evidence were challenged and debated. More importantly, and more damaging to the progovernment press, were reports and evidence presented in the Costa Rican media—including television documentaries, investigative reports, and news stories—which were quickly publicized in Panama's opposition media. Again and again, these more credible sources flatly contradicted official government statements and press reports.

The PDF experienced its first major shock as an institution over the Spadafora crisis. The officers soon experienced even greater shocks:

- A defection and exposé by the chief of staff, Col. Díaz Herrera, in July 1987
- A coup attempt by reformist majors followed by their arrest, torture, and a purge in March 1988
- The creation of a paramilitary force, the Dignity Battalions, outside the institution
- The purge of more than one hundred officers and men suspected of disloyalty
- The creation of an advisory structure, the Strategic Military Council (CEM), to rival the general staff
- A second coup attempt in October 1989, followed by a much more repressive purge

These events contributed to the disintegration of the PDF as an institution. That disintegration was not complete, however; many officers and men beyond Noriega's inner circle remained loyal, if not enthusiastic, members of the PDF. And, as two coup attempts revealed, the officers who did seek reform did not intend to diminish the political power or status of the PDF. Leaders of the March 1988 coup had made contact with two prominent oppositionists, and these officers might have supported some reform. Later, however, the very limited reform the October 1989 coup was likely to produce was one reason President George Bush was reluctant to provide more support. Neither coup was initiated to restore civilian rule. Instead, both coups were designed to preserve the military regime.

Noriega was determined to survive; a crucial element in his domestic power base was having officers and armed troops under his direct control. Throughout 1987–1989, Noriega subordinated the long-term interests of the PDF as an institution to his temporary personal power needs.

Noriega and his loyalists used the PDF, media, and PRD to stonewall the opposition and weather the storm the Spadafora crisis caused. During the Spadafora crisis many parts of the PDF cooperated enthusiastically in stifling dissent. In the process of handling the Spadafora crisis, several repressive tactics were developed:

- Bullying and threatening oppositionists and the people, through public announcements and telephone calls
- Launching a disinformation campaign to discredit the opposition, the Spadafora family, and Costa Rican sources
- Pressuring witnesses to retract damaging testimony and creating false witnesses
- Launching a cover-up, with false public statements, doctored documents, and a public relations offensive
- Stonewalling a legal investigation
- Manipulating the legislature
- Mobilizing progovernment demonstrations and playing dirty tricks to sabotage opposition events
- Intimidating and harassing opposition journalists
- Completing a truncated self-investigation, yielding a clean bill of health for the PDF

These tactics were used and expanded during subsequent crises, particularly Díaz Herrera's defection and the 1989 election (see Chapter 6).

The Spadafora Crisis: A Trial Run for the Opposition

Just as Noriega and the PDF flexed their power and developed strategies to constrain the opposition during the Spadafora crisis, oppositionists also developed power resources and strategies as they pressed their cause. During this crisis the opposition began to learn a significant lesson: how to overcome factional and political differences that had hindered coordinated actions in the past. Habits of cooperation gained in 1985 were repeated and expanded during the next five years. In this respect, the Spadafora crisis provided an opportunity for the opposition to build upon the coalition it had formed during the 1984 election campaign. Opposition party leaders took a major developmental step in 1985 by using the ouster of the presidential candidate they had campaigned against the year before to challenge the legitimacy of Noriega's regime.

The role played by the Spadafora family was crucial in facilitating cooperation among various groups—political parties, the Church, journalists, legislators, and other activists—during the six months the crisis lasted, from September 1985 to February 1986. The family planned and participated in symbolic protests and used religious events to keep the Spadafora crisis alive as an unresolved issue (see Chapter 5). These included the funeral itself, with several processions on that day at regular intervals to commemorate the burial; a hunger strike by Hugo's brother, Winston Spadafora; marshalling of evidence about the case and against the PDF; economic strikes; mass rallies; and symbolic protests, including candlelight vigils, chaining two members of the Spadafora family to a streetpost in front of the Papal Nunciature and conveying the keys to President Delvalle, and a human-chain protest spanning several miles. Throughout the Spadafora crisis, the family and opposition leaders stuck to two clear themes based on their conviction that PDF officers and Noriega were guilty: demanding a thorough investigation, independent of the PDF and the attorney general's office, and exposing the government's complicity in a cover-up and abuse of power.

The Spadafora family's leadership provided a focal point and a series of events around which political opposition groups could coordinate supportive activities. The Spadaforas, rather than any one of several traditional opposition figures, were in the premier position; this facilitated cooperation among rival opposition leaders and groups.

The Spadafora crisis demonstrated an opposition movement in the process of pioneering and practicing the techniques of nonviolent conflict. Symbols of their cause were developed, publicized, and authenticated. Rituals were performed, in repeated attempts to enlarge and expand the opposition movement. Techniques for mobilizing audiences and crowds and for building an organized opposition were ventured.

Learning to Struggle

Miguel Bernal often said, in explaining the nature of citizen protests and political behavior, that Panamanians needed to learn to struggle. This need stemmed in part from the ban on political activity that had been in place from 1968 to 1978 and in part from a sixteen-year hiatus in presidential elections. Opposition leaders had lacked opportunities and incentives to form coalitions prior to 1984. Many oppositionists were experiencing their first opportunities to protest. The opposition's learning process began in 1984, and the theft of its electoral victory was a bitter lesson.

Two lessons stand out in the transformation the opposition experienced during 1984–1989: (1) learning to broaden its base of support, at the follower level, and to expand its agenda to encompass the concerns of new followers; and (2) learning to work, at the leader level, with former enemies when they turned against Noriega's regime. Both lessons were difficult, particularly the latter, and both took time to learn.

Outsiders often criticized the opposition for being fragmented. Disunity among secondary leaders resulted from a leadership gap created by the presence of one dominant, but aging and problematic figure of presidential stature, Dr. Arnulfo Arias (see Chapter 4). Disunity was also a heritage of having, instead of one umbrella opposition party, several small, distinct, opposition groups, each with its own leaders who had to learn to work as a coalition. Disunity was also a function, particularly after 1987, of trying to function in an environment fraught with rumor, threats, and suspicion, as well as Noriega's pervasive intelligence gathering. Tomás Herrera, a civilian leader, summarized the problem: "It is very difficult to fight a dictatorship, very difficult. There are all kinds of risks, all kinds of threats."[5]

As major figures—Col. Díaz Herrera, PRD leader José Blandón, President Arturo Delvalle—defected from the regime, the traditional opposition leaders faced a new problem: how to accommodate these new allies. Each of these defectors had been very close to Noriega; each had participated in and supported repression of the opposition. For traditional oppositionists, these new allies were very hard to embrace. The process of deciding whether to work with a series of former enemies made the opposition, at the leadership level, appear to coalesce and fragment as new players either worked with or parallel to the opposition.

The opposition's next chance to learn, after the Spadafora crisis, was provided by Col. Díaz Herrera's break with Noriega (see Chapter 6). The overwhelmingly and unexpectedly large wave of popular protest ignited by Díaz Herrera's confessions and accusations demonstrated substantial opposition to the regime. This wave of protest was much larger and broader than the popular response the Spadafora crisis had provoked. Opposition party leaders, along with newly politicized businessmen, professionals, and civic leaders, found themselves out on the streets among students, taxi drivers, and various elements of the lower class. All, irrespective of background, could wave white handkerchiefs, beat pots and pans, and honk horns. As demonstrations became routinized during the next two years, and as people learned to struggle together, the opposition broadened.

Significant in this process was the formation of the National Civic Crusade (NCC). In its tactics, the NCC drew upon the symbols used and the tactics developed during the Spadafora crisis. To that inventory it added the strength of some 200 member organizations ranging from Kiwanis and Rotary Clubs, to auto dealers' associations, to students' and workers' organizations. A typical week's schedule of activities in 1987 included the following:

> Tuesday, 1 Sep—White Day at the University. Participate by papering the whole campus and rejecting the attempts to close the University of Panama.
> Wednesday, 2 Sep—La Chorrera, 1600 local time, Civic gathering at Feuillet Park. Join the people of Arrijan, La Chorrera, and Capira.
> Thursday, 3 Sep—Teachers' march.
> Friday, 4 Sep—March of the civic clubs for Panama's civic and moral values. Will begin at 1500 local time from the Holy Trinity Church in Bethania (across the street from Momi) toward El Carmen Church.[6]

But the NCC also brought its own challenge to the opposition movement—working with additional individual leaders, many of whom were new to the opposition movement.

Thus, as time passed, the opposition learned to struggle and to integrate former enemies and new friends. This process was uneven, but it gained a focus and the impetus of practical necessity during the 1989 election campaign.

The Opposition Wins

Prior to the 1989 presidential election, the United States did not consider the Panamanian opposition to be capable of running the country. The United States treated the opposition as a very junior partner during the ouster crisis, particularly during negotiations over Noriega's removal in 1987–1988. The United States took this approach partly to maximize its own interests and flexibility, but also because officials in Washington seemed to be waiting for a Philippines-style peoples' uprising on the streets of Panama. When Panama's nonviolent opposition confronted PDF riot squads and Noriega's Dignity Battalions, it retreated in the face of brutal repression. After a time of apparent quiescence, leaders and followers mobilized again, when a new opportunity or cause arose. But neither leaders nor followers were inclined to transform their nonviolent movement. Instead, oppositionists repeatedly said that they would not lead their people to be slaughtered. For U.S. officials and other observers, the fact that Panama's protesters could be cowed was frustrating and disappointing.

In Panama's political culture, tradition and inclination combine to make retreating from superior force a normal reaction. Noriega's was not the first regime to employ military and paramilitary force to repress dissent. The reaction pattern that developed historically was to retreat and fight another day. In this context, the government could successfully dampen, if not destroy, opposition activity. When the contest shifted into the electoral arena, however, the opposition was better positioned to fight.

Lessons in struggle, coalition politics, and organization paid off in a substantial "victory" for the opposition in May 1989 (see Chapter 6). Two fundamental changes resulted from the election: (1) the opposition gained a legitimacy it had previously lacked, along with potent symbols that redefined Noriega's image in Panama and in Washington; and (2) Noriega appeared to have lost control of the political process—he disappeared for a while, scrambled to recoup, then launched another brutal crackdown, and in the process he lost PRD support.

The nullification of the election and its aftermath created a crisis that allowed mediation by the Organization of American States (OAS), a step that recognized the opposition as a player equal to the government. This considerably strengthened the opposition and inadvertently provided a continuing reason for the opposition to keep working together as a coalition.

Finally, the 1989 election provided for the United States an answer to the question, "What is the alternative to Noriega?" By polling an overwhelming majority of votes, the opposition slate provided an obvious answer. An unproductive debate in Washington that had required projection and speculation about alternative coalition governments or transitional figures could finally be dropped. After May 7, the answer was simple: the Endara slate is the alternative. Guillermo Endara and his two vice-presidents were installed in office just moments before the U.S. invasion began in December 1989.

Noriega's Power Curve

An analysis of internal developments focused on Noriega's domestic power base reveals a man struggling to solidify his position. He was dealing with increasingly unreliable and less useful instruments. Except for the loyal military forces he could directly control, the bases of Noriega's regime disintegrated during 1987–1989. Had he been less resourceful and less determined to use whatever means were required to stay in power, he might have been toppled in 1988.

During the spring of 1988, the combined efforts of domestic opposition and U.S. pressure almost broke Noriega's resources and his determination. The combination in quick succession of a series of internal crises and external pressures severely weakened Noriega's position. In the space of three and a half months the following pressures were applied:

- December 30, 1987: Assistant Secretary of Defense Armitage visited Panama to tell Noriega it was time to "step back," clearly signaling that his departure was expected soon. This message was from the Department of Defense, not State; it was stronger than earlier signals.
- January 14, 1988: Noriega fired José Blandón, who had just negotiated a deal to remove him from power. This cost Noriega a formerly close adviser and PRD official, and indicated that a key player from his inner circle had not only defected but also tried to arrange Noriega's departure.
- February 4, 1988: Noriega was indicted on drug trafficking charges in two U.S. federal courts.
- February 25, 1988: President Eric Arturo Delvalle tried to fire Noriega. Noriega had to use extraordinary measures to get the Assembly to remove Delvalle and appoint a replacement. The United States continued to recognize Delvalle. Such manipulation won points for the opposition and further weakened the PRD and the legislature itself.
- March 1, 1988: The opposition began a strike that forced banks to close. This was reinforced by a financial squeeze strategy orchestrated, with the help of a Washington law firm, by Gabriel Lewis and other opposition leaders. The U.S. Department of State cooperated, making

Delvalle's government the sole legal recipient of U.S. payments to Panama.

- March 7–15, 1988: Presidents from neighboring states undertook a diplomatic initiative designed to achieve Noriega's removal and established a timetable for restoring democracy.
- March 16, 1988: PDF majors attempted a coup.
- April 8, 1988: President Ronald Reagan applied stiffer economic pressure, invoking sanctions under the International Economic Emergency Powers Act.

These events constitute repeated and serious challenges to Noriega's regime. The most crucial time was February 25–March 16, 1988—two and a half weeks when the U.S. government, the PRD, the opposition, and, most importantly, the PDF all exhibited a willingness to remove Noriega. Even after the March coup failed, economic pressures were still having a strong effect. By late March, the PDF and government workers—Noriega's primary constituencies—were experiencing reduced pay and payless paydays. Critics of the Reagan administration, particularly those who tried to get stronger economic sanctions during the first three weeks of March, argued that a potent economic blow delivered during this window of opportunity could have knocked Noriega out.

A State Department spokesman commented on the conjunction of events, saying,

> [Noriega] seems to be among the few who don't recognize the message that the Panamanian people are sending. That message continues to grow—demonstrations, strikes underway today—for the sixth straight day, I believe, more calls by the Delvalle government, by the opposition groups, by the Civic Crusade. It's clear in all of this that the people who continue to suffer, unfortunately, are the people of Panama. That includes the Defense Forces and their families.[7]

The Panamanian people did, in fact, seem to be giving their all, both in terms of businesses participating in the strike and people demonstrating on the streets. In terms of Panamanian political culture, this was a significant showing. Catholic bishops called for Noriega's resignation. The Civic Crusade and opposition parties signed a joint statement, indicating their agreement not only on the need for Noriega to depart but also on transitional steps toward a new regime.

The list also reflects a concerted effort of coordinated and parallel actions taken by organized oppositionists in Panama and in the United States, people on the streets, officers opposed to Noriega, neighboring presidents, and the U.S. Department of State. Concerted pressures were being applied from almost every available quarter. Throughout these weeks, President Reagan called repeatedly for the people of Panama and the PDF to rid themselves of

Noriega. This was the only time between 1986 and 1989 when all these players were active in a coordinated fashion, and when economic pressure was occurring simultaneously with diplomatic initiatives. Whether additional U.S. pressure, either from the Pentagon or in the form of early application of economic sanctions, could have removed Noriega in 1988 remains a matter of speculation. If a window of maximum opportunity were to be identified, however, this would be it.

Noriega, however, was willing to ride out the economic storm and to use force to intimidate the opposition. As the strike wore on, support in the business community began to slip. The combined internal and external economic pressure was not severe enough to make Noriega decide to leave. Moreover, Noriega was able to obtain sufficient cash to endure the toughest weeks of the financial squeeze. Alliance patterns of the 1980s and Noriega's foreign connections allowed him to patch together the resources he needed to survive. Explanations from the decisionmaking level of analysis address the question of why the Reagan administration was not better able to take advantage during this pressure period and why Noriega was able to survive (see Chapter 3).

By May 1989, Noriega had few power resources on which he could rely. Numerous members of the PDF had voted against the government's slate of candidates in the election. Although loyal officers and men were willing to commit the fraud and repression Noriega ordered after the election, the numbers of PDF who voted for the opposition shocked observers and Noriega. The military's party, the PRD, split over how to respond; as a support structure, the PRD was already weakened, and the election made it even less useful. Much of the middle class had turned against Noriega, joining the Crusade or going into exile. As a referendum, the election measured the low level of Noriega's support. Politically, he was left with loyalists who served in his government but who could hardly be said to govern.

While Noriega's power curve was declining, the power of Panama's opposition forces was rising. The opposition experienced three significant periods of activity associated with three major events, interspersed with occasional and lesser actions: Díaz Herrera's defection in June 1987, the Delvalle firing/March coup period, and the May 1989 elections. Each time, the opposition took to the streets in greater numbers, more broadly representative of society, and more determined to succeed. Noriega's violent response was also more severe in each instance, and the fact that he could use force to subdue popular protest ensured his survival.

During the last months of 1989, Noriega retained his job but he had lost most of his power. He retained control over the National Assembly and could get declarations passed and statements made. He retained command over much of the PDF and over the Dignity Battalions, which he could use to maneuver and to retaliate. He could force people off the streets, but he could not remain in office much longer. In December, the context changed. New elements of uncertainty were added to a previously measured but increasingly escalating war of nerves between U.S. and Panamanian military forces. Noriega made a preemptive power play and whipped up anti-U.S. hostility, igniting a crisis situation that appeared to be spiraling out of control. That crisis dynamic, analyzed in detail in Chapter 3, culminated in a steady erosion of Noriega's power base.

Notes

1. My analysis of Panama is informed by the work of Steve C. Ropp, Richard Millett, William L. Furlong, Lester Langley, and Walter LaFeber.

2. These terms are somewhat confusing because different opinion analyses have coined different labels for the successors to the cold war containment consensus of the 1940s through the 1960s. Moreover, once the cold war consensus, which was shared by a large majority of U.S. citizens and elites, broke down, competing belief sets emerged. None of these gained the degree of majority support that containment views did; competing minority viewpoints make it very confusing to talk about a foreign policy "consensus" during the 1970s and 1980s.

3. For an analysis of cold war and post–cold war assumptions reflected in the treaty ratification debate, see Furlong and Scranton, *The Dynamics of Foreign Policy Making*, chap. 3. For an analysis of public opinion polls reflecting alternative components of the foreign policy consensus, see Moffett, *The Limits of Victory*.

4. The process was not entirely linear, nor did each administration from 1965 to 1977 endorse these ideas as strongly as Carter's did; see Scranton, "Changing United States Foreign Policy."

5. Personal interview, Panama City, August 1990. Herrera was an organizer of the National Civic Crusade.

6. "Civic Crusade Announces Week's Activities," FBIS-LAT-87-172, September 4, 1987, p. 9.

7. U.S. Department of State, "Daily Briefing Report," March 28, 1988, p. 12.

3

Dealing with Noriega: Decisionmaking Level of Analysis

Explanations at the decisionmaking level of analysis focus on the characteristics of individuals and their influence on policy. This level considers questions about choices: what options were considered and what choices were made. Of particular interest are perceptions and misperceptions, motives and aims, bargaining calculations, and views of the national interest. This level also considers the policymaking process and the impact process exerts on options and choices. Insights are gained from analyzing leadership styles, patterns of routine and crisis decisionmaking, and bureaucratic and interagency politics.[1]

Throughout the years that they sought to remove Gen. Manuel Noriega, U.S. officials insisted first that they would not use force to achieve that end, and later that force would be used only as a last resort. Nonetheless, in December 1989, President George Bush and his advisers reached that undesired point, saying that they had no choice but to use massive military force against the Noriega regime. The United States ended up exercising the one option that it had persistently avoided and least preferred. The decisionmaking level of analysis considers the structure of the crisis between Noriega and the Reagan and Bush administrations and suggests explanations for Noriega's staying power and the Bush administration's decision to invade.

Initially, the United States had hoped to nudge or coax Noriega out of power by offering him a deal; various negotiating initiatives were assayed between late 1986 and May 1988. The decisionmaking level of analysis uses a bargaining perspective to assess the deals the United States and others offered, the signals and resources that were used to support the offers, and Noriega's considerations in rejecting them. Noriega's motives and choices are also addressed at this level. Why did he not accept a deal that would allow him to step down with his reputation and wealth intact? Could such a deal, in fact, have been constructed? Why was he so determined to stay in power, irrespective of the costs and risks? Only Noriega can provide definitive answers, but this level suggests possible explanations for the inefficacy of negotiations in this case.

Bureaucratic politics is another dynamic that the decisionmaking level considers. Commentators repeatedly noted the debilitating effect on U.S. policy of conflicting organizational missions and vested interests in Panama and the region, jurisdictional conflicts, and resulting differences in organizational perspectives on Noriega and his activities. During negotiations for Noriega's removal, Panamanians repeatedly complained that they were getting mixed signals from the United States. This level of analysis considers the impact of organizational differences, interagency consensus building, and a lack of involvement by senior advisers and the president until very late in the crisis.

Structure of the Crisis

A crisis, by definition, entails threat, surprise, and a short amount of time to respond. The shift from routine expectations about another country to severe threats, uncertainty about events, and time constraints is what makes a crisis so serious. This shift, and the change in stakes for both parties that a crisis creates, pulls policymaking out of routine channels and into the highest councils of government. In the United States, crisis decisionmaking is associated with National Security Council (NSC) meetings, a president closeted with a few senior advisers, and Congress and the media relegated to the periphery.

U.S. Panama policy did not follow this pattern until the October 1989 coup attempt failed. Up until that point, from 1986 until late 1989, Panama policy was made through routine (noncrisis) channels. Although the issue was labeled a crisis in the press, and the term "ouster crisis" was used by participants, analysts, and reporters, policy was not made as though a crisis were under way. This was not a classic crisis; instead, like the 444-day Iranian hostage "crisis," the Noriega ouster crisis was prolonged. If press exposés about drug trafficking are taken as the precipitants of the crisis, the ouster crisis lasted forty-two months, from June 1986 through December 1989. If Col. Díaz Herrera's confession in June 1987 is considered the precipitant, the duration is thirty months.

Panama policymaking exhibited an unusual pattern: prolonged crisis management at the working level until a more severe precipitant triggered classic crisis management behavior. Panama policymaking during the period from 1986 to October 1989 fit the prolonged pattern, whereas policymaking during October–December 1989 came closer to classic expectations. Events during the weekend of December 15–17, 1989, constituted the final precipitant that created a change to an immediate, "true" crisis, with suddenly heightened threat perceptions, surprise at the turn of events, and a sense that time was quickly running out. Decisionmaking by the Bush administration between December 17 and 19 came closest to models of crisis management. Interaction patterns between the United States and Panama during this last phase also fit expected bilateral crisis behavior.

The Prolonged Crisis, June 1986–October 1989

The ouster crisis involved several U.S. initiatives that had related impacts and consequences in Panama: several rounds of negotiations to engineer Noriega's removal, a disjointed covert paramilitary operation, governmental and private economic pressure strategies, and covert and overt support for the opposition during the 1989 election. These were pursued serially, with one approach being initiated after another failed, rather than as a planned sequence of escalating pressures.

During a classic crisis, time constraints may force premature closure on debate, creating an ill-founded consensus and foreclosing consideration of more appropriate choices. During the prolonged ouster crisis, however, perceptions of plenty of time to ease Noriega out contributed to the Reagan administration's lack of consensus over what means to use to remove Noriega. U.S. Panama policy was not even processed as a crisis during February 25–March 16, 1988, when Noriega's regime experienced several debilitating shocks in rapid succession. Failing to shift into high-level crisis management during this crucial three weeks may have denied the Reagan administration an opportunity to deliver a knockout blow to Noriega. The combination of time constraints, different interagency procedures, and personnel who would have been involved if NSC-centered crisis management had been used might have yielded a consensus to implement a unified, concerted, tough pressure strategy.

In this respect, the Reagan administration placed itself in a no-win situation: it had declared a crisis but was not behaving as if a crisis were under way. The severity of administration rhetoric, particularly announcements of Noriega's imminent departure, did not match the administration's decisionmaking or its initiatives. Noriega—correctly from his vantage point—paid more attention to U.S. actions than rhetoric. He perceived latitude to evade and temporize, which he used to his full advantage.

Several reasons can be suggested for the persistence of working-level decision patterns despite the opening of a window of opportunity in early 1988. One concerns U.S. expectations about what an uprising against Noriega should look like—namely, a Philippines-style revolution. The prevailing concept held by U.S. officials of their role seems to have been to apply pressure behind the scenes, prepare an exile option, and negotiate the terms of Noriega's exit, concerning his own status, the status of the military, and a transition government. Panama's role, according to this conception, was to flood the streets with protesters who would stand up to the military and thereby convince some officers that the tide had turned and that they must overthrow Noriega. This argument suggests that until events confirmed that the Panamanian opposition was "serious," or until officials' expectations changed, decisionmaking would remain at the working level.

Another reason U.S. Panama policymaking did not get pulled into the White House during 1987 and 1988 was that the president's high-level advisers disagreed over options. Until a consensus emerged at the senior level, Panama policy would remain at the working level despite changes in the situation in Panama. Several Washington insiders have commented on this tendency in the Reagan administration: Reagan was loathe to settle a dispute between senior advisers. He would neither order the warring parties to settle their differences nor make a decision himself that would tip the balance. Thus, if senior advisers disagreed, interagency review procedures for reaching a consensus would not be used.[2] Instead, decisionmaking would remain at the working level: one department would get grudging approval for a watered down initiative; other departments (or parts thereof) would contribute minimal support. Leaks to the press and Congress by various participants to disrupt or derail an initiative were common.

U.S. Panama policy was affected by this tendency during 1987 and 1988. Secretary of State George Shultz and Assistant Secretary for Inter-American Affairs Elliott Abrams advocated military and paramilitary operations to remove Noriega. Admiral Crowe, the chairman of the Joint Chiefs of Staff (JCS), and National Security Adviser Frank Carlucci vigorously objected. When the Department of State initiated negotiations, these were accompanied by a reassurance strategy, rather than coercion. This bargaining strategy required the U.S. military in Panama to withhold pressures on Noriega. Some military officers strongly disagreed with this approach, believing that Noriega would be more impressed with a high-pressure strategy that included vigorous psychological operations and supporting military leverage.

Fundamental disagreements existed about the probable success of U.S. paramilitary operations in Panama and of covert actions by Panamanians, as well as about the best incentives and threats to use to influence Noriega. Until a consensus could be reached on these questions, the administration could not mount a concerted, forceful strategy to back up either a diplomatic or covert initiative. Lack of such a consensus was one source of mixed signals from the Reagan administration. Under an "activist" NSC system, the NSC adviser might have decided such disagreements or forced the issue. Stung by the findings of the Tower Commission report about NSC involvement in the Contra war, however, the NSC was particularly concerned with avoiding additional adventures. Both Carlucci and his successor, Gen. Colin Powell, preferred a more neutral, procedural role as adviser and for the NSC. A negative consequence of that choice was that without presidential intervention serious disputes among advisers were allowed to fester rather than be resolved. As a result, decisionmaking remained at the working level.

A factor that contributed to disagreements among senior advisers, principally from the departments of State and Defense, was interpersonal conflict involving Assistant Secretary Abrams. Once the Iran-Contra scandal broke, Abrams and the activist options he was advocating (the two cannot really be separated) were viewed with misgivings in the Department of Defense. Some Washington columnists asserted that Defense's opposition to State positions was actually due to the fact that Abrams was their advocate. Veterans of bureaucratic battles had accumulated grudges against Abrams and were suspicious that his ideas owed more to his need, as a policy entrepreneur, to find a new issue once the Contra war began to wane.

The March 1988 coup attempt might have pulled policymaking into a crisis mode if the attempt had lasted longer than a few hours. The majors' coup was quelled so quickly on the morning of March 16, however, that it had no process ramifications in the United States.

Later in 1988, a U.S. presidential election year, the fact that Vice-President Bush was campaigning for the nomination for president, and later for election, exerted a minor effect that further contributed to working-level status for Panama policy. In and of itself, this political factor would not have been sufficient to keep policy at the working level if other factors had pulled decisionmaking into a classic crisis mode. Potentially negative political ramifications were considered by Bush's staff. Some reporters have argued that political considerations inserted by these staff into interagency debates contributed to back-burner status and working-level treatment for U.S. Panama policy.[3] Given the markedly negative media tactics that characterized the 1988 campaign, Bush's advisers may well have feared that Noriega could become the centerpiece of a "Willie Horton" commercial directed against Bush. The Democratic candidate, Michael Dukakis, tried to make an issue of Bush's involvement in the policy of working with Noriega, but with little effect.[4]

The impact of electoral considerations on U.S. Panama policy was not significant. Such political considerations certainly did not stop the two federal indictments against Noriega from being unsealed on February 5, 1988. Political factors probably did contribute, however, to Bush's public opposition, during negotiations with Noriega held in the spring, to a deal that would drop the indictments. The impact of electoral considerations was probably negligible after negotiations with Noriega ended on May 25, 1988. After that point, the Reagan administration had run out of nonmilitary options. A new diplomatic or economic initiative was not likely to have been tried during the next few months, even if 1988 had not been an election year.

Panama policymaking by the Bush administration remained at the working level for many months. Options short of force had been exhausted or were under way, so a new presidential initiative was not likely. The focal point of the Bush administration's efforts between January and October 1989 was the May 1989 presidential election in Panama. This elicited covert and overt actions: assistance to opposition candidates and organizations in Panama and to external election observer groups. Both secret and official election assistance could be easily and appropriately managed at the working level; neither required a change in Panama policymaking.

An additional factor that contributed to managing Panama policy at the working level was the cautious, pragmatic style deliberately cultivated by the Bush administration during 1989. Although Bush said on several occasions that he reserved the right to use force if U.S. lives were threatened in Panama, his administration continued the existing official position that military intervention was not to be used to remove Noriega.

Even after the opposition "won" the May election only to be brutally repressed, the Bush administration retained its cautious approach. Bush declined to initiate either negotiations or a covert operation to unseat Noriega and install the opposition presidential candidate, Guillermo Endara. Instead, the administration supported regional diplomacy and mediation by OAS, along with continuing the sanctions that already were in place. Unexpected events in Panama and harsh criticism at home finally shifted the Bush administration into another decision pattern.

The October 1989 Coup Creates a Crisis

Although the United States had been calling for another coup since the very day the previous one occurred—March 16, 1988—the Bush administration appeared surprised at the course of events on October 1–3, 1989, and seemed to be caught off guard as the coup progressed (see Chapter 7). Although the administration gave limited support to the coup, U.S. officers in Panama were not authorized to block a third road, which was used by loyal forces, or to prevent air transport of troops who came to Noriega's aid at the Comandancía.

During these fast-breaking events, normal crisis procedures were not used—a fact that featured prominently in congressional and press criticism of the administration's handling of the October coup. That criticism, which was biting and personal, and the postcoup review of decision procedures that it engendered, shifted U.S. Panama policy into a different decision pattern. The attention of the president and senior advisers was engaged, a serious review of options was completed, and decisions about preparing new options were made by the president.

Personnel changes affected these deliberations. Many of the participants who had disputed U.S. Panama policy during 1987 and 1988 were gone, and a different combination of senior advisers considered Panama policy in October 1989. Some of the new participants had vested interests in self-correction, particularly NSC Adviser Brent Scowcroft and White House Chief of Staff John Sununu. Sununu, in particular, let it be known that the Bush team was determined not to get caught unprepared again.

The most important decision that resulted from these postmortems concerned the status of the military option. Although this option was not placed directly on the table in late October, the decision to revise and prepare plans to use military force to remove Noriega constituted a significant difference in the choices considered, and the level at which they were considered, before and after the abortive October coup.

The decision to prepare military options resulted from changes in senior advisers' perceptions that occurred during and after the attempted coup. Most significant were the views of President Bush, NSC Adviser Scowcroft, and Colin Powell, who now served as chairman of the Joint Chiefs of Staff. All three had previously taken the position that Panamanians must remove Noriega, probably through a coup accompanied by popular protest; U.S. pressure would be applied as part of the removal, but Panamanian, not U.S., force must remove the general. The failure of the October coup challenged their assumptions that Panamanians could overthrow Noriega themselves and the success of any coup backed with only passive U.S. military support. After Noriega's postcoup purge, the Bush administration judged prospects for another coup to be quite low, but it was determined to be ready in case another coup occurred, or if events, particularly retaliatory actions against U.S. personnel, required the use of military force.

Contributing to the decision to prepare military options was a reevaluation of Noriega and conditions in Panama, with the conclusion that the situation was more likely to worsen than improve. A war of nerves between U.S. and Panamanian military forces reached a new intensity after October 3; U.S. personnel and facilities seemed to be at greater risk than before the attempted coup. The administration perceived a new level of threat, and Noriega was judged to be willing to exploit his ability to provoke and harass U.S. forces and personnel to the maximum. The prolonged ouster crisis became more like a classic crisis as provocative episodes continued in Panama during November and early December, and observers in the administration and the press suggested that it would be only a matter of time before something happened. Threat perceptions increased during October and November; time appeared to be growing short. The only missing ingredient for a true crisis was an unpleasant surprise. The structure of the situation, as it approached the characteristic dynamics of a true crisis, was narrowing the options available to each side.

The Final Crisis, December 15–19, 1989

In December 1989, the United States ended up exercising the one option— massive military force—that had been deliberately kept off the table throughout the ouster crisis in Panama. Numerous explanations have been offered for this change.

Foremost among these is the concept of a situation spiraling out of control. The incidents of the weekend of December 15–17, including violence initiated by both countries, were not much different from the most severe of hundreds of previous incidents in the war of nerves. Nonetheless, the December 15–17 incidents were perceived and handled differently. Once a spiral was perceived, the likelihood that the United States would use force increased significantly.

One reason for this shift arose from a change in the Panamanian context: Noriega made a power play through his National Assembly and seemed, on December 15, to have whipped up so much anti-U.S. hostility that some of his military forces went out of control. Although Noriega's intentions in obtaining additional legal powers were not clear, the Assembly's action was perceived by the Bush administration as a step in a more dangerous direction. The death of Lt. Robert Paz and the brutal treatment of two U.S. witnesses to the shooting that led to his death constituted a fundamental change in Bush's perception of the situation. Whether Noriega intended to provoke the United States or not, the Bush administration felt provoked and responded as if provoked.

A second reason that brought the administration closer to the use of force arose from a change in the U.S. context: the United States was ready to use massive military force if it had to do so. Precautionary steps, particularly the removal of as many U.S. civilians as possible, had been taken; equipment had been pre-positioned; readiness exercises had been practiced. This does not suggest that the option determined the policy; rather, the option made the policy possible when the context in Panama provided a precipitant.

Both of these reasons involved an element of frustration for Noriega: neither the United States nor the opposition would give up. Neither one had been able to deliver a knockout blow, but neither one would go away. Noriega then took a risky step, his power play. Fatigue, from using elaborate security precautions so long, probably played a role in his decision, along with accumulated frustrations of a two-year war of nerves with U.S. forces in Panama and an escalating confrontation with Washington.

The ouster crisis was equally frustrating for the United States. The Bush administration perceived the United States as having tried every available means to remove Noriega. The White House was frustrated and embarrassed over criticism of its handling of the October 1989 coup only two and half months earlier.[5] President Bush expressed personal frustration that Noriega would not comply with U.S. exhortations that he leave Panama. U.S. officials' frustration led to a conclusion that if Noriega actually threatened U.S. lives, Bush would have no choice but to take him and the military out. During the forty-eight hours that culminated in the decision to invade,

Noriega issued one taunt too many; whether Noriega was in complete control or not, Bush had had enough.

During those few days, the United States and Panama seemed to be headed for a collision. The pattern of events and perceptions passed a threshold beyond which neither side could de-escalate. Once this more acute stage of the crisis began on December 15, both sides' choices seemed to be limited to more hostile actions; "limited choices" made a more severe confrontation unavoidable.[6]

Bargaining With Noriega

A bargaining perspective can be used to consider the offers the United States made to encourage Noriega to leave and the resources used to support those offers. The sequence of offers was frequently criticized in the press. Considering just the elements of the deals offered, the progression was from weak to tough to less tough positions: (1) the nudge—it is time to step back; (2) the golden parachute—please go and take your money, punctuated by indictments that threatened the sanction of going to jail; and (3) the coax—please go for a while, and keep your money in exchange for not dropping the indictments (see Chapter 6).

If Noriega truly had wanted to bargain with the United States, this progression toward a compromise in his favor should have yielded a solution. Each U.S. offer was closer to Noriega's objectives of protecting his reputation, wealth, and the PDF. But for each step in the progression there was a mismatch that allowed Noriega to either play for time while seeking other objectives, or to misinterpret U.S. intentions and thereby misunderstand the U.S. offer.

The Nudge: Mismatch in U.S. Signals

When the United States first attempted to nudge Noriega out, he was in a strong bargaining position and he had not yet become "the issue." At this point, Noriega could have left office with his dignity and sense of machismo intact. He was not convinced, however, that he had to leave. The United States was sending mixed signals. The nudge suggestion was only one message; Noriega's direct communication with CIA Director William Casey and NSC staff aide Oliver North suggested that he not only could, but should, stay in power, and that they considered his continuance valuable. At the moment when it would have been easiest to arrange an exit with honor, Noriega did not take the "step back" message seriously. Part of the Reagan administration thought it was sending a clear signal; other parts undermined that signal and sent a conflicting message. Had reinforcing messages, particularly from the Pentagon and the CIA, been sent and had additional resources been applied to demonstrate the seriousness of U.S. concerns, Noriega might have perceived the nudge differently.

A nudge is, in essence, a weak instrument. This tactic might have worked *if* Noriega concluded, based on his own evaluation, that his situation was only going to deteriorate and that positive values could be gained by his departure. During 1986 and 1987, that conclusion was not yet apparent. The United States hoped that Ferdinand Marcos's ouster from the Philippines would have a salutary effect—an example Noriega would want to avoid. But this message was not convincing to Noriega. Neither the opposition movement nor dissident officers seemed to present a viable threat to his position. The nudge did not succeed in convincing Noriega that he must go.

The Golden Parachute: Mismatch of Incentives

A similar problem affected the golden parachute approach initiated by the United States in July 1987. Noriega seemed to be fishing for an offer; one of his top advisers, José Blandón, made an approach that Noriega apparently authorized. As the Reagan administration pursued the details of a deal, however, the negotiating field got so crowded that signals were difficult to perceive clearly. Too many deals were on the table and too many parties were involved. In such a crowded negotiating field, Noriega could take the initiative and change the game into a contest among bidders. He could keep the various parties—the Department of State, Blandón, Admiral Murphy, various opposition factions in Panama, the Church—busy while he remained in power.

The longer this process continued, the more determined Noriega became to remain in power. The more he became the issue, the more he resisted pressures for his removal. This pattern suggests another mismatch—one between Noriega's incentives to stay and U.S. incentives for him to go. By the time the case against Noriega was so strong that the Reagan administration mounted a united front, Noriega's own personal stakes in remaining in power were engaged and he could not back down. Previously, before Noriega reached that position, U.S. stakes were not sufficiently engaged for the Reagan administration to make a strong and concerted demand for his removal. By late 1987, as Noriega's stakes became more clear and his determination to stay increased, the Reagan administration was at a disadvantage. The administration could not muster a consensus that the time had come for Noriega to depart.

At an earlier moment, probably in late 1986, Noriega might have been persuaded to leave. But a significant decisionmaking dynamic prevented the United States from seriously considering the issue of his departure at the highest levels. That dynamic involves what can be described as a "glass ceiling" between the working level and the top level of the executive branch: an invisible wall that filters agenda items, preventing all but the most pressing or politically sensitive issues from consideration by senior officials.[7] Without a full-blown crisis, working-level officials find it almost impossible to push a policy problem through the glass ceiling to obtain a decision, especially one that involves change or possible costs. When Noriega might have been quietly, but forcefully, pressured to leave, U.S. Panama policy was neither a crisis nor a salient issue. Instead, the message from the working level to senior advisers was that Noriega was headed for trouble and that something should be done now. That message bounced off the glass ceiling; it could not get through the competition of much more pressing issues that crowded the agenda.

The Coax: Mismatch between Bargaining and Political Realities

The coax-him-out approach attempted after Noriega was indicted in February 1988 suffered from a different mismatch. In this case, the U.S. initiative was hampered by a mismatch between bargaining necessities and domestic political realities. By May 1988, when the coax deal was placed on the table for the last time, the status of the drug issue precluded the Reagan administration from offering a deal that Noricga could not refuse. The United States could not meet the one condition that Noriega seemed to want: assuring Noriega that the administration would drop the indictments in favor of his temporary exile. By the time Noriega was indicted, the drug issue was so salient, and Noriega's image was so tarnished, that a coax deal may have been politically impossible for the United States to offer. Concomitantly, even if such a deal was offered, Noriega may not have believed that the Reagan administration would really deliver its part of the bargain. Electoral politics contributed to the saliency of the drug issue and to presidential and congressional candidates' fears about negative ramifications of ignoring Noriega's indictments. Noriega's reputation was so connected to drugs in the U.S. media in 1988 that a deal trading an exit for indictments might not have been politically feasible even in a nonelection year.

Although it is impossible to make a definitive assessment, most of the evidence points to a conclusion that Noriega was not interested in bargaining for his departure during 1987 or 1988. Instead, he used negotiations for "nonsolution" bargaining; that is, he bargained for time, not for a deal.

The Noriega Factor

As a bargainer, Manuel Antonio Noriega was one of the shrewdest and most cunning leaders the United States has ever tried to influence. Noriega withstood three years of U.S. pressure, outlasting economic, diplomatic, and covert initiatives, and outmaneuvering the United States during direct and indirect negotiations and third-party mediation efforts. Until he miscalculated in December 1989, issuing one challenge too many, and appeared to lose control over some elements of the PDF, Noriega had succeeded in frustrating every U.S. effort to engineer his removal. What made Noriega such a formidable adversary?

One explanation concerns a relative imbalance of will between U.S. officials and Noriega. Noriega was more determined to succeed and more motivated because of his direct stake in the outcome. In addition, Noriega had one main adversary and could focus single-mindedly on the removal/survival game. In the United States, most officials, especially senior advisers, had additional and often more pressing concerns. Until late 1989, Noriega held bargaining advantages on all these dimensions.

Noriega believed in being a tough bargainer. He viewed the world in terms of winners and losers, and considered flexibility to be a losing strategy. Standing firm and playing for time, outwaiting and outwitting the opponent were his hallmark. Noriega's own writing on strategy and psychological warfare emphasized ways to confuse and wear the adversary down; he stressed the importance of timing and subterfuge.

> Through strategy we try to trick the enemy with cunning and skill and overcome him more easily than by a direct attack with masses of soldiers, that is, without battle. Militarily, surprise can complement the psychological operation. . . .
> Strategy is the first and foremost version of psychological warfare that strictly speaking, is natural to a man fighting for his life.[8]

Noriega's operating style and personality worked, until very late in the game, to his advantage. He presented himself as tough, he acted tough, and, not surprisingly, he proved to be a tough opponent. One side of that toughness involved ruthless, reprehensible conduct, such as his actions toward Dr. Hugo Spadafora and Maj. Moisés Giroldi. Until 1988, such conduct appeared to be an irregular pattern in his career, a recurring exception to his usually selective application of force. Commentators often remarked, especially in comparing the PDF with the military in El Salvador, that Noriega directed force at one target and only occasionally to send a message to a broader audience. As PDF commander, his use of force was seen as relatively restrained, selective, and impersonal, designed to deter through psychological impact.

Beginning in 1988, the pattern of Noriega's use of force changed. As his power position grew more precarious, his use of force grew less selective, less restrained, and more geared toward retaliating and punishing whole crowds. And as the Spadafora and Giroldi killings demonstrated, Noriega began taking opposition personally, holding grudges, and taking satisfaction in revenge.

Noriega's central personal value was machismo, a value that was strongly reinforced by his experience in the National Guard and his view of Panama's national dignity. As he assumed greater power but also faced greater opposition, these three values—his personal machismo, the military institution, and Panama's dignity—seemed to fuse into one for Noriega. On several occasions he said, "Virility is proven by staying in power." In a bargaining situation, he was not able to give in or back down. This provides a clue to his assessments of deals offered by the United States and the opposition.

The characteristic that most enhanced Noriega's bargaining ability was his inscrutability. Panamanians, U.S. officials, and analysts found him incredibly hard to "read." His intentions in initiating or responding to negotiations were particularly obscure. Noriega consistently demonstrated an ability to do the unexpected; no one, for example, predicted that Noriega would surrender to the Papal Nuncio. Compared to the U.S. government, Noriega could much more easily maneuver without revealing his true intentions. This ability, and his skillful use of timing, allowed him to gain an upper hand throughout his negotiations with the United States and the opposition.

Bureaucratic Politics and U.S. Policy

If the Noriega factor represents many of the advantages a single individual bargainer can hold, policymaking in the Reagan and Bush administrations illustrates the bargaining disadvantages of large, complex organizations. And, whereas Panama's bargaining power was strengthened (until the invasion) by its decision process, the U.S. process of formulating and executing policy weakened its bargaining ability. Noriega could stifle dissent, but disagreement within the Reagan administration was clearly broadcast to Noriega. The United States was not able to penetrate Noriega's inner circle; Noriega, until early 1988, cultivated allies within the U.S. executive branch. These connections enabled Noriega to exploit the interagency consensus-building process and bureaucratic routines to his own advantage.

Organizational Routines and Interests

One bureaucratic routine frequently cited by Noriega's defense lawyers and critics of U.S. policy was the sending of letters to Noriega from DEA Administrator John Lawn, congratulating Noriega, as commander of the PDF, on contributing to specific enforcement missions. Such letters are sometimes called "attaboys," to indicate their function of conveying thanks whenever cooperation or joint operations occurred. Noriega received many of these, but they were only formalities and entailed no endorsement whatsoever of Noriega's regime. Each one stood for a joint operation or PDF fulfillment of a DEA request. Thus the letters also reflected a record of consistent contributions by Noriega's regime to the statistics used by DEA, the Office of Management and Budget, the White House, and Congress to measure success in drug enforcement. Although he was clearly part of the drug problem, Noriega was careful to comply with DEA requests. He turned the U.S. operational definition of success in the drug war to his best advantage. Noriega understood this aspect of the U.S. policy process and made sure that the DEA was on his side.

Much more important, as a signal of U.S. approval and as a valuable ally for Noriega, were messages of support from CIA Director Casey and NSC staff aide Oliver North. These men, and others who used Noriega as an intelligence and operations asset, contributed to Noriega's conviction that he need not take "official" criticism seriously (Chapter 5).

Unity of Objectives, Disunity over Means

The characteristic that best depicts the U.S. decisionmaking process from 1987 to October 1989 is unity of objectives (Noriega must go) and disunity over means. Until legal indictments were well under way in late 1987, no bureaucratic actor, except the Department of State, had a vested interest in Noriega's removal that was strong enough to yield a serious commitment to that objective. Instead, given the security concerns discussed in Chapter 1, several organizational participants were predisposed to work with Noriega rather than agree that he was becoming a liability. The CIA, important parts of the Pentagon, the DEA, and the NSC gained tangible benefits from Noriega's remaining in power.

As negative press coverage accumulated and congressional pressure mounted, the administration felt pressure to do something. But none of the institutional players, except for Assistant Secretary of State Elliott Abrams, were predisposed to turn negative information into a case for an initiative to oust Noriega prior to 1987. Instead, although Noriega was heading for trouble, the situation was not serious enough to warrant his removal or a search for alternatives, and agencies allied with Noriega took the position that he could be redirected or reformed, and that he could be part of the solution.

During 1986 and 1987, the State Department's position in favor of stronger pressure and even the use of military action to remove Noriega was countered by two very strong arguments raised by the CIA and the Pentagon. The first concerned an alternative to Noriega. Who would run the military? Díaz Herrera, who was second in command until May 1987, was a logical alternative, but he had been portrayed to the United States by Noriega as a dangerous leftist and an unstable character. That option vanished in June 1987. The only acceptable alternative then seemed to be to wait for an unspecified and unknown "reformist element" in the PDF to come forward and act. Consequently, the United States signaled it had no quarrel with the PDF and encouraged a coup. Then, the March 1988 coup failed.

By the time an interagency consensus was achieved on reaching out to an officer the United States would prefer—Col. Herrera Hassan—Congress, with some prodding from dissidents in the executive branch, was predisposed to block the covert operation known as Panama 3. Interagency support for Panama 3 was thin and fragile. Press coverage of congressional opposition to the covert plan contained many leaks from the executive branch. Such bureaucratic conflicts were reinforced by personal disputes. One of the worst of these, a sharp disagreement between the chairman of the Joint Chiefs of Staff, Admiral Crowe, and Assistant Secretary Abrams, reached the pages of *The New York Times* (see Chapter 6).

Opposition from the Pentagon and the CIA to options involving military force advocated by the Department of State was also based on concern for military base rights worldwide and with ramifications in Panama if an operation failed and Noriega retaliated against the large U.S. community there. SOUTHCOM and the Pentagon consistently took the view that Noriega, if he chose to do so, could do much more damage to U.S. interests and personnel than the United States could do to him. The caveat to this position was that the option of using massive military force was off the table. Once the Bush administration decided to consider that option, and "cleared the decks" for action by removing as many U.S. citizens as possible, Noriega's relative damage advantage was substantially reduced.

Notes

1. My method of analysis combines policy process and cognitive variables and is informed by the work of Charles O. Jones, Richard C. Cottam, Michael Brenner, Charles F. Hermann, Glenn Paige, Robert J. Art, Richard Jervis, and Robert Axelrod. My approach to bargaining and negotiations is shaped by the work of William I. Zartmann and Robert Wendzel. My understanding of Panama policymaking also has been assisted by Anthony Lake's analysis of the Carter administration's policy toward Nicaragua (Lake, *Somoza Falling*).

2. Bert A. Rockman argues, for example, that during Reagan's second term, unlike the first, the White House was "devoid of mediators and brokers" (Rockman, "The Style and Organization of the Reagan Presidency," p. 25).

3. See, for example, Madison, "Passing the Torch," p. 1732. Frederick Kempe makes the strongest argument about Bush's staff influencing decisions on U.S. Panama policy in *Divorcing the Dictator*, pp. 335–340.

4. Dukakis said, for example, Bush has "been part of an administration which has given us this kind of thing, and it seems to me he's got to explain it. The best I can determine, he's defended our relationship with Noriega" (cited in an interview in "If New Taxes Needed," p. 1855).

5. Some commentators emphasized a desire to overcome a "wimp factor" as contributing to Bush's decision to invade Panama. Although the term was used frequently in the press prior to the invasion, I do not believe that label had much of an effect and prefer to consider charges of wimpishness and ineptness in

handling the October coup as part of a general feeling of frustration about Noriega's tenacity.

6. L. L. Farrar, Jr., applied the concept of "limited choice" in an analysis of multiple explanations for the outbreak of World War I. He argued, as I do here, that this factor operated in a setting in which system and decisionmaking dynamics also affected the use of force; at the most advanced stage of that crisis, as in Panama policy, the structure of the crisis situation reached a point that precluded a negotiated outcome or de-escalation. See Farrar, "The Limits of Choice."

7. Anthony Lake has documented similar obstacles in his analysis of U.S. Nicaragua policy during the Carter administration.

8. Noriega, "Psychological Operations," p. 6.

4

Three Men and Their Legacies

Three men played critical roles in Panama's recent history and politics: Dr. Arnulfo Arias Madrid, Gen. Omar Torrijos Herrera, and Gen. Manuel Antonio Noriega Moreno. All three were strong figures and developed reputations as authoritarian strongmen. Arias was an old-style *caudillo*; Torrijos and Noriega were military dictators. Each, in his own way, was macho and proud to be so.

Arias, Torrijos, and Noriega had uneven relations with the United States. Each was nationalistic and quarreled with the United States in the process of asserting Panama's demands for independence. Each man, even Arias, worked with the United States when it suited his own purpose. Torrijos and Noriega were, at times, close friends of the United States. In fact, the first half of the Noriega years, 1982–1986, was a period of close collaboration. Once the United States decided to sever its connections to Noriega, however, U.S.-Panamanian relations reached their lowest point in decades.

All three men, in different circumstances and in differing degrees, were at odds with the commercial elite that governed Panama, with only a few interruptions, from 1903 to 1968. Panama has not been as well known for its oligarchy as have El Salvador and Nicaragua. Nonetheless, Panama has had an identifiable and powerful commercial elite that has been dominated by a few upper-class families of Spanish descent. The men belonging to these families became politicians, diplomats, and professionals. Their prestigious club, the Union Club in Panama City, became a symbol of oligarchic power. Arias, Torrijos, and Noriega opposed their dominance and their conception of politics.

These three men were powerful at different times. Arias was primarily a man of the 1940s, although his political career continued for four more decades. Torrijos governed during the 1970s, and the 1980s were the Noriega years. Each left legacies that outlasted their tenure and that continue to shape Panamanian politics today.

49

Arnulfo Arias

Arias, called Fufo by friends and admirers, was born on August 15, 1901, two years before Panama's independence from Colombia. His early years coincided with those of the republic and its founding event, the 1903 Hay–Bunau-Varilla Panama Canal treaty. Arias earned an M.D. at Harvard University and practiced medicine in Panama, but he soon gravitated to politics. He and his brother, Harmodio Arias, were active in a middle-class, mestizo movement that opposed the power of the oligarchs and the United States in Panama. As president from 1931 to 1935, Harmodio Arias promoted government services for rural constituents and politicization of the middle class.

Arnulfo Arias also promoted these aims during his political career, although he pursued more extreme directions, which even his brother would not support.[1] Politically, Arnulfo was best known for opposing two foes: the United States and Panama's oligarchs. Much of Arias's life was devoted to the nationalist cause of renegotiating the 1903 Panama Canal treaty. Arias wanted to gain what the 1903 treaty had given away: Panama's effective sovereignty and control over its most precious resource, the canal and Canal Zone. His doctrine was *Panameñismo*: Panama for the Panamanians. In 1968, one of Arias's first actions as president was to demand negotiations leading to the immediate return of the Canal Zone to Panama. That achievement was not to be his legacy, however. Instead, Omar Torrijos, his rival and enemy, achieved the historic role of renegotiating the 1903 treaty.

Arnulfo Arias's legacy was domestic. His personalist leadership style made a lasting impact on the country. He dominated the strongest opposition group that existed from 1940 to 1988; in the process, he stifled the development of a new generation of leaders for that group and preempted the political space where other opposition groups might have mobilized. Concomitantly, his adversarial relations with the military undermined his ability to remain in power once he managed to win the presidency.

Arias and the Military

Arias has often been described as the grand old man of Panamanian politics, as a perennial presidential candidate, and as the opposition figure from 1940 to 1988. He won three presidential elections, in 1940, 1948, and 1968, but he never served a full term. He claimed to have also won in 1964, although the official result had him losing by more than 10,000 votes. According to some assessments at the time and more recent official acknowledgments, he also won in 1984, although that election was awarded to the military's candidate.

As the strongest opposition figure to challenge Panama's oligarchs during the 1940s and 1960s, Arias was able to win elections, but he was unable to govern successfully due to his inability to work with the oligarchs or the police, or to effectively subordinate either group to his will. His adversarial relations with the oligarchy and later with the National Guard repeatedly caused his premature departure from office. President Arias was first overthrown in 1941, when he was opposed by his cabinet, his brother, and the United States. The oligarchy denied his 1948 victory; he was removed from office by José Antonio Remón, the commander of the National Police. Remón reinstated Arias in 1949, only to oust him again in 1951. Arias's tenure as president was even shorter in 1968: he was overthrown by a colonel's coup on his eleventh day in office. Arias then fled into the Canal Zone and eventually into exile in the United States. He returned to Panama during the early 1980s to wage another campaign for the presidency. His victory in the 1984 election was denied by the military, who stole the election in favor of their own candidate. This marked the second time that Arias won the votes but not the election. Thus, he was overthrown or denied victory at least four times, usually due to his adverse relations with the military. When he died in August 1988, Arias was seriously considering running for president in the 1989 election. Despite his advanced age of eighty-seven years, Fufo Arias wanted to take another shot at Noriega's military regime.

Arias the Politician

Arnulfo Arias was a complex political leader who espoused different and sometimes opposite causes during his long career. His ardent nationalism incorporated extreme anti-U.S. and anti-Communist strains along with strong patriotism. Nonetheless, he offered on several occasions to work with the United States to renegotiate the 1903 treaty, arguing that he was the only Panamanian leader who could deliver Panama's side of the bargain. While in office during the 1940s, he espoused fascism and racism; he opposed and persecuted minorities, particularly English-speaking West Indians, whom he wanted to deport in order to purify Panama's racial structure. He was not just pro-Nazi in rhetoric; he organized Panamanian boys and girls into Clubs of Urraca, named after a local hero but modeled on Hitler's *Jugend*.[2] After the war, he took repressive measures, establishing a secret police and goon squads and closing down the press. Yet, Arias also took liberal positions, notably his support for women's suffrage, and he sought to represent mestizo campesinos and urban workers.[3]

An excerpt from Arias's 1940 inaugural speech provides a sample of the more authoritarian themes associated with his politics:

> The words democracy, liberty, liberalism, are so bandied about nowadays that they have no meaning. . . .
> The "demagogic concept" that all men are free and equal is biologically without foundation.

> Panama should give "opportunity to every citizen in accordance
> with his merits, his patriotism, his moral and physical worth, and his
> capacity for work."
>   The concept of liberty as an inalienable and unlimited right of the
> individual must give way to the more modern concept of liberty
> conditioned by the social exigencies of the community.
>   The concept of individual property must likewise yield to the more
> modern and advanced concept which assigns to property a social
> function.
>   The family must likewise be subject to regulation in order that it
> may co-operate efficiently with the state in the education of the child.[4]

These sentiments, and his stridently anti-U.S. views made Arias unlikely to
gain U.S. support. When Arias was overthrown in 1941, U.S. officials
welcomed, and probably encouraged, his removal. Although Arias maintained
ties with some U.S. politicians, no postwar administration ever preferred him
to a sitting government, whether it was civilian or military.

Changes in the National Guard

As Arias's career progressed, his opposition to the military increased, partly
because the military became a different and stronger institution. Steve Ropp
characterized the military of Arias's early political years, from the 1920s to
the 1950s, as having an "outlook that perhaps bore closer resemblance to that
of the Chicago police than to other Latin American armies."[5] That police
force was transformed and expanded by President Remón during the mid-
1950s, in order to create a National Guard that would be his own power base.
Remón further developed the Guard during his presidency.

   During the years leading up to Arias's 1968 campaign, a young Omar
Torrijos and several like-minded officers advocated changes in the National
Guard. These included several colonels who would play leadership roles
during the 1980s: Florencio Flórez, Rubén Paredes, Roberto Díaz Herrera,
and Manuel Antonio Noriega. They, like many officers throughout the
hemisphere, supported a national security doctrine that incorporated economic
development and civic action as military functions. These objectives clearly
conflicted with Arias's plans for the Guard and its reformist colonels. The
National Guard that Arias faced in 1968 was also a more programmatic
opponent than the National Police of the 1940s. The officers associated with
the revolution of 1968 articulated a view of Panama's domestic conditions
and prospects.[6] They also were pragmatic, recognizing that Arias's
inauguration meant that they were going to be removed from power. Lt. Col.
Omar Torrijos and Maj. Boris Martínez led a coup d'état on October 11,
1968. Arias fled into the Canal Zone and later took up residence as an exile
in the United States.[7]

   Under Torrijos, the Guard was further transformed into an institution
with a domestic mission and distinct constituencies. Between 1968 and 1981,

the year Torrijos died, the military was transformed into a more complex organization, oriented toward civic action and service delivery. Thus, Panama's National Guard became multifaceted: a police force plus a newer, more effective and professional army, with a stronger sense than the police of its institutional interest and national development mission. Concurrently, an undetermined number of officers established networks for receiving "bonus" payments through a variety of legal and illegal activities, originally including arms and liquor smuggling and prostitution, and later expanding into drug trafficking and money laundering. These activities, and numerous government contracts and businesses under government control, connected additional "constituents" to the National Guard. Traffic in contraband was by no means new to the isthmus. During the 1970s, these networks were institutionalized under one man's control, first under Torrijos and even more so under Noriega.

When Arias campaigned for the presidency in 1984, he faced an even stronger military adversary. A renamed Guard—the Defense Forces of the Republic of Panama—had become the government under the command of Gen. Manuel Antonio Noriega. Earlier, Torrijos had created a political party, the Democratic Revolutionary party, to institutionalize the Guard's political base and to support and control candidates who would participate in the "civilianization" process. The PDF selected Nicolás Ardito Barletta for the PRD to sponsor in 1984, and Noriega was so determined to maintain the regime with minimal civilian disruption that he orchestrated massive fraud in order for Barletta to win. But despite its many connections and beneficiaries, the PDF could not deliver enough votes on election day. It took ten days of manipulation of the electoral count to deny Arias the 1984 election.

Arias and the Opposition

As the military became increasingly entrenched, beginning in the 1950s and accelerating after 1968, opposition to the regime centered on Arnulfo Arias. He built his own political party, the Authentic Panameñista party, but this personalist organization did not incorporate additional opposition groups. Instead, several other, weaker political parties developed: the Christian Democratic party; the National Liberal party; and MOLIRENA, the National Liberal Republican Movement. The Christian Democrats, established in 1964 to contest that election, developed a distinct program, but the party was relatively small and relegated to a distant, secondary role as long as Arias was alive. The Liberals were a stronger, older political party, but they were often factionalized.

This was Arnulfo Arias's political legacy: as long as he lived, *he* was the one national figure who could amass enough votes to contest an election against the military. Although Arias never held power more than two years, he dominated Panamanian politics for more than fifty years.

Fufo Arias was an incredible campaigner. Wearing distinctive white suits, sunglasses, and a beret, he could mesmerize crowds with his anti-U.S., anti-military, strongly nationalistic rhetoric. Even though Arias was eighty-two years old during his 1984 campaign, he drew large, enthusiastic crowds, especially among the poor. A report at the time asserted that "his presence at the head of the ticket is alone worth 200,000 votes (out of a total of perhaps 700,000)."[8] In 1988, when an opposition coalition was forming, Arias continued to campaign. By then, he was frail, almost blind, and barely audible, but his presence at an opposition rally was guaranteed to boost attendance.

However, Arias's larger-than-life presence filled the political landscape and stifled the development of the next generation of leaders. He did not deny them space—he did not have that power—but his presence, the Fufo legend, his contacts, and his popularity so dominated the political scene that other leaders seemed to be weaker men, relegated to the background. His very existence limited their potential.

Omar Torrijos

Opposition to the military regime during the 1970s was deliberately stifled by Torrijos. General Torrijos considered political parties to be tools of the oligarchs, and he therefore banned them. He denied his critics the only event that could galvanize an effective opposition, namely elections, for sixteen years. With their organizations banned, the press stifled, and elections denied, opposition leaders and parties went into a holding pattern. By 1984, when the military was ready to allow parties and elections, politics was dominated by a new strongman: Gen. Manuel Antonio Noriega.

The Torrijos Years

The 1970s were the Torrijos years.[9] Omar Torrijos had played a secondary role in the military coup that ousted President Arias. He soon became a central figure in the military junta, eliminated his rivals, and withstood a coup attempt in 1969 with handy assistance from Colonel Noriega. The United States initially distanced itself from Torrijos, but by the time of the coup attempt the Nixon administration was ready to collaborate and cooperate with Torrijos. Once solidly in control, Torrijos had the National Assembly grant him extraordinary powers to serve, until October 1978, as maximum leader of the revolution (this was the same title that Noriega bestowed upon himself just prior to the U.S. invasion). A constitution that institutionalized the 1968 revolution was passed in 1972. Article II specified that the civilian government was to act in "harmonious collaboration" with the military, creating a legal basis for the Guard's continuing involvement in politics. Despite civilianization plans that Torrijos announced in 1978, the military remained in control throughout his tenure, from 1969 until his death on July 31, 1981. Torrijos's years in power spanned a period longer than that served by any elected president in Panama's history.

Democratization and Demilitarization

In 1978, Torrijos initiated plans for civilization to democratize and demilitarize the regime. Constitutional amendments to provide for a transition from military to civilian rule were passed that year, and a six-year civilization schedule was set. Local representatives were to constitute a national assembly that would legislate and prepare for election of a national legislative council in 1980. Between 1980 and 1984, this council would formulate new national election laws and implement preparations. National elections would be held in May 1984, followed by elections for mayors and municipal authorities in June.

These plans for democratization benefited Torrijos's image among U.S. senators visiting Panama during early 1978 as they considered how to vote on the pending Panama Canal treaties. Progress in civilization undercut the argument made by treaty opponents that the United States could not "hand over" the canal to a military dictatorship. In this context, Torrijos pledged to President Jimmy Carter that he would restore democracy to Panama. Similarly, Torrijos wrote a letter to Senate Majority Leader Robert Byrd in which he described repeal of penal decrees and restoration of constitutional guarantees for public activity. Torrijos added, "I am keeping my word. Please transmit this to your colleagues in whom I have full confidence."[10] Soon, exiles, including Arnulfo Arias, began returning to Panama.

Torrijos carried out his own withdrawal from office and formal power. He supported the selection of a civilian president, Aristides Royo, and relinquished his extraordinary powers as maximum leader, as scheduled, in October 1978. Royo and his vice-president, Ricardo de la Espriella, were elected indirectly, by the National Council, to serve from 1978 to 1984.

The opposition gained access to media, with radio stations being more accessible than print or television. A daily tabloid, *Ya*, began publishing in July 1979, and the major daily, *La Prensa*, first was published on August 10, 1980.[11] Criticism about restrictions on the press persisted, however. At one point Torrijos complained to visiting journalists, "so many United States leaders seem to know more about Panamanian newsmen than Panamanian newsmen do." But, he continued, "Panamanians do not use newspapers for opposition, we use the *radio*, and there are over *fifty* radio stations in Panama. *The government has only one!*"[12]

Parties were reactivated, in no small part because Torrijos planned to create a new party to represent the military, its interests and constituencies. This party, the PRD, was the first one to garner the 30,000 signatures required to be legally registered. Arias reactivated and registered his Panameñista party, but refrained from contesting the 1980 election. About 60 percent of the eligible voters turned out to vote. The PRD campaigned for all nineteen elected seats on the National Legislative Council and won ten. Christian Democratic party candidates won two seats, and the Liberals won five. Two independent (nonparty) candidates also won seats. Thus, in its first electoral test, the PRD won a majority.

International observers from the United States and neighboring states found long delays at some *mesas* (vote tables) and some instances of voters not being registered where they thought they were. Overall, however, the observers judged the 1980 election to be relatively free and fair. The official U.S. assessment drew this conclusion:

> The election demonstrated the government's willingness to accept public criticism and its ability to run limited, open and fair elections. Government-regulated facilities (radio, TV and press, as well as some transportation) were provided for all candidates and the campaign, with minor exceptions, was free from repression or interference.[13]

Other sources did not make such rosy assessments, especially because the main opposition party and its leader—the Panameñistas and Arnulfo Arias—refused to participate.

Many changes broadening political activity were significant, but several fundamental barriers to free expression remained in force from 1978 throughout the 1980s. These had a negative, chilling effect on the opposition. The 1972 constitution guaranteed freedom of speech and the press, but laws prohibited and punished actions damaging a person's reputation, the security of society, public security, and public order.[14] Similarly, the right of peaceful assembly (without arms and for a legitimate purpose) was limited: demonstrations could legally be prevented or halted if they interfered with traffic, threatened public order, or violated the rights of third parties.[15]

The opposition felt constrained by the regime, but political activity endorsed by the government did not materialize as planned. The PRD faltered and failed to meet Torrijos's aims. Richard Millett characterized the PRD as "an opportunistic, corrupt body covering a wide range of ideologies but incapable of mustering majority support and increasingly dependent on the military for access to power and government positions."[16] Neither pro- nor antigovernment forces developed much political strength.

Between 1980 and 1984, the civilianization process appeared increasingly likely to yield "elections without surprises"[17] designed to legalize military rule through a dominant military party and a facade of representative democracy.

Torrijos left two legacies: (1) new Panama Canal treaties and (2) *Torrijismo*, a military dictatorship with a populist, leftist approach to politics that adamantly opposed the oligarchy and embraced the poor, rural sectors, workers, and students. For many years, the latter so defined Torrijos's image as a feisty but pragmatic Latin soldier-diplomat, that the dictatorial side of his tenure was ignored by U.S. policymakers and in the U.S. press.

New Panama Canal Treaties

That the 1978 Panama Canal treaty and the Treaty Concerning the Permanent Neutrality of the Panama Canal were achievements of the first order cannot be denied. From a historical perspective, and as a case of bargaining and conflict resolution through diplomacy, the 1978 treaties marked significant changes in U.S.-Panamanian relations and the future of the Panama Canal. Presidents Johnson, Nixon, Ford, and Carter advocated those negotiations throughout fourteen difficult years. Torrijos and these U.S. presidents, particularly Jimmy Carter, exerted considerable effort and suffered substantial political costs to achieve new treaties.[18] Torrijos's role in pushing the negotiations to a successful conclusion will guarantee him a prominent place in history. Nonetheless, the treaties were not considered perfect, either in the United States or Panama. In the process of "selling" the treaties during ratification processes in both countries, accuracy about treaty provisions, Torrijos and his government, and long-term U.S. intentions took second place to the sales job both governments felt pressed to perform.

Torrijos's Domestic Legacy

Almost a decade after his death, a balanced assessment of the Torrijos years is still difficult to achieve. What is increasingly apparent, however, is that Torrijos's domestic legacy is mixed. He extended government benefits and representation to previously excluded sectors; this is the positive legacy of the revolution of 1968. At the same time, he quashed traditional civilian political activity and expanded the power and functions of the National Guard. In addition to making the Guard more powerful, Torrijos also set in motion the pattern of corruption and abuse of civil rights that Noriega later accelerated. Although Torrijos advocated demilitarization in 1978, his civilianization schedule was slowed and finally derailed entirely by Noriega.

The programmatic thrust of the Torrijos revolution was to redistribute economic and political power to those sectors neglected by the oligarchs: labor involved in traditional canal-related commerce, workers in new agroindustries, peasants, and a growing number of government workers.[19] Many new programs were initiated: significant investment at all levels of education and health care; construction of roads; and passage of a labor code, agrarian reform, price and rent controls, and export quotas. To create jobs, Torrijos expanded the public sector, making the government the country's largest employer. By 1986, government workers numbered 160,000 in a country of some 2,100,000 people. Counting family members as well, journalist Adelaide Eisenmann estimated that some 750,000 Panamanians came to depend for their livelihood on government jobs.[20]

Expansion of the public sector was financed through borrowing, a strategy that gave Panama the highest per capita foreign debt in the hemisphere. Although this strategy could be sustained for a while, the dire consequences of deficit spending and international borrowing contributed in 1985 to the demise of the first president elected since the military took power in 1968.

Although Torrijos redirected the domestic agenda and thereby raised living standards for previously unserved citizens, he also established a securely based, long-lived military dictatorship. He forced many opponents into silence or exile; others reached an accommodation with the military regime, separating their business activity from political concerns.

After almost a decade of military rule, the U.S. government described the situation in Panama in 1977 this way:

—The Torrijos Government is basically authoritarian—it *can* legally abridge many rights (even it if normally *chooses* not to), and it *can* act extra-legally without significant independent oversight from within its own system (even if it normally shies away from this except under extreme provocation). This capability is itself a significant repressive factor.
—While not common, abuse of authority does exist, particularly by lower-level police. When it occurs, the system often seeks to ignore it, or cover it up.
—Exile for political reasons is used by the Government even if other forms of political repression are rare.[21]

Concerning exiles, professor and journalist Miguel Antonio Bernal estimated that some 300 Panamanians went into exile during the Torrijos-Noriega years.[22] Thus, along with expanded services for many, the Torrijos revolution also brought repression and authoritarian rule. For this reason, Torrijism has aptly been characterized as "spending freely while carrying a big stick."[23]

The power of the National Guard increased during the Torrijos years; concomitantly, so did corruption. Many officers became involved in legal and illegal businesses to supplement their incomes, and as the years passed the military became increasingly dependent on such business connections. One reporter asserted that by 1985 the military had become "an unshakable parasite" devouring Panamanian society.[24]

Ropp considered the transformation of the National Guard to be one of Torrijos's most significant legacies.[25] Torrijos himself realized that the role of the Guard must change. An integral part of his civilianization plan, therefore, was a progressive reduction in the role and influence of the military in politics. The 1984 election was supposed to constitute a dual challenge:

for civilians to move into the political arena and for the military to pull back from its hegemonic position. As in other Latin American countries, in Panama "return to the barracks" did not mean a complete withdrawal from politics. Instead, Torrijos's plan envisioned two changes: moving from direct to indirect military governance through the PRD and significantly reducing top officers' daily involvement in politics.

How far Torrijos actually would have taken the demilitarization process will never be known. Torrijos unexpectedly died in an airplane crash late on the night of July 31, 1981. Some sources claim that the weather was bad that night and that the pilot was inexperienced; others deny this version. Rumors persist that the crash was not accidental. In 1987, when Col. Roberto Díaz Herrera turned against Noriega, he accused Noriega of staging the crash to kill Torrijos. In 1990, the well-known investigative reporter, Seymour Hersh, found sufficient evidence for him to assert that Noriega was responsible. Hersh reported that a remote-controlled bomb was used to blow up Torrijos's plane. Hersh asserted that this was the same sort of device that Noriega was suspected of using to bomb the plane of the president of Ecuador earlier in the year. A U.S. official who participated in an investigation of the incidents emphatically told Hersh, "Noriega knocked off Torrijos. He pulled the equivalent of a major coup."[26] The record about these episodes remains incomplete.

When Torrijos died, he left no designated successor or transition plan for the military. It had been rumored that in 1980, in conjunction with the anniversary of the 1968 coup, Torrijos was ready to step down, and that "paperwork for the change . . . reportedly has already been initiated" to promote Col. Florencio Flórez.[27] Torrijos may have been facing resistance to civilianization, which he successfully assuaged; he may have been bluffing or he may have reconsidered. Whatever his reasons, Torrijos did not step down, and as a result his unexpected death was followed by a period of jockeying for power. Flórez, the most senior officer, emerged as the successor and commander of the National Guard. The Torrijos years came to an abrupt, unfulfilled end.

Torrijos and Noriega

Torrijos and Noriega are often compared. Both built careers in the military that allowed them the power, wealth, and prestige they would never otherwise have obtained. Both were very ambitious. Torrijos seemed able to gain enough of what he valued; Noriega seemed driven to acquire more and more. Both loved the military institution and had great contempt for civilian politicians; both disparaged civilians' abilities and motives for governing. Both lost touch during their last years in office, proving themselves unable to govern, with Noriega's excesses causing the demise of the military regime.

After stepping down in 1978, Torrijos continued to wield considerable influence, but during 1980 and 1981 he became increasingly withdrawn and dispirited. Perhaps the aftermath of successful treaty negotiations could not sustain his interest; perhaps his civilianization process was too fractious or failed to capture his attention to the extent the negotiations had. For reasons that remain unclear, Torrijos became progressively more disengaged from matters affecting the government and the Guard. As a result, the democratization process began to languish even before Torrijos's death.

Noriega also proved unable to govern Panama. Noriega gained and consolidated power, expanded the military, and survived repeated U.S. attempts to remove him from office. Noriega's excesses, however, caused the demise of the PDF. During 1988 and 1989, Noriega became increasingly consumed with his confrontation with the United States. When he appeared to lose touch with reality and lose control of the PDF, the United States intervened.

As a leader, Torrijos was often described as disorganized, taking ad hoc initiatives, and being irritated by detail. He was further described as emotional, as a romantic, and as a man who perceived himself as the defender of the people. Noriega was more organizationally inclined, keen on detail, and immensely interested in tactics and psychological warfare. His power and potential were succinctly summarized, with considerable foresight, in a 1974 U.S. military intelligence report:

> Subject's [Noriega's] leadership qualities, though effective, are limited to sheer force and weight of position. Subject has a strong will for power, and will exercise the power necessary to gain his objectives. Despite his rank, Subject is for all practical purposes, the number two man in the country, and as such, his influence is second only to TORRIJOS.[28]

This report aptly characterized Noriega's leadership style and also implied the problem that would plague his last years as commander: Noriega became a power addict. Once he acquired overwhelming power, he sought still more, along with opportunities to exercise his power. His last few years and months in office were a series of power contests; he played most of these with consummate skill, except for the final episode that triggered the U.S. invasion.

Neither Torrijos nor Noriega was ideological; neither perceived the world in East-West terms. Both were strongly patriotic, nationalistic, and more concerned with maximizing Panama's options and asserting its sovereignty and dignity than with Marxism or anticommunism. Torrijos often said he was neither with the Left nor with the Right. Nonetheless, he had programmatic interests. Noriega had a different agenda, coming to power after the revolution was already in place. In addition to occupying a different place in the revolutionary cycle, Noriega was more concerned with using the system for maximum personal gain. Torrijos also used the system for personal gain, and both men were rumored to take a "share" or "percentage" of legal and illegal business activities, but Noriega's tenure lacked the programmatic element that gave Torrijos's record more balance.

Former U.S. Ambassador Jack Vaughn described Torrijos as "a consummate politician. He was very shrewd politically. In terms of all different elements of his constituency, he would be the world's greatest charmer, he could be conciliatory, he could be a man of seemingly big vision, and he could be very cold blooded."[29] Noriega, Vaughn said, "lacks a lot of the suave, sophisticated moves. He's much better in the smoke filled room with pistols on both hips. He is one tough hombre and not a very good politician. You don't have any doubt about where he is—just look in those eyes of his."[30] Vaughn's characterizations were made in 1986, just after an investigative report appeared detailing much of what we now know about Noriega. Vaughn's comments were critical, but they did not "demonize" Noriega or Torrijos. Some post-invasion coverage so focused on the "sleaze factor" that even journalists have complained. Recent studies are seeking to assess both military strongmen and their legacies in Panama, but an adequately balanced assessment may not be possible for many years.[31]

Journalist James LeMoyne characterized both men in 1985. Noriega, he said, "lacks the popular touch and appears to be more feared than respected." Torrijos, on the other hand, combined "a unique blend of military authoritarianism with a populist conscience"; he "seized power . . . and manipulated it better than almost any other Latin American political leader."[32] Such characterizations anger Panamanian oppositionists, many of whom feel that the U.S. press and government deliberately covered up Torrijos's repressive and corrupt activities. Guillermo Cochez, a Christian Democratic party legislator, wrote that Torrijos was "just as authoritarian—and, his foes assert, just as corrupt" as Noriega, but that President Carter "tolerated his indiscretions" and allowed the CIA to work with him "every bit as much" as the Reagan administration worked with Noriega.[33]

A U.S. diplomat who served in the region was adamant on this point: Torrijos was every bit as bad a character as Noriega; the difference was that he got better press and was in power at a time when the United States was interested in having him look as good as possible.[34] Similarly, a U.S. embassy officer who served in Panama characterized U.S. policy as a "passingly useful white-washing of Torrijos" who, he asserted, would have been targeted by the Carter administration had the new Panama Canal treaties not been a higher priority.[35] Members of Congress who opposed the canal treaties tried to raise these issues without success during 1978; congressional investigations during 1986–1989 of human rights violations and drug trafficking charges were more effective (see Chapter 6). After the December 1989 invasion, U.S. media substantiated accusations that charges against

Torrijos and Noriega were covered up during the Nixon, Ford, Carter, and Reagan administrations.[36]

Manuel Antonio Noriega

If assessments of Torrijos are still marred by the gloss of the 1978 treaty ratification campaign, assessments of Noriega are even more flawed by affective invective, spin control, media hype, and lurid curiosity. As Carla Robbins recently said, "I've met Noriega, and I'm willing to believe almost anything about him. *Almost* anything."[37] Not everything, however, that has been suggested since the invasion bears up under close scrutiny.

Noriega's background was much more disadvantaged than that of Arias or Torrijos. Noriega grew up a child of poverty on Panama's tough streets.[38] There he developed a style of maneuvering others and selling information that became his trademark. A student who attended the same high school later recalled Noriega's role as class "snitch." The main offense against school rules committed by boys at that time was to smoke cigarettes. Noriega never went on escapades with the other boys, and he never got reprimanded, but whenever one of the other boys did, they suspected Noriega of being the informer.[39] Noriega cultivated this role as snitch, or intelligence asset, with several U.S. agencies and several rival governments. He was not embarrassed or shy about this role. "*Sapo*" is slang for "snitch"; Noriega kept and displayed a large collection of *sapo* figurines.

Early in his career, Noriega got into trouble for losing control in outbursts of violence and for his abusive and humiliating treatment of prisoners, particularly Arnulfistas. Much of Noriega's reputation for cruelty was earned, but part of Noriega's negative image was deliberately fostered. As head of G-2, the Guard's intelligence division, Noriega found it useful to cultivate the popular image of being the regime's "enforcer." A U.S. intelligence report written in 1986 described this tactic: "Noriega deliberately cultivated the image of a man of intrigue and sinister deeds."[40] Later, as commander of the PDF, and while he contemplated running for president, Noriega tried to erase this image.

Noriega's Legacy

Only a preliminary assessment of Noriega's legacy can be offered today. One theme that will probably stand the test of time concerns opportunities lost, for institutional transformation and economic growth, during the Noriega years. Instead, the country and society were derailed by Noriega's struggle for power at the expense of social, political, and economic development. Another legacy concerns the cost of the U.S. invasion to Panama, physically and financially in the short term, and in damage to Panamanian political culture and national identity in the long term.

Initially, Noriega had tried to create a different legacy. He tried to emulate Torrijos, to present himself as Torrijos's successor, and to gain legitimacy through associations with the 1968 revolution. Noriega's speeches, particularly prior to 1988, contained numerous references to the revolution and *Torrijismo*. The following example illustrates Noriega's efforts and also the surrealistic quality that characterized Noriega's self-promotion.

Torrijos, in his day, had staged elaborate, spectacular celebrations to mobilize and demonstrate his popular support, and to set some traditions for his regime. Noriega devoted considerable effort and $3,000,000 to duplicate such an event on August 12, 1986, the third anniversary of his taking command.[41] Noriega donned the symbols of peace and protest: he appeared attired in white civilian dress, calling himself the "General of Peace," and had flocks of doves released during a military parade. Meanwhile, troops from Battalion 2000, one of the crack units created to defend the canal, appeared in procession in full combat gear at the Cinco de Mayo Plaza. Buses had transported people from outlying provinces, totally disrupting bus service in Panama City, but bringing thousands of attendees. To boost attendance, bus and taxi drivers were given gasoline and "forgiveness" of traffic tickets; at the rally, plenty of free food, liquor, and music were provided; T-shirts and caps were given away.

But all these enticements drew only about 100,000 people, not the 400,000 the government claimed. Reports from the U.S. embassy cataloged reactions: "[excised] said that not even those on the stand—including President Delvalle, seemed to pay attention to, or refrain from talking to each other, during General Noriega's speech." Noriega and Delvalle both made "highly nationalistic" speeches "defensive" of the PDF, but according to another observer there was an "almost complete lack of enthusiasm or even polite interest in the words of the only two speech makers."

This account illustrates several of Noriega's dilemmas. He inherited Torrijos's system, but not his leadership style, motives, or allies. Even if Noriega had been more like Torrijos, that system itself was flawed and headed for financial and political trouble. Noriega managed to acquire power at a moment when the system was scheduled for reform, but in a direction he did not want to take. The August rally was an attempt by Noriega to generate popular appreciation for and loyalty to himself and the PDF. U.S. analysts drew this conclusion:

> Quite apparently, General Noriega and his immediate subordinates feel that they will not be able to dismount from the tiger, i.e., turn over political power to a civilian government in the near future. Unlike General Torrijos, General Noriega is believed to have presidential ambitions. How to reconcile his presidential ambitions with the FDP's

[PDF's] intention to retain the real power seems to be one of the
principal dilemmas Noriega faces.[42]

Much of the Noriega years were devoted to managing this dilemma, first
through eliminating rivals in the PDF and changing that institution, then
through civilian presidents behind whom he continued to control the regime.
When officers turned against him and staged two attempted coups, Noriega
responded with purges and consolidated power over the PDF in his own
hands.

A U.S. Legacy?

Panamanians often accuse the United States of creating, endorsing, and
maintaining Torrijos and Noriega in power. More accurate would be an
accusation of turning a blind eye to militarism and human rights abuses in
Panama, looking the other way when evidence of trafficking in drugs and
arms surfaced, and ignoring suppression of civic and political freedoms. The
United States did not create Torrijos, Noriega, or the Panamanian military,
although the United States was responsible for expanding the National Guard.
During the 1950s, U.S. concern with containing communism coincided with
President Remón's aim of transforming the National Police into a more
powerful organization. The United States encouraged and funded that
transformation during the 1950s and 1960s.[43] Beginning in 1968, successive
U.S. administrations, led by Democrat and Republican presidents, worked
with the military regime and accepted the favors Torrijos and Noriega
provided. The United States did little to prevent Torrijos and Noriega from
consolidating their power, and did not consider military dictatorship a
significant problem until late in the 1980s. The Noriega years are a decade of
increasingly close and then increasingly hostile U.S. relations with Panama's
military regime.

Notes

1. A brief character sketch such as this cannot contain a full account of
these events. Ropp, *Panamanian Politics*; and LaFeber, *The Panama Canal*, chaps.
3 and 4. For a Panamanian source that treats Arias's early years, see Linares,
Enrique Linares en la Historia Política chaps. 21 and 22. Jorge Conte-Porras
covers Arias's career through the 1984 election in *Requiem por la Revolución*.
2. John Gunther, *Inside Latin America*, p. 149.
3. Ropp, *Panamanian Politics*, pp. 21–24.
4. Quoted in Gunther, *Inside Latin America*, p. 148. Conte-Porras, *Requiem
por la Revolución*, pp. 524–533, provides the full text, "Discurso Inaugural."
5. Ropp, "Panama," p. 131.
6. Ropp correctly points out that the National Guard at this point did not
have a unified ideology, and that its officers did not comprise a single political
group (Ropp, "Panama," p. 132).

7. Former Ambassador William Jorden provides a lively and detailed account of these events, and of Torrijos's ascendancy, in his *Panama Odyssey*, chapter 6.

8. U.S. Department of State, Confidential Panama 00816, pp. 1–2.

9. LaFeber (*The Panama Canal*) and Jorden (*Panama Odyssey*) provide detailed descriptions and analyses of these years; Jorden's personal recollections and interviews provide a valuable portrait of Torrijos. Graham Greene provides a character sketch from Torrijos's later years in *Getting to Know the General*. Two Panamanian views are provided by José de Jesús Martínez in *Mi General Torrijos* and Juan Materno Vasquez in *Omar Torrijos*. A U.S. novelist and journalist, R. M. Koster, and the Panamanian columnist Guillermo Sánchez, have collaborated on a treatment of both Torrijos and Noriega (Koster and Sánchez, *In the Time of the Tyrants*).

10. "Letter from General Torrijos (Translation)" Appendix 11, in U.S. Congress, *Report of the Senatorial Delegation*, p. 10.

11. U.S. Congress, *Country Reports*, 1981, p. 503.

12. Quoted in Peters, "Panama's Genial Despot," p. 68.

13. U.S. Congress, *Country Reports*, 1981, p. 506. This is also the source for the turnout figure, election results, and the assessment of international observers.

14. Ibid., p. 503.

15. Ibid., p. 504. The constitution also required a twenty-four–hour notice prior to demonstrations.

16. Millett, "Looking Beyond Noriega," p. 49.

17. The phrase comes form Rouquie, "Demilitarization and Institutionalization," p. 465.

18. See Jorden, *Panama Odyssey*; LaFeber, *The Panama Canal*; Furlong and Scranton, *The Dynamics of Foreign Policymaking*; and Scranton, "Changing United States Foreign Policy."

19. Steve C. Ropp provides a thorough analysis of constituencies and coalitions during the Torrijos years in *Panamanian Politics*, chaps. 4 and 5. See also Millett, "Government and Politics," especially pp. 192–201, for a recent assessment. For a study of the early Torrijos years, see Priestley, *Military Government and Popular Participation in Panama*.

20. U.S. Congress, *Human Rights and Political Developments*, p. 77.

21. U.S. Department of State, "Fact Sheet: Torrijos' Government and Human Rights," p. 2.

22. Bernal, "Panama: A Prescription for Progress," p. 26.

23. James LeMoyne, "The Opposition Takes Cover in Panama," *The New York Times*, October 13, 1985.

24. Ibid.

25. Ropp, "General Noriega's Panama," p. 421; see also Ropp, "National Security," especially pp. 220–224.

26. Hersh, "The Creation of a Thug," pp. 88, 90.

27. U.S. Department of Defense, Confidential [number excised], "Weekly Intelligence Summary for 11–17, October 1968," October 17, 1980. Apparently the issue of replacing Torrijos with Flórez at this time concerned reversing a leftward drift epitomized by the government's electoral reform, a direction that Colonel Paredes, in particular, was reported to oppose.

28. U.S. Department of Defense, "Biographic Information on LTC Manuel Antonio NORIEGA Morena," p. 2.

29. Testimony in U.S. Congress, *Human Rights and Political Developments*, p. 76.

30. Ibid.

31. Koster and Sánchez's *In the Time of the Tyrants* is significant in this regard, both for the assessment that an activist journalist like Sánchez-Borbon can provide, and for presenting the consensus view, held roughly one year after the invasion, by a significant element in Panama's attentive public. The authors are known, however, for occasionally sensationalist and acerbic commentary.

32. LeMoyne, "Opposition Takes Cover."

33. Guillermo Cochez, "Can Noriega Still Play His Marxist Card?" *Wall Street Journal*, February 12, 1988, p. 13.

34. Confidential interview, Little Rock, Arkansas, February 1990.

35. Miller, "Panama and U.S. Policy," p. 130.

36. "The Noriega Connection," Frontline Report, aired on PBS, January 30, 1990.

37. Robbins, "Growing Pains in Panama," p. 29.

38. Two recent accounts provide very detailed treatments of Noriega's background and early and formative years: Dinges, *Our Man in Panama*, chap. 2; and Kempe, *Divorcing the Dictator*, chaps. 3–5.

39. Confidential interview, Little Rock, Arkansas, April 1990.

40. U.S. Department of Defense, Confidential [excised], "193rd Infantry Brigade (Panama) Weekly Intelligence Summary for MR 31-86 [7–13 Aug 86]," August 15, 1986, p. 2.

41. See ibid., pp. 1–3, for the following account.

42. Ibid., p. 3.

43. See Ropp, "National Security," p. 221; Ropp provides a more extensive treatment of this process in his *Panamanian Politics*.

5

Live and Let Live:
Play Ball with Noriega

Between 1980 and 1986, the United States was willing, if not content, to live with the military regimes of General Omar Torrijos and General Manuel Antonio Noriega. The United States had reached an accommodation with military rule in Panama early in the Torrijos years.[1] The Nixon, Ford, and Carter administrations worked with the Torrijos regime to achieve new Panama Canal treaties. Collaborative relations continued after Torrijos's death, and U.S. policy can be characterized as a "play ball" strategy, in which the United States maintained working relations with a military regime that became increasingly entrenched. The Reagan administration pursued strategic objectives in the region while minimizing the flaws of Panama's military regime. Officials mentioned democratization in Panama as a goal of U.S. policy, but this objective took a distant second place to U.S. security concerns.

The Military Succession

The death of General Torrijos left the officer corps of the National Guard temporarily in disarray during the summer of 1981. Four colonels soon developed a powersharing agreement to provide for the long-term interests and stability of the Guard and, needless to say, their own careers. "*Secreto Plan Torrijos: Cronograma-Compromiso Historico de la Guardia Nacional*" (Secret Plan Torrijos: The National Guards's Historic Compromise Timetable) was signed on March 8, 1982. Rubén Dario Paredes would take the first turn as general, replacing Florencio Flórez as commander-in-chief; then Paredes would retire in 1983 to run for president, with the Guard's backing, in 1984. Colonel Armando Contreras was to command from 1983 to 1984, and then Noriega was to take his turn, serving from 1984 until July 31, 1987. Finally, Colonel Roberto Díaz Herrera would command the Guard until July 31, 1988.[2] The 1989 presidential election was not mentioned in the document, but the prevailing expectation was that one of the Guard commanders would run for office to succeed Paredes.

Thus, at the beginning of 1983 a post-Torrijos transition was under way. The military institution appeared cohesive, but many observers expressed doubts about the future. These focused on Noriega, who was known to be powerful and power-hungry, but who had not yet made his intentions clear. Noriega was described by a reporter in November 1982 as "the biggest question mark in Panama's political future."[3] During 1983, it became apparent that Noriega had his own plan, along with ample ambition to carry it out.

First, Noriega ousted General Flórez, moving "swiftly, surprisingly, and efficiently" to remove him from office on March 3, 1982.[4] When asked why this sudden change of leadership occurred, Noriega's immediate reply revealed his motive: Flórez, he said, "did not have the capacity to be the commandant and was not listening to me." Realizing his blunder, Noriega quickly corrected himself, saying that he meant that Flórez "was not listening to the GN [Guardia Nacional] staff." When pressed further about the timing of Flórez's ouster, Noriega replied, "You are familiar with the principle of war called surprise." The United States concluded that Noriega had made a deliberate and calculated move against Flórez.

Noriega was not acting alone, however. U.S. military analysts reported that Contreras, Díaz Herrera, and Paredes also agreed that Flórez should go.[5] Each then took his turn moving up the hierarchy. Contreras retired on December 12, 1982. Paredes took over and was given the rank of general after just seven weeks in office as commandant. Noriega was promoted to chief of staff; Díaz Herrera was promoted to deputy chief of staff and head of G-2 (intelligence), the position Noriega vacated.

In assessing these events, the U.S. 470th Military Intelligence Group concluded that Flórez's ouster and the resulting promotions of the Guard's top leaders amounted to a solidifying of Paredes's position. Concurrently, they noted, Noriega "certainly has improved his situation."[6] But Noriega had plans for further improvement, plans that would soon call for him to move against Paredes.

Noriega Takes Command

Noriega's career was steadily advancing. On July 31, 1983, he was promoted to brigadier general. Two weeks later, on August 13, 1983, he assumed command of the National Guard. In his address that day, Noriega made several "promises" and "commitments": "to restructure the Guard" to prepare it for canal defense responsibilities, to make "internal development and civic action . . . part of the Guard's new face, . . . to subordinate the Guard to the constitution and the president, and to withdraw the Guard from a direct role in public administration," to hold "free and honest elections in 1984," and to maintain "public tranquility to permit an orderly electoral process."[7]

Noriega lost no time in addressing his first promise, restructuring and expanding the Guard, which was renamed the Defense Forces of the Republic of Panama. Enlarged military powers were specified in Law 20, which was passed in October 1983. Law 20 gave the PDF the power to close down the press if it were deemed offensive, and gave military personnel extraordinary power to detain and arrest civilians.[8] The law also limited the president's power to appoint military officials to higher ranking positions by requiring the consent of the PDF commander for such appointments. The Military Organic Law also expanded the power of the military and its involvement in government, consolidating various administrative and security functions under the PDF.

The full implications of these changes were unclear at the time, but Steve Ropp concluded in 1986 that Law 20 itself was a clear and significant signal that the PDF would not be demilitarized "in any meaningful sense."[9] Thus, Torrijos's plans for civilianization, a process of increasing democratization and returning the military to the barracks, were altered in 1982 and 1983. The officers' powersharing agreement and Noriega's reorganization indicated that a revised institutional interest, combined with Noriega's personal ambitions, was supplanting Torrijos's plans.

The promises and commitments Noriega announced in his speech on August 13 were received skeptically by U.S. officials. The U.S. embassy described reactions in Panama as ranging from "extreme skepticism" to "satisfaction, even optimism."[10] The embassy's assessment reflected the complexity of the situation:

> Did Noriega mean it? That is the question that has pervaded the political scene since Friday's ceremony. Many observers, who are accustomed to regarding Noriega as a sort of diminutive Darth Vader, scoff at his assurances about taking the Guard back to the barracks and assuring free and honest elections in 1984. They insist that what happens in 1984 will depend on how Noriega sees his own interests and those of the guard at that time. Other less cynical observers would agree that the outcome depends on how Noriega sees his own interests and those of the Guard. . . . In any event, Noriega's speech was an eloquent and very public commitment from which he might find it difficult (though not absolutely impossible) to extricate himself.[11]

Events soon proved the wisdom of this caveat. In August 1983, however, embassy officials hoped that momentum, along with public endorsements and U.S. encouragement, would keep the PDF on Torrijos's course toward civilianization.

The U.S. commitment to democratization could also be questioned. Official statements from Washington emphasized holding elections on schedule, but the Reagan administration's overriding priority at that time was to contain the Sandinista revolution in Nicaragua. The National Bipartisan Commission on Central America (the Kissinger Commission) conducted site visits during the fall, visiting Panama during October 9–16, 1983. Commission members met with Noriega and Nicolás Ardito Barletta, the banker who would soon replace Paredes as the military's presidential candidate. They also met with more than fifty Panamanians, ranging from PDF and government leaders to representatives of civic, labor, church, and social groups. Although Panamanians stressed their domestic concerns, the Kissinger Commission was more concerned with Nicaragua and El Salvador. Those priorities forced Panama policy into the background.[12] Not only did the United States view Panama as an asset in the Contra war, but the need to have stable allies in the region caused the United States to ignore early danger signals about the PDF. In October 1983, the United States did not see Panama as part of the problem in the Caribbean Basin; Panama was considered to be relatively successful and stable, and it provided a model for its violence-ridden neighbors by preparing to hold national elections following a period of military rule. Moreover, Panama was part of the U.S. solution to conflicts in Central America; along with Honduras, Panama served as a forward base in the Contra war.

Transition to National Elections

The 1984 presidential election in Panama was heralded as a significant step in that country's history. Its outcome would be the clearest indicator of the extent to which the PDF was willing to support civilianization. The campaign period was watched closely by citizens, military officers, and politicians for indications of relative strength and intentions.

Paredes's Candidacy and Withdrawal

One of the earliest contestants to emerge was General Paredes, who resigned from the PDF on August 12, 1983, in order to become a candidate. He expected to have an easy campaign and victory; few observers predicted otherwise.

The extent to which Paredes was committed to Torrijos's plan for democratization remains nebulous. In November 1982, Paredes had compared the process of demilitarization to releasing one's grasp of a dangerous snake: "If you have a viper in your hands and you want to release it, you put it on the ground and pin its head with a stick. . . . Then you move away quickly."[13] After assuming office as commander, Paredes had frequently promised that the Guard would surrender all political power after the election, but such statements should be considered as precampaign rhetoric rather than real plans. Paredes shared Torrijos's and Noriega's disdain for civilian politicians, referring to them as "politickers, not politicians." Paredes distrusted politicians' motives, particularly their commitment to represent the poor, and referred instead to the Guard as "the public in uniform."[14]

No one was surprised when Paredes officially announced his candidacy. His campaign, however, was much shorter than expected. Within a month his campaign collapsed, due to lack of popular support for his national unity message and opposition from General Noriega, who now commanded the Guard. Cables from the U.S. embassy reported that Paredes's candidacy had been "disinflating" for some time, a downward trend that actually accelerated after he declared his candidacy.[15]

Because Paredes had advanced from the police tradition in the Guard rather than the army, he was associated with the Guard's more conservative elements. During his campaign he tried to maximize support by appealing to conservatives, his natural constituency, in and outside of the military and the PRD. That strategy, however, alienated important PRD constituents with more leftist views.[16] After a center-right coalition failed to materialize, Paredes was not able to rally the PRD behind his candidacy.

Paredes released a lengthy withdrawal statement on September 6, 1983. This was described by U.S. observers as "pure Paredes—wandering, emotional, and vague."[17] At this moment, Noriega decided to act. In case Paredes's announcement ignited popular support that might encourage him to resume his campaign, Noriega sent him a terse telegram designed to quash his ambitions once and for all. Noriega congratulated him for making a decision "in the highest tradition of the service, and as a contribution to peace and democracy."[18] The pleasant language was deceptive; Noriega actually was making a power play against Paredes, shutting him out of politics and the new PDF.

Paredes angrily accused Noriega of breaking the power-sharing agreement, but to no avail. Noriega and President Ricardo de la Espriella quickly removed all of Paredes's supporters from the cabinet. As commandant, Paredes had treated de la Espriella with contempt; this and de la Espriella's own ambition to remain in office would have prompted him to favor Paredes's demise and support Noriega's power play. Nonetheless, de la Espriella was a junior player during these events. Privately, he admitted to being "the administrator of a ship of state steered by the Guard."[19]

Noriega proved to be Paredes's main opponent, just as the two had competed throughout their careers. Both wanted to achieve the two top power positions in Panama—PDF commander and president—backed, of course, by a military power base. Noriega, however, was not willing to wait for Paredes to take his turn. Paredes had many positive personal qualities; he was "intelligent, competent, ambitious, with good judgement and leadership ability."[20] During Paredes's ascendancy, he was described in a U.S. Defense Department cable as "one of the leading contenders for political dominance in the post-Torrijos era" and as having "a wider power base than his nearest rival in the Guard" (Noriega).[21] Despite these assets, Paredes was not able to build the political and institutional base he needed to mount a successful campaign and to keep Noriega in line. Instead, Noriega turned Paredes's weaknesses to his own advantage.

Several months after his withdrawal announcement, Paredes still longed to be president; he decided to run independently of the PDF, as a candidate for the Popular Nationalist party (PNP). He attracted 15,976 votes in May, which compared favorably with minor party candidates but left him far behind the major contenders.[22] Later still, when Noriega faced public accusations of corruption and drug trafficking in 1986, Paredes would call for him to resign for the good of the service, but his power base was still too weak for him to challenge Noriega.

De la Espriella's Campaign

As the campaign progressed, additional signs of PDF reluctance to return to the barracks accumulated. Already, two presidents who had not supported the military's plans to win the 1984 election had been removed. President de la Espriella had moved up from the vice-presidency in July 1982, when General Paredes had ousted President Aristides Royo. Royo had been removed, in large part, to improve Paredes's election prospects. Thus, de la Espriella's chances for remaining in office were uncertain, especially if the PDF decided that he should be removed.

The PDF objected to de la Espriella because he kept acting like a candidate despite the fact that they had placed him in office as a transitional figure. To his "old banking friends," de la Espriella appeared to be a "master cajoler, delicately nudging and tugging at the Guard" toward democratization.[23] Some of their confidence was justified. A State Department report described de la Espriella's administration positively: "access to decision-making positions in the Government broadened to include technocrats and independents, and even a few members of opposition parties, where before most positions were reserved for official party adherents" in the PRD.[24] In marked contrast, his political opponents considered de la Espriella to be a "puppet incapable of wresting from his boss [the PDF] anything more than what the boss wants to surrender."[25]

For his part, de la Espriella enjoyed the office enough to want to remain president, either by postponing elections or heading the PRD ticket. However, the constitution prohibited succession and required an incumbent to wait for at least two presidential terms to pass before seeking reelection, so de la Espriella's candidacy depended on changes in these provisions. The military signaled that he was getting out of line by calling, in public, for elections to be held on schedule. When legislation was passed that would have allowed de la Espriella to run, the PDF forced him to veto it.

Tensions between de la Espriella and the PDF continued to build. De la

Espriella refused to reorganize his cabinet to include representatives of the coalition of parties backing the PDF candidate. Although the PRD's nominating convention had not yet been held, the PDF had already made clear its decision to support Nicolás Ardito Barletta, a vice-president of the World Bank. Then de la Espriella refused to release government funds that the PDF considered to be part of their candidate's war chest.[26] He also refused to grant government workers time off to attend Barletta's welcoming ceremony, which was scheduled for February 13, 1984.

Despite these warnings, de la Espriella continued to act like a candidate. Finally, when an opposition coalition coalesced around Arnulfo Arias on February 11, just two days before Barletta's return, Noriega moved against de la Espriella. Now that it faced an opposition slate headed by Arias, the PDF had to gain maximum unity. Arias's first campaign proclamation "denounced the current civilian and military leadership . . . in bitter and uncompromising terms."[27] He even went so far as to say that Law 20 "must be completely changed," and that "Senor (sic) Noriega" would have "to head for prison." In order for Barletta to win, de la Espriella would have to go, and on February 13, 1984, Noriega forced him to resign and exit the political scene.

The press portrayed these events as a sign that the military did not want to diminish its political role. Clearly, the PDF was intent on picking its own candidate and using government resources for his benefit.[28] Nonetheless, many observers were surprised by de la Espriella's ouster, including Vice-President Jorge Illueca, who was sworn in as president the same day.[29] Noriega took the precaution of advising the U.S. military in advance of these events. A PDF spokesman telephoned the commander in chief of U.S. SOUTHCOM, headquartered in Panama City, around noon to assure him that matters were well in hand and that no U.S. interests were jeopardized, including holding elections on schedule.

The ouster drew no adverse comment from Washington. Instead, official U.S. reactions stressed concern that the election be held as scheduled. In private, the message was the same. Ambassador Briggs requested authorization to convey the following in a letter from President Reagan to President Illueca:

> Dear Mr. President: I send you cordial greetings on your assumption of the office of the president of the Republic of Panama. You know the importance my administration and the American people attach to the genuine exercise of democracy, and I therefore wish to express satisfaction over your declaration, on assuming office, that Panamanian national elections will take place as scheduled in May of this year.[30]

Once again, the United States was willing to play ball with the military regime, this time in the hope that 1984 would bring to power a civilian who "might somehow kindle democratization."[31]

Barletta's Candidacy

One reason for this mild U.S. response was its positive assessment of the PDF/PRD candidate. Technically, the United States was neutral toward all candidates and the outcome of the election. Privately, officials were relieved that Barletta was running. They were well aware that the PRD was controlled by Noriega, and that as the military's candidate, Barletta would operate under certain constraints. Nonetheless, Barletta had additional credentials that made him attractive to the United States. As an adviser to Torrijos, Barletta had worked closely with the Carter administration during ratification of the 1978 canal treaties. As a vice-president of the World Bank, he had gained additional expertise in international finance, building upon a career that included positions as Panama's minister of planning and economic policy, director of the Department of Economic Affairs at the OAS, and as a member of the Inter-American Committee of the Alliance for Progress. Barletta also had personal connections to the Reagan administration through Secretary of State George Shultz—Barletta earned his Ph.D. in economics from the University of Chicago while Shultz was on the faculty. Given Panama's $4 billion foreign debt and worsening economic situation, U.S. officials considered Barletta to be a good choice.

Even if Barletta had not had these positive attributes, the United States was not likely to support the civilian opposition in 1984. None of its candidates appeared viable. The main candidate from the civilian sector, Arnulfo Arias, was now eighty-two years old; moreover, he remained as antimilitary and anti-U.S. as ever. Most importantly, the United States feared that even if Arias were elected, he would be overthrown again, and this would hardly contribute toward Panama's democratization. Thus, lacking an alternative and being predisposed toward Barletta as a competent banker, diplomat, and close friend of Secretary Shultz, the United States remained officially neutral but privately pleased with the PRD's choice. Once President Illueca indicated that elections would be held as scheduled, the United States did not object to de la Espriella's unceremonious ouster.

Why did the PDF choose Barletta? An obvious reason is pragmatic. Barletta had international financial connections, friends in Washington, and a reputation for *tecnico* leadership that the PDF needed in order to salvage Panama's deteriorating economy. Realizing that truly stringent measures would be required, the PDF wanted to bring in an outsider to administer the unpleasant "cure." One reporter wrote that Noriega was worried "about keeping Central America's political violence off Panamanian soil." He continued, "One way to do this, the Guard believes, is to speed up economic progress by letting responsible civilians run the country."[32]

Another reason for choosing Barletta was political: the PDF either disliked or positively abhorred the other candidates—Arias was anathema and de la Espriella had never been a serious contender. Paredes's campaign had fizzled, and he had moved too far to the Right. President Illueca had differed, publicly, with the PDF over their participation in CONDECA, a multilateral regional defense organization.[33] None of these men, therefore, were acceptable to the PDF.

In addition to seeing Barletta as more compatible with their corporate, institutional interests, the PDF considered him to be more malleable. Barletta had lived and worked outside of Panama during the past six years. He had connections in Washington but no independent power base or natural constituency back home to rival the PDF/PRD power base. This was a crucial matter for the PDF. They were interested in a president who could manage the economy and Panama's debt; they wanted to hire a manager, not to establish a rival power center.[34]

Events were well orchestrated on February 13, 1984. De la Espriella was ousted in the morning, Illueca was sworn in around noon, and Barletta's airport arrival ceremony began at 2:30 that afternoon. Coincidentally or not, a city-wide power failure limited media coverage of the afternoon's events. A reporter found it "mysterious" that Illueca's inauguration speech was carried on television but not mentioned at all in official newspapers.[35]

The 1984 Election

As the first presidential election in sixteen years, and with Arias running once again, the 1984 election looked like a contest between old rivals. The two major presidential candidates seemed to represent "ins" and "outs," with Arias, the old nationalist, standing against the new nationalists, personified by Barletta and Noriega. In fact, both coalitions were broader than that, but the election was dominated by one overriding domestic issue: which side would rule and, as a result, how far would the military go in stepping back to the barracks?

The government's slate also included two vice-presidential candidates, Eric Arturo Delvalle, a wealthy industrialist from the Republican party, and Roderick Esquivel, a physician and member of the Liberal party. In addition, three other parties were associated with UNADE (the Democratic National Union), yielding six parties that ran progovernment legislative candidates. The opposition coalition, ADO (Opposition Democratic Alliance) comprised Arias's Panameñistas, Christian Democrats, and the National Liberal Republican Movement (MOLIRENA). Carlos Rodríguez and Ricardo Arias Calderón ran as first and second vice-presidential candidates.

From the U.S. perspective, the election initially appeared to be a great success. First, it was held on schedule, on May 6, 1984. Second, the campaign marked the first time in history that two perennial issues— relations with the United States and Panama Canal treaties—did not figure in a presidential campaign. A U.S. diplomat interviewed in January 1984 emphasized this change: "our relations with Panama today are as good as historically possible." Similarly, Dennis McAuliffe, administrator of the Panama Canal Commission, said "relations between the two countries have never been better. In retrospect, the first half of 1984 would mark the high-point of positive U.S.-Panamanian relations during the Noriega years."[36]

Preelection reports suggested that the procedures enacted during 1982–1984 to ensure a free and fair national election would achieve that result. Events on and after election day, however, were tainted with fraud. The vote count was stopped early and then suspended three days later, on May 9. When results from sixteen of forty districts were tabulated, Barletta had 139,761 votes and Arias had 133,502.[37] Both candidates were claiming victory, Barletta by 8,000–10,000 votes and Arias, according to 86 percent of the *mesas* the opposition surveyed, by 2,000 votes. When many challenges to the validity of many tables' counts were made, the National Board of Vote Examiners declared itself unable to proceed, and turned the process over to the National Electoral Tribunal. On May 12, the tallies stood at 319,671 for Barletta and 314,714 for Arias,[38] but the trend, with challenges, was favoring Arias. On May 16, the Tribunal declared Barletta's victory. Of some 640,000 votes cast, they found Barletta the winner by 1,713 votes.[39] The process looked suspicious: the announcement came ten days after the election, and one of the three members of the Tribunal abstained.

Rumors of fraud spread as soon as the count was stopped on election night, May 6. Arias quickly made a public announcement, accusing the PDF of stealing his victory. The United States made no adverse comment, as the Reagan administration reportedly was concerned with instability. If Arias fought back, perhaps by mobilizing demonstrations, this could spark a violent response by the PDF, which might threaten the security of the Panama Canal. Such fears were not entirely unfounded. On May 7, two people were killed in demonstrations, and more than forty were injured in a shootout outside the building where votes were being counted. Election-related violence did not subside when Barletta's victory was announced. On May 30, riot police closed the opposition's headquarters on Avenida Balboa and arrested 100 of Arias's supporters.[40]

The role the PDF played in perpetrating the fraud was confirmed three years later, when Col. Roberto Díaz Herrera, Noriega's second in command, confessed that he was ordered to steal the election on Barletta's behalf. In 1984, however, the United States lacked the inclination, and Panama's oppositionists lacked the power, to challenge the fraudulent outcome.

Barletta insists to this day that he actually received enough votes to win, without fraud, by a comfortable majority. On several occasions he showed reporters and visitors crumpled, yellowed pages of vote tallies that added up to a 10,000 vote margin in his favor.

Election results aside, Barletta apparently hoped that he could manage the military, rather than vice versa. Although he had been in Washington for the past six years, he had also worked closely with Torrijos, so he was well aware of the military's power. When questioned after the election about his relationship to the PDF, Barletta replied, "I am not a lackey of the Defense Force"; instead, he saw himself as "someone trusted by the military who can bring democracy to Panama."[41]

How far was Barletta willing to go to promote democracy? Soon after his victory was announced, Barletta said, "One must treat the military well so that the military will treat the government well."[42] Whatever his commitment to democratization, his first priority was economic recovery, which he pursued with fervor. By the time his first real showdown with the military occurred in September 1985, Barletta's economic austerity measures and assertive political style totally alienated his supporters. When Noriega and Díaz Herrera later decided that Barletta had to go, the president had no allies to come to his aid. Although Barletta began his term hoping to act independently, the PDF disposed of him when he was no longer useful and violated their interests.

U.S. Relations with Barletta

Barletta hoped to hit the ground running when he took office in October 1984. He began preparing the way for U.S. assistance at preliminary meetings in Washington on July 26, 1984. He outlined his aims to Secretary of State Shultz: "strengthened democracy through a government of national reconciliation, economic recovery and growth, honest and efficient government and a foreign policy built on a continued special relationship with the US."[43] The rhetoric could not have pleased the United States more. Assistant Secretary of State Langhorne Motley wrote, "We see in his moderate approach our best opportunity to build the political stability our interests in Panama need."[44]

U.S. Interests

Motley made a succinct argument in Barletta's favor in a briefing memorandum for Secretary Shultz: "We want to assist him, because of Panama's intrinsic importance as the site of the Canal, a major US base complex, and massive US investment; we want to [excised] help to preserve the political tranquility that our interests in Panama require."[45] Basic national interests, which had guided U.S. policy toward Panama for decades, were identified with support for Barletta's administration: the strategic value of the canal, U.S. bases in Panama, stability, and political tranquility. Self-interest, particularly in canal security and the hope of negotiating an agreement to allow U.S. bases in Panama after the year 2000, appeared to require playing ball with Noriega's candidate and a regime dominated by the PDF. The primacy of security concerns was distorting U.S. views of and hopes for domestic developments in Panama.

Barletta was inaugurated on October 11, 1984. Secretary Shultz attended the ceremony and spoke positively about Panama's future. He approached the visit with two goals: "to demonstrate the importance we attach to democracy and civilian primacy," and "to develop effective working relations with the incoming Barletta administration and agreement on major objectives."[46] The major objectives the Reagan administration had in mind were continued Panamanian opposition to Cuban and Nicaraguan threats in the region and support for U.S. initiatives to strengthen provisions in the *Acta* being negotiated through the Contadora peace process. On these and broader issues, the Reagan administration saw "an essential parallelism between Panama's national security interests and those of the US in the region."[47] Former President Jimmy Carter, who had worked with Barletta on the 1978 canal treaties, happened to be in Panama during the inauguration; his presence further strengthened the appearance of U.S. support for Barletta.

Barletta's Administration

The day before the inauguration, Noriega pledged that the PDF would "respect the civilian government" and he called on the opposition to "rein itself in."[48] He continued:

> We call on all Panamanians to provide [Ardito Barletta] support. . . . We are retiring from the first line of defense, but we are not retiring from the heart of the Panamanian people. . . . Fellow Panamanians, remember that today starts the phase of full democracy, but his democracy will have a positive balance in the way in which the governors and the governed join together in a respectful and Christian way.[49]

Meanwhile, between 300 and 400 riot police, wearing Doberman insignia and armed with hard rubber truncheons and rifles, clashed with some 1,000 demonstrators, arrested at least fifty people, and injured dozens of others.[50] The next day, some 1,000 demonstrators chanted "fraud, fraud" while Barletta was being inaugurated.[51]

Aid from the United States soon skyrocketed, in part because Panama qualified for assistance under President Reagan's new Caribbean Basin Initiative (CBI). Total U.S. economic assistance went from $7.4 million in 1983, and $12.0 million in 1984, to $74.5 million in 1985. Of the 1985 figure, most of the aid ($66.4 million) came in the form of AID (Agency for International Development) grants. Military assistance did not change drastically: $5.5 million in 1983, $13.5 million in 1984, and $10.6 million in 1985.[52]

As expected, Barletta took stiff measures to repair the economy. To reduce the deficit, he cut back government spending. According to one report, he fired some 15,000 government employees, many of whom had been added to the payroll as patronage in conjunction with the 1984 election.[53] Barletta also instituted a wage freeze to bring Panama's labor costs closer to regional rates and a tax increase. He was forced to repeal the tax hike in February 1985 when an unprecedented number of protesters—150,000 out of a population of about two million—took to the streets.[54] In response to demands from the World Bank and International Monetary Fund (IMF) that labor laws be changed to make the economy more competitive, Barletta submitted revisions in the labor code. To increase foreign investment, Barletta made tariff structures less protective of domestic industry, removing an advantage the commercial sector had long enjoyed.

Aside from the technical merits of these measures, the common complaint was that Barletta's policies were too favorable to the IMF and the banks to which debts were owed, and too hard on Panama. But from Barletta's perspective, the problem was too staggering for half-measures. In 1985, the amount due for repayment to the IMF was $700 million; the government's deficit for the year was $100 million.[55] The country's foreign debt was $3.7 billion, requiring a $400 million annual interest payment—an amount that constituted 35 percent of Panama's export earnings.[56] By December 1984, the foreign debt reached $4.6 billion.

Facing these economic realities, Barletta felt he had no choice but to implement austerity measures. Their cumulative effect, however, was to injure and enrage each group whose support Barletta needed to remain in power: government workers, labor leaders and workers, industrialists, and, finally, the PDF. Barletta's assertive, executive political style was not well received in Panama's more consensual civilian political circles. A U.S. banker said Barletta "has been holier than the pope, approaching the job like an economist rather than a politician . . . in his single-minded concentration on debt problems he has almost totally neglected the need to build a base of political support."[57] A Christian Democrat party legislator, Guillermo Cochez, was slightly more diplomatic, saying that Barletta's "technical knowledge of international economics proved useless without complementary practical political experience."[58]

Noriega and U.S. Interests

During 1983–1984 several U.S. agencies were working very closely with Noriega and the PDF. Noriega had been restored to the CIA payroll in 1981, and as the Reagan administration became increasingly active in supporting the Contra war, U.S. officials made additional contacts with Noriega. On December 11, 1983, Vice-President George Bush met privately with Noriega in Panama. The vice-president reportedly raised U.S. complaints about money laundering in Panama and also asked for Noriega's help for the Contras. Ambassador Everett Briggs, who attended the meeting, later said that Bush's request was not for military assistance, but for diplomatic support, especially to counter Sandinista positions at the Contadora peace process.[59] Noriega apparently interpreted the meeting, however, as a signal that his help in Central America would be rewarded. Subsequent investigative reports have substantiated extensive activities by Noriega, encouraged and supported by the CIA from at least 1983 to 1986, in support of U.S. objectives in Central America.[60]

During these years, Noriega deliberately and actively promoted several U.S. interests. He addressed the problem of calls for democratization from the Department of State through Barletta's candidacy and election. For a Reagan White House determined to fight Communist insurgencies in Central America, Noriega provided arms, a supply network, and cash donations. For a DEA fighting drug traffickers and money launderers, Noriega appeared to cooperate in arrests, raids, and in tracking funds. For the CIA, he provided intelligence on Cuba and other targets.[61] Noriega cultivated positive relations with U.S. departments and agencies during the 1980s even more diligently than he had during the Torrijos years, when he headed the National Guard's intelligence division. He was also actively cooperating with Mossad, the Israeli intelligence agency, in his activities in Central America; his relations with the Israelis were related, in ways that are not entirely clear, to his involvement with the CIA.

Noriega also tried to improve his public image. He made public appearances, such as a speech at Harvard University as part of a Conference on the Military in Central America held in February 1985. His public relations strategy was designed, according to U.S. military analysts,

> to offset his and the PDF's dismal reputation and to create a personal image as: a peacemaker (e.g., defender of the Contadora Process), a defender of democracy (e.g., he told his Harvard audience that the PDF had returned democracy to PN) and an opponent of Communism (e.g., his recent offer to defend Costa Rica against Nicaragua).

Those analysts concluded that because Noriega's efforts were making little headway at home, he was seizing "every opportunity to make his wholesome pronouncements overseas or before foreign correspondents."[62]

In fact, Noriega's image was becoming more, not less, tarnished. A series on drug trafficking in the *Miami Herald* in February 1985 portrayed him and the PDF as key players in the international drug market. Similar press reports appeared elsewhere. A 1985 staff report for the House Foreign Affairs Committee described the PDF as "the axle around which the wheel of corruption in Panama turns."[63] Arnulfo Arias charged that Panama was being headed by a drug dictatorship.[64]

The "Play Ball" Strategy

Despite a fraudulent election and continued domination of Panamanian politics by a military regime, the United States chose to play ball with Noriega and Barletta. From the U.S. perspective, current democratic deficiencies were minor concerns compared to the seemingly insurmountable task of renegotiating the Panama Canal treaty that had dominated bilateral relations from 1964 to 1978. After visiting Panama in January 1984, Georgie Anne Geyer wrote that new treaties made good relations between the United States and Panama possible.[65] This comment was made almost twenty years to the day after the 1964 flag riots that had left four U.S. citizens and twenty-two Panamanians dead in the wake of protests demanding Panamanian sovereignty over the canal and Canal Zone. Moreover, in January 1984, Panama seemed to U.S. officials to be in a much better condition than its neighbors. Geyer confirmed this perception; in stark contrast to Nicaragua, El Salvador, and, increasingly, Guatemala, she described Panama as "calm, serene and stable."[66] Geyer typified the view also shared by the Reagan administration when she concluded that resolution of the sovereignty question through new canal treaties had contributed significantly to Panama's relative tranquility. From the vantage point of October 1984, the situation in Panama did not look that bad to the United States. At worst, the process of democratization was being slowed down. Perceptions were lagging behind events during 1984, but during 1985 and 1986, those perceptions changed.

The Drug Trade

Several events occurred in 1984 that indicated the extent to which significant elements of the PDF and Noriega's business connections were involved in international narcotics trafficking. The significance of these events was not recognized in Washington, however, until 1986 and 1987. During 1984, while Panama's government and military endorsed true democracy and demilitarization, an altogether different transformation was occurring: the PDF was becoming a "narco-military" institution. Opposition journalist and publisher Roberto Eisenmann used this term to describe PDF involvement in drug trafficking and protection activities, ranging from loading, transporting, and guarding shipments of drugs and cash, to providing security for drug lords and their associates in Panama, to participating in drug deals and protection arrangements.

The year 1984 was notable for its presidential election, but this was also a year marked by three major drug developments.[67] A very large cocaine processing plant in Darién province bordering Colombia was busted by U.S. and Panamanian authorities. This revealed an unexpectedly large operation located in Panama under PDF protection. The bust caused a crisis in

Noriega's relations with the Medellín cartel that reportedly necessitated mediation by Fidel Castro to restore Noriega to the cartel's good graces.[68] As additional PDF involvement in drug trafficking and double dealing by the cartel were exposed, Noriega needed to sacrifice a fellow officer to take the heat. The second event was the "Melo affair," in which Col. Julián Melo Borbua, who was responsible for overseeing the Darién operation, was accused of drug trafficking; he was dishonorably discharged from the PDF but never prosecuted.[69] Finally, 1984 was also the year Colombian drug lords, accused of murdering Justice Minister Rodrigo Lara Bonilla, spent a month hiding out in Panama. Thus in May, while the election was heralded as restoring democracy, the PDF was hosting and protecting Pablo Escobar Gaviria, the Ochoa family, and more than 100 "accountants, bodyguards, lawyers, and families."[70] Noriega reportedly received part of a $4 million bribe from the cartel for these services.[71] At the time, these events did not penetrate Washington's consciousness. In 1986, they surfaced in investigative reports and congressional hearings, but it took two years for U.S. perceptions to catch up with Panamanian realities.

A Turning Point in U.S.-Panamanian Relations

The years 1983 and 1984 look, in retrospect, like a high point in U.S.-Panamanian relations. Ratification and implementation of the 1978 canal treaties had changed the tenor and focal point of the relationship from controversy with the United States over a new canal treaty to controversy at home over civilian-military relations. Implementation of the treaties was progressing well. The negative consequences of involving Panama in the Contra war, and the PDF's growing involvement in international narcotics trafficking were not yet salient issues in U.S.-Panamanian relations.

Instead, in marked contrast to El Salvador and Nicaragua, Panama appeared to be a model its néighbors could emulate. An election had been held, and Noriega's steps to strengthen the military, although under way, were not yet considered a problem by Washington. In fact, when Panama was certified for Carribean Basin Initiative (CBI) aid in November 1984, the major issue that Congress treated as a serious obstacle was not democracy, human rights, or narcotics trafficking, but the government's failure to crack down on piracy of video recordings.

The United States had looked forward to a Panamanian election in which complaints about U.S. canal policy would not be the primary issue, and in which Panama would join the regional trend toward replacement of military regimes with civilian government. Subsequently, the United States backed Barletta strongly and ignored questionable aspects of the election, according to Richard Millett, "on the belief that this would strengthen ultimately a transition to civilian government, that this was a capable and a relatively honest individual even though he lacked a political base of support."[72] The year 1985 clarified the direction Panama's domestic development was taking and diminished the likelihood that U.S.-Panamanian relations could remain on an even keel until the canal was turned over in December 1999. Millett asserts that the United States faced a "real crisis" during 1985, "when it became quite obvious that Dr. Barletta could not act independently" and he was finally ousted.[73] The United States had backed the only apparent alternative and hoped for the best; in the process, the Reagan administration lost both Barletta and hope that democratization would proceed. By late 1985, Barletta was gone, along with hopes for Panama's demilitarization; factions wracked civilian groups; and Noriega was expanding his control and the PDF's power.

What were the objectives of U.S. relations with Panama? A consensus administration position was stated by several State Department witnesses in 1986:

1. maintain and implement the canal treaties and maintain use of our bases;
2. assure in the long term transit across the isthmus for U.S. commerce and military;
3. promote the legitimate use by U.S. firms of Panama as a major center of regional and global finance, commerce and trade;
4. deny the use of Panama to U.S. adversaries;
5. protect the large investments by U.S. individual and corporate citizens in Panama;
6. assure the welfare of U.S. citizens in Panama.[74]

Objectives 1, 2, and 4 linked Panama to global U.S. security concerns— concerns that the Reagan administration defined in anti-Communist and antileftist terms. The greater the threat the administration identified with Cuba and Nicaragua, the more important U.S. security interests in Panama appeared to be.

Administration witnesses either added promotion of democracy in Panama as an additional objective or stressed it as a condition required to promote and protect other U.S. objectives. Democratization was often identified with stability, another long-term U.S. objective for Panama. Deputy Assistant Secretary of State Elliott Abrams expressed this connection: "Protecting and advancing these interests requires stability in Panama. . . .We have long felt that stability can only result, in the long run, from constitutional order and responsive civilian political and governmental institutions."[75]

Testifying before Congress in 1986, Assistant Secretary of State Elliott Abrams assessed the political situation in Panama this way:

The systemic problem in Panama is . . . the excess of military or police

> involvement in government. . . . There is just too much military involvement in what should be civilian decision making to say flat out that Panama is a democratic country. It has many democratic institutions, it has an enormous amount of personal freedom. I guess I would put it this way: it's the freest country that isn't a democracy, if you don't call it a democracy.[76]

This was scant praise indeed, but it reflected the dilemma the United States faced when it considered Panama in its regional context. Despite the negative developments that occurred in 1985, Panama still had no death squads like El Salvador did, and no leftist movement comparable to the Sandinistas. Panama had emerging problems, but it lacked an immediate crisis that could propel the situation onto the front burner in Washington.

Seymour Hersh flatly stated that officials in the Reagan administration and previous administrations "overlooked Noriega's illegal activities because of his cooperation with American intelligence and his willingness to permit the American military extensive leeway to operate in Panama."[77] These officials referred to Noriega as "a valuable asset" who was "providing sensitive information" about Nicaragua.[78] In 1985, for example, Noriega engineered an operation to blow up a Sandinista arsenal in Nicaragua; he also gave $100,000 for the Contras.

Thus, just as canal policy had taken precedence over democratization goals during the Nixon, Ford, and Carter administrations, so too did regional security concerns take precedence over Panama's demilitarization and drug enforcement during the Reagan administration. Commitment to one overwhelming priority distorted U.S. policy on secondary objectives.

When asked in 1986 if U.S. policy toward Panama had changed after Barletta's ouster, Richard Millett replied, "I don't think you can say the policy has changed particularly . . . but certainly the difficulties in carrying out that policy have increased tremendously."[79] The process of changing U.S. Panama policy was just beginning in 1985. By the end of the year, the equation balancing U.S. national interests and the favors Noriega could provide versus his growing liabilities was starting to shift against the general. The U.S. National Security adviser, Admiral John Poindexter, was sent to Panama in December to tell Noriega to "cut it out," meaning the drug trade and close relations with Cuba. This was supposed to be a tough, direct signal. Other officials, however, were maintaining a pro-Noriega stance. According to documents produced at Lt. Col. Oliver North's trial, Noriega traveled to London to meet North, then an NSC staff aide working for Poindexter, to discuss operations to support the Contras. North reported to Poindexter that Noriega had offered to assassinate Sandinista leaders, an offer that Poindexter quickly rebuffed. North recommended taking Noriega up on other offers, such as sabotaging Nicaraguan facilities, including an oil refinery, airport, and an off-loading facility at Puerto Sandino.

Trouble on the Horizon

In December 1985, Guillermo Cochez reviewed the year and noted that not a week had gone by "without protest of some kind, involving strikes, arrests and injuries."[80] At the beginning of 1985, protests were directed against President Barletta and his stringent economic policies. In mid-September, demonstrators decried a brutal, politically motivated murder of a popular opposition figure, Hugo Spadafora. Two weeks later, when President Barletta was "resigned by" (a verb meaning to be forced out by) the PDF, protesters supported Barletta and his call for an investigation of Spadafora's death. The year revealed the weakness of civilian authority, the limits of domestic economic reform as a solution to the debt crisis, and the determination of the PDF to protect its institutional interests. The events of 1985 made the U.S. "play ball" strategy more difficult to sustain; these events fueled opposition to that strategy that was already mounting in the press, in the Congress, and, finally, in the executive branch.

Spadafora's Murder

On September 13, 1985, a long-time opponent of Noriega, Dr. Hugo Spadafora, was murdered and beheaded by PDF officers. The brutal killing of this popular figure sparked demonstrations in Panama, where it was widely assumed that Noriega was responsible for the torture and death of Spadafora.[81]

Who was Spadafora? He was a medical doctor, a political activist, a romantic revolutionary, and a guerrilla fighter. He had participated in revolutionary causes in Guinea-Bissau, Nicaragua (with Edén Pastora's Contras), and, of course, Panama. Although he opposed the military revolution at first, he soon warmed to Torrijos; he later served as vice-minister of health and joined the PRD. Soon after Torrijos's death, Spadafora began to criticize Noriega, who then headed the intelligence division (G-2) of the National Guard. In December 1981, Spadafora said he "didn't believe that clean elections could take place" in Panama with Noriega in charge of G-2 and his brother Luis in charge of the Electoral Tribunal.[82] These remarks were not made in private; instead, Spadafora made these direct, personal accusations on radio and television broadcasts and in newspaper interviews. Cables from U.S. Army intelligence reported that Noriega and Spadafora were moving toward a "head on confrontation."[83] Embassy cables described a "blood feud" between the two men as "notorious."[84]

Spadafora began compiling detailed evidence about drug trafficking and corruption—names, dates, amounts of shipments, and bribes paid. He even took his evidence to U.S. DEA officers in Panama. He also took political action, reportedly maneuvering with Aquilino Boyd to support General Paredes's candidacy. Spadafora's critical comments about Noriega became increasingly pointed as the years passed. In 1984, he said, again in public, that it was a "national disgrace to have Panama governed by an international drug trafficker." He became so openly critical in late 1985, that Noriega "is known to have told several aides 'I want that guy's head'."[85] For several weeks prior to the murder, government-controlled newspapers "vilified Spadafora and predicted his doom, in particular his death by beheading."[86]

On the night of September 17, 1985, the following report was cabled to Washington from the U.S. embassy:

> 2. Summary: A decapitated corpse presumed to be that of Dr. Hugo Spadafora . . . was found on September 14 or 15 in Costa Rica near the Panamanian border. . . . On present evidence it is impossible to know who committed the murder, or even if the corpse is that of Spadafora. Nevertheless, eyewitness reports that Spadafora was taken into custody by the Panama Defense Forces (FDP) [PDF] on September 13, if confirmed, will likely create a wide-spread presumption in Panama that the FDP was indeed responsible. End Summary.[87]

The cable went on the convey the "story":

> 3. A variety of television and newspaper reports in Panama indicate that on September 14 or 15 a decapitated body presumed to be . . . Spadafora, was found in Rio Robito, located at Laurel, Costa Rica, some 14 kilometers from the Panamanian border town of Paso Canoa. . . .
> 4. According to a statement issued by Spadafora's father . . . Spadafora travelled from San José, Costa Rica to Paso Canoa on September 13, and crossed the border on that same day. Reportedly Hugo Spadafora, after lunching at noon on the Panamanian side of the border, boarded an eastbound bus at 12:15 p.m. This bus was stopped and inspected at an FDP [PDF] guardpost between the border and Concepción, Panama, but was allowed to proceed. However, according to Carmelo Spadafora, the bus was stopped again by the FDP near Concepción, and Hugo Spadafora was detained. As he was taken on foot to the FDP offices, Spadafora reportedly made a point of calling out his name and waving his identification to passersby.[88]

Six hours later, confirmation came from the U.S. embassy in San José, Costa Rica, that Spadafora's body had been found, partly covered with a canvas bag bearing the words "Domestic U.S. Mail J 460." The San José embassy cabled Washington:

> [Excised] informed us September 17 that a headless body found floating in a creek in southern Costa Rica two days ago is that of Panamanian internationalist and Pastora protegé Hugo Spadafora. [Excised] source posits that the killing was done in Panama . . . the body was probably brought into Costa Rica on a train and was dumped near the border.[89]

The manner of Spadafora's death, particularly the targeting of a political opponent, and, more importantly, the deliberate humiliation and brutal torture inflicted upon him, were events previously beyond the pale in Panamanian politics. A Senate report described the murder as "unique in Panamanian history both in the sadism of the torture and in the brutality and cold-bloodedness of the killing."[90] Spadafora's murder exceeded the expected norm for PDF brutality. As more and more became known about the case, protests sprang up against the military regime. Spadafora's murder became a symbol for what was happening in Panama's public life; as *The Washington Post* put it, "Panama's painful progress toward democracy was thereby 'beheaded,' too."[91]

Barletta's Ouster

President Barletta called for an investigation of Spadafora's death and allegations of PDF complicity. Those actions, in conjunction with a power struggle between Díaz Herrera and Noriega, caused the PDF to oust this increasingly unpopular president.[92]

Barletta spoke out about the murder as soon as the remains were identified. Taking a strong stand in response to "a wave of horror and indignation sweeping the country," Barletta made a televised address to the nation on September 18.[93] He condemned the murder and reported that he had spoken with President Monge to ensure Costa Rican cooperation in the "exhaustive" investigations he had ordered Panama's civilian and military authorities to conduct.[94] Oppositionists and Spadafora family members called for an independent investigation, charging that neither the military nor the district attorney's office, which depended on the PDF for investigative work, could be trusted. Barletta made another public statement on September 19, the day Spadafora's body was returned to Panama, but he did not take further steps to launch an extraordinary investigation. He sent a message to Spadafora's father saying that he had "given instructions that those responsible for the murder be brought to justice."[95] Carmelo Spadafora was not satisfied; Barletta's claim lacked credibility. When Carmelo told the crowd assembled for Hugo's funeral about Barletta's message, people responded with catcalls.[96]

Barletta was in a bad spot. Politically, he was calling for an investigation, trying to calm the situation with tough rhetoric. Legally, he was prohibited by the constitution from taking any decisive action, including naming an investigative commission. His attempt to take control of the issue by taking a hard line so early was causing him trouble on both sides: the PDF felt betrayed, having expected him to defend the institution, and the opposition felt that he was not doing enough.

The United States was also in a delicate position. In view of the "apparent culpability" of Noriega and the PDF, the embassy and

SOUTHCOM agreed that "to the maximum degree possible, we will keep our distance—especially publicly" from the military.[97]

Noriega, it was rumored, would return to Panama from Paris on September 20 or 21; his return was then postponed until September 25. Meanwhile, the PDF stonewalled an investigation and launched a cover-up to discredit opposition claims and protect the military institution from further damage. Barletta began to backpedal. On September 22, he sent an official petition to Attorney General Manuel José Calvo, asking him to establish an advisory commission to assist the public prosecutor.[98]

In this last move, petitioning Calvo, Barletta failed to adequately balance competing pressures, at least from the PDF's vantage point. As one source told the U.S. embassy:

> The last straw as far as the FDP [PDF] was concerned had occurred when Barletta called FDP Deputy Chief of Staff Justines and read to Justines his letter to the Attorney General. . . . Justines had not rejected the letter, but had asked Barletta to add a paragraph to the letter praising the FDP. Barletta had agreed to this but when the letter was published on the following day (September 23), no such paragraph was included. This had incensed Justines and others and sealed Barletta's fate.[99]

Having done all he felt he could accomplish in Panama, Barletta then departed for a United Nations meeting in New York, where he was scheduled to give a speech about foreign debt.

On September 25, General Noriega returned to Panama. The next night, Barletta returned, called home by the PDF but also acting on his own determination to resolve the situation. Barletta was taken directly from the airport to the Comandancía, where he was held for fourteen hours. Díaz Herrera, other PDF officers, and PRD leaders applied the pressure. At one point Barletta talked by telephone with Assistant Secretary of State Abrams, who assured him of U.S. support and urged him to resist military pressure.[100]

While Barletta was being held, pressure was also applied against the opposition, particularly the press. Oppositionists asked the U.S. embassy for an informal show of support, and officials paid a visit to *La Prensa* on the evening of September 26. Their pictures with editor Rubén Dario Carles were featured prominently in the next day's edition.[101] The embassy received members of Spadafora's family, who brought documentary evidence that implicated the PDF in the killing. Such gestures could not help Barletta, however, who remained under PDF control at the Comandancía.

When Barletta emerged to make a televised address at 2:45 P.M. on September 28, 1985, he announced that he was "separating himself" from his office.[102] Barletta said that he had been told by party officials, legislators, and the PDF that "they could no longer work with my presidency."[103] After making his speech, Barletta went home.

Despite the vigorous objections of Ambassador Briggs, PDF officers insisted on resigning Barletta. Millett confirmed the application of U.S. pressure and that it was "ignored."[104] Beyond that pressure, the United States did little. As former Ambassador Ambler Moss put it, "Shultz made no move to help save the Barletta presidency with a show of U.S. support."[105]

One reason the United States was relatively powerless was the PDF's strong determination to cover up Spadafora's murder. This fit an ongoing pattern of shielding excesses committed by individual officers that might damage the institution. In the Spadafora case, the military was adamant about having its own way. Noriega himself made this clear when he said that "slanderous attacks" should not be made against the PDF and that "outspoken generals" should "keep their mouths shut."[106] The PDF was notoriously serious about affronts to its dignity. By law, anyone could be jailed for thirty days without a hearing if they were accused of "lack of respect" by a member of the PDF.[107] Because excesses of much smaller dimensions were routinely covered up, such a strategy was even more likely in response to the more threatening Spadafora case.

Four sources—Panamanian journalist Guillermo Sánchez-Borbon, U.S. journalist James LeMoyne, U.S. embassy officer David Miller, and former NSC staff member Norman A. Bailey—suggested another reason. They asserted that Barletta's ouster was also, if not more importantly, motivated by Noriega's need to distract attention from a military coup attempted by Col. Díaz Herrera during the Spadafora crisis.[108] Díaz Herrera later admitted that he and two other officers (Marcos Justines and Elías Castillo) considered a coup, but that they changed their minds.[109] Díaz Herrera initially confessed, "I caused . . . the ouster of Barletta . . . to justify . . . what I had plotted against Noriega."[110] He later recanted the coup claim, further confusing the issue. Miller later wrote that Barletta's ouster was a means for Noriega "to a) shift attention away from the coup and the Spadafora murder; b) anoint a replacement more politically effective (for Noriega) than Barletta; and c) blame the ousted economist for the nation's woes."[111]

Bailey, the former NSC staff member, suggested another reason for Spadafora's death. He asserted that Noriega was reported to have attended a high-level meeting in Cuzco, Peru, just prior to Spadafora's death. At that meeting, according to Bailey, Noriega was "asked to eliminate Spadafora," supposedly because he was drawing adverse attention to the drug trade.[112]

Some commentators at the time stressed economic and domestic policy concerns as motives for Noriega's decision. Barletta's vigorous application of IMF austerity measures had not just left him politically isolated; they had also hurt the PRD and the military regime generally. Bailey reports that this argument was also advanced by the Department of State as a reason for opposing more forceful negative responses that were advocated by "other agencies" in the executive branch.[113]

Working with Delvalle

Barletta was replaced by his vice-president, Eric Arturo Delvalle, on Saturday, September 28, 1985. Delvalle was widely described as a "front" for Noriega, and the presidency was characterized as a "revolving door" through which occupants were resigned by the PDF after losing favor. Some observers used the analogy "kleenex presidency" to refer to the military's use and disposal of incumbents. The chief opposition newspaper made a play on Arturo Delvalle's nickname "Tuturo"; instead, they called him "Tutorno," meaning "it's your turn."

Delvalle is difficult to describe, in part because his role and objectives changed during the years of his presidency, from 1985 to 1989. His political background was in the relatively small Republican party. As the heir to a fortune made in the sugar business, he was a member of the elite commercial class. He was also a business executive, a graduate of Louisiana State University. At first, Delvalle seemed much more pliant than Barletta; nonetheless, he soon advocated similar policies, but without provoking the PDF. Several years later, when he ordered Noriega to resign, Delvalle would become known as Panama's president-in-hiding. During 1985 and 1986, however, he managed to placate both the PDF and the United States.

One of Delvalle's first official actions was to restore subsidized prices for milk, rice, and petroleum. Ironically, despite the fact that he immediately reversed Barletta's unpopular policies, Delvalle soon found himself implementing the same austerity measures that Barletta had instituted.[114] He, too, was forced by budgetary and debt requirements to take tough actions against the unions.

Even more incongruous were statements by U.S. officials, particularly Assistant Secretary Abrams, praising Delvalle for having the political skills and independence from the military to make the National Assembly actually enact measures that they had rejected from President Barletta.[115] Abrams even went so far, in June 1986, as to say, "President Delvalle has proved to be more forceful than most observers had predicted. . . . There are a number of decisions that President Delvalle has made where we have a variety of reasons to think that he did so in opposition to the military establishment."[116]

Other assessments of Delvalle's administration were much harsher. A Christian Democrat legislator stated that PDF "meddling in public affairs" actually increased, "particularly in promoting themselves and defending their privileges through those daily papers and radio stations that they control."[117] *The New York Times* reported that diplomats and U.S. officials said in February 1986 that "they believe [the PDF] is becoming entrenched and may not be willing to withdraw from government any time soon."[118]

At this point, one observer commented critically that the United States was dealing "carefully with Panama, avoiding any open censure of the military's tough, behind-the-scenes rule that could jeopardize the American position here."[119] Bailey is even more biting in his criticism. He attributes the lack of forceful U.S. action to a "case of intellectual paralysis brought on by a high degree of ignorance of and insensitivity towards [sic] Panama and the region in general."[120]

Official statements did soft-pedal the issue. The reaction of the Department of State, quoted above, was weak. Other official statements referred to the ouster as a "setback on the road to democracy." Press guidance from the embassy summarized the U.S. position:

1. The U.S. government has been shocked to hear of the resignation of Panamanian President Nicolás Ardito Barletta. Dr. Barletta is someone of international stature, highly respected in many countries, including the United States.
2. U.S. Government Policy has been to support constitutional, civilian and democratic government in Central America and elsewhere. It therefore views with considerable concern the sudden change of government in Panama, and hopes that the circumstances which forced this event will be clarified.[121]

Ambassador Briggs used a public speech in Panama to send a stronger negative signal to the military, pointedly referring to democracy as requiring "the rejection of arbitrary authority from above or from the military."[122]

The most tangible message to Noriega and the PDF involved the loss of $14 million in U.S. military aid. These funds had been earmarked for Panama, but they were sent instead to Guatemala, where an elected civilian president had just taken office. Millett confirmed that the United States made some critical, if temporary, moves that "badly disrupted relations between our ambassador" and the Panamanian government.[123]

Behind the scenes, a follow-up message was conveyed to Noriega from the White House by National Security Adviser Poindexter in December. This was the "cut it out" message mentioned previously, which Noriega later claimed had been an ultimatum that he must support the Contras or else. This provided the rationale Noriega later used to explain why the Reagan administration had turned against him: his refusal to do the bidding for the Contras. In December 1985, however, Noriega was sufficiently worried about his meeting with Poindexter that he flew to Washington for a meeting with CIA Director Casey. Casey, according to subsequent reports, reassured Noriega, telling him that he was "too valuable an intelligence source to lose."[124]

In the context of 1984–1986, Barletta's ouster was treated by the Reagan administration as just another round in Panama's long-running game of "musical executive chairs."[125] Although he was the first elected president in sixteen years, Barletta was Panama's fourth president in the past five years. The United States was soon working as closely with Delvalle as it had with Barletta, reflecting the persistence of a "play ball with the powers that be" strategy. The objective of democratization was taking a distant second place.

Noriega Becomes The Issue

Spadafora's murder and Barletta's ouster served as salient events that provided ammunition for two investigations in the United States,[126] which were initiated separately—one by Congress and the other by an investigative reporter. Their combined impact moved the United States toward reinterpreting its objectives, and toward considering Noriega and his PDF as incompatible with U.S. security interests and Panama's democratization.

Seymour Hersh, the Pulitzer Prize–winning journalist well known for accurate investigative reporting, was working on a story about Panama. When his report, a three-part series in *The New York Times*, appeared in June 1986, it sparked a temporary surge in coverage. Two of his headlines summarized the story: "Panamanian Strongman Said to Trade in Drugs, Arms, and Illicit Money" and "U.S. Aides in '72 Weighed Killing Officer Who Now Leads Panama."[127]

NBC's "Today" program ran a feature on Noriega's drug connections and the Spadafora killing; the issues were treated in depth also on the "McNeil-Lehrer News Hour." Noriega and U.S. policy toward Panama were the subject of a flurry of editorials around the country. Taken together, these reports portrayed Noriega as a man playing dirty games, games contrary to the U.S. national interest. Coming only a few months after the corruption scandal exposed by Ferdinand Marcos's ouster from the Philippines, these reports made Noriega seem like another rich, corrupt dictator whose faults the United States had overlooked to protect its own security interests. The charges against Noriega, however, were much more serious: taking bribes to send drugs into the United States, hosting and protecting cartel leaders, arming terrorists abroad, and torturing enemies at home. Most of the allegations made against Noriega during the next two years, and much of the evidence, were detailed in these reports.

The Charges

What evidence did Hersh report? He asserted that Panama was "extensively involved in illicit money and drug activities," that Noriega was "tied" to Spadafora's murder, that Noriega "has been providing intelligence information simultaneously to Cuba and to the US for the last 15 years," and that Noriega was "a secret investor in Panamanian export companies that sell American technology to Cuba and Eastern European countries."[128] To insiders, none of this was news. In fact, a similar report by Knut Royce, published in the *San Antonio Light* almost exactly a year before, had documented the same charges. Royce cited equally devastating comments, including this assessment by a senior law enforcement official in Washington: "Not only is it [Panama] the center for laundering proceeds but it's a center for cutting up the deals, for making payments, for meetings, it's like the corporate center for drug trafficking."[129] In February 1983, a Senate staff study on money laundering had concluded that the PDF "provides warehousing for narcotics on their way north, assures the release, for bribes received, of drug traffickers arrested and guarantees nonarrest of offenders wanted elsewhere who have paid a kind of local safe conduct fee."[130] But in 1983 and 1985, political conditions did not favor agenda status for issues of drugs, corruption, and repression in Panama; in 1986, conditions were conducive, and U.S. Panama policy was taken off the back burner for the first time since 1979.

Whether by design or coincidence,[131] Hersh's allegations were published the very same day that Noriega was in the United States to receive a Panamanian medal of honor at the Inter-American Defense Board, comprised of U.S. and Latin American militaries. Noriega left early, without his medal. Noriega did not think the timing was coincidental; he felt personally affronted and that the PDF had been insulted as an institution at the very moment that its commander was being honored. A PDF spokesman denied all of Hersh's charges.

Hersh's report did, in fact, directly implicate Noriega. He cited a recent classified Defense Intelligence Agency (DIA) report as concluding that Noriega, through his top associates, "maintains tight control of drug and money-laundering activities by his associates" in the PDF.[132] The DIA report also concluded that Noriega himself was "deeply involved" in illegal business.[133] Most of the evidence, according to an official "who had extensively reviewed the most sensitive intelligence available" (National Security Agency communications intercepts), concerned arms trade and drug trafficking. On the Spadafora case, Hersh cited an official with first-hand information who said the DIA is "known to have intelligence demonstrating that General Noriega ordered the killing."

In Washington, officials were seriously concerned. Administration witnesses, particularly from the DEA and the Department of State, were grilled at two separate congressional hearings on June 19, 1986.[134] An additional hearing was held on July 23.[135] Committee staff prepared a six-page chart detailing allegations and evidence against Noriega and the PDF. The charts had three columns: allegations, source(s) where each charge was reported (primarily the Hersh series but also Royce's 1985 series), and the person (or agency) to which allegations and evidence were attributed.[136] This presentation made a devastating case against Noriega. Evidence spanning four years of investigative reports was arrayed across six pages; for each charge, multiple sources were cited, including confirmations in press reports, government documents, and officials' statements.

Witnesses from the DEA tried to point out Panama's positive contributions to drug enforcement, citing marijuana eradication programs and compliance with extradition requests. But the congressmen in attendance were more concerned with cocaine trafficking and money laundering—areas where the DEA readily admitted Panamanian cooperation did not meet their needs or expectations. The State Department's main theme was taken from a public statement by U.S. Ambassador Arthur Davis after he was "summoned" to meet with Panama's foreign minister, Dr. Jorge Abadía Arias:

> The United States Government is aware of the articles about Panama that have appeared recently in newspapers in the United States. I do not wish to speculate about the allegations themselves. The Government of Panama has issued its observations on the stories' charges. The United States respects the sovereignty of the Government of Panama, and intends to continue working with its duly elected officials and representatives in pursuit of our shared goals. High on that list of goals is the combatting of narcotics activity in its various forms. In this regard, the Government of Panama and the United States have worked in the past and continue to work closely with President Del Valle and through him with other Panamanian officials with promising results. We are now preparing, for example, to resume talks on a mutual legal assistance treaty which we hope will lead to concrete measures of particular value in the area of illicit narcotics traffic and the fruits of this criminal activity.[137]

This was relatively tough language for the Department of State to use. The Panamanian government's response was characterized as "observations," a very neutral term implying no justification whatsoever. The mention of "duly elected officials" with whom the United States would continue working pointedly excluded the unelected PDF, which controlled official liaison positions with DEA and other U.S. enforcement agencies.

The statement also strongly stressed an issue on which the United States now expected some positive action, namely the Mutual Legal Assistance Treaty (MLAT). Progress on this issue was emphasized by DEA witnesses as essential to their work and as an important indicator of Panama's commitment to effectively prosecute the drug war. At the same time, however, the statement tried to convey a "balanced" view, noting past cooperation and refusing to "speculate" about the allegations. At both hearings, State Department officials refused to be drawn into a discussion of these charges, arguing either that the United States had no concrete evidence or that such a discussion would not serve U.S. interests. Richard Wyrough, coordinator for Panama affairs and deputy director of the office of Central American affairs, said this most plainly: "We do not believe our interests would be served by added public speculation on this matter. At the same time, we believe our interests demand that we work with the Government of Panama to ensure the fullest cooperation on such important matters as narcotics control."[138]

What Wyrough did not stress was the fact that the relevant part of the Panamanian government with which the United States would continue to work was the PDF. Deputy Assistant Secretary of State for Inter-American

Affairs James Michael made virtually the same statement when he testified at another hearing.[139] There, several committee members were bothered that the administration was continuing to do business as usual with the PDF. They were convinced that Panama was substituting cooperation in extradition for effective enforcement against cocaine trade and money laundering. Members referred to Panamanian cooperation as a set up and as a strategy to "buy you [DEA] off."[140] One expressed the idea slightly more tactfully, but equally to the point: "If the [Hersh] story is true, is it not also probably true that it does not make a tinker's dam if the Panamanians eradicate every marijuana plant in the isthmus as a token of how cooperative they are, because it is a drop in the bucket about what is probably happening?"[141] These congressmen were ahead of the administration in diagnosing the situation in Panama, but they lacked the ability to redirect U.S. policy.

An Inconclusive Policy Review

At this time, officials in the Reagan administration were articulating a consensus position: the United States would discretely signal its displeasure while making clear that the name of the game was still to play ball with Noriega. This reflected an imbalance of bureaucratic power between advocates of change and the status quo. A leak to *The Washington Post* cited a CIA study that was creating a split in the intelligence community between those who favored "overlooking" the problem and those who argued that Noriega's vices could no longer be "ignored." This story also cited a senior Reagan administration official as admitting that "in the past, we've needed" Noriega, but that Hersh's charges might force a reevaluation of the relationship.[142] Another source, former Ambassador Moss, described the administration as experiencing "considerable . . . repercussions" and undertaking a "new look" at U.S. Panama policy. Nevertheless, by September 1986, the review yielded few viable options, and therefore no change in U.S. policy. The decision reached through interagency deliberations was to maintain the status quo. Moss summarized the consensus position: "Let's, for the moment, let well enough alone while encouraging democracy as best we can."[143]

In Panama, Noriega scoffed at Hersh's allegations. He commented that his problems with Washington were "not serious." "There have been opinions and criticisms," he said, where the United States displayed "an excessive readiness to accept the complaints of the opposition." But in Noriega's view,

> the United States and Panama need each other . . . the U.S. cannot change its policy to suit the ego of certain functionaires, and Panama cannot get into a fight with the United States in response to their complaints. The United States has certain strategic priorities in this region, and Panama is a part of that.[144]

In an interview televised on CNN on June 13, 1986, Noriega said, "it is not the United States as a constituted governmental organization that is behind these maneuvers, (but rather) the traditional enemies of the sovereignty and nationalism of the Republic of Panama."[145] Concerning the charges against him, Noriega flatly stated, "it would be 'really imbecilic, totally imbecilic' to believe the U.S. press accusations." When he was asked about the Spadafora case, Noriega simply said, "It is of no interest to me."[146]

President Delvalle, however, went on the offensive: "We are not going to let the name of Gen. Noriega or this government to be stained."[147] The president of the PRD, Rómulo Escobar Bethancourt, characterized the Hersh story as "an attack on the party, the government and the country."[148]

Noriega replied in more detail in an interview published the following week. Noriega told reporter James LeMoyne that he "was the victim of a political campaign by his enemies in Panama who, he said, had manipulated American officials and news organizations to join in attacks against him."[149] Noriega provided some insight about the Spadafora case when he said, "I ask you who has been hurt by the death of Spadafora." Other responses were flagrantly misleading. On the issue of money laundering, he asserted that the PDF "could not be engaged . . . because bank transactions and banking regulations were outside of its control."

What really had been going on in Panama? What did U.S. officials know, and when did they know it?

Congress Investigates the Issues

As the evidence cited at congressional hearings demonstrated, the "story" about Noriega and the PDF had been reported in great detail since 1983. Congress's focus on these allegations had also begun before the Hersh series transformed the story into a salient political issue. Earlier, but with much less press attention and public exposure, a few congressional staff and senators had started to study the situation in Panama. It is from these investigations, by congressional committees and the press, that much of the case against Noriega was made public.

Winston Spadafora, Hugo's brother, tried to recruit congressional allies to publicize Hugo's assassination and to oppose Noriega. Frederick Kempe credited Spadafora's meeting with Sen. Jesse Helms with precipitating the senator's investigative hearings on Panama on March 10 and April 21, 1986. Congressional sources also credited Helm's staff specialist on Latin America, Deborah DeMoss, for the hearings and Helms's subsequent activities on Panama policy. Kempe reported that testimony by Norman Bailey, a former NSC aide, on March 10 covered not only fraud in the 1984 election, Barletta's ouster, and Noriega's corruption and drug trafficking, but also implicated the PDF and characterized it as a barrier to democratization.[150] Attracting no public attention at the time, Helm's hearing did spark the interest of Sen. John Kerry, whose subcommittee dealing with international narcotics later launched an exhaustive investigation covering Panama, neighboring countries, and the Medellín cartel.

All this negative coverage had an effect on the Reagan administration. Electoral fraud, growing repression, and stalled democratization had not been salient issues during 1984 and 1985. During 1986, concern over Noriega's faults was beginning to take precedence over the favors he could provide the U.S. government. By July 1986, reports indicated that demands were growing for the administration to "do something" about Noriega, but without a viable alternative this pressure found no clear focus and yielded no plan. Noriega's opponents in Panama were seen as unrepresentative of the people who would have to take to the streets to achieve a "Philippines solution." The civilian opposition was also seen as badly divided and poorly organized; if they could not get their act together, they could not constitute an option. With no prospects for immediate change in Panama, the administration's concern was reported to center on "a calm transition" in implementing the Panama Canal treaties.[151]

Panamanian Assessments

Two Panamanians offered critical assessments of the first five years of the decade. Roberto Eisenmann described the government as "an autocratic military kleptocracy covered by an ever smaller democratic fig leaf," capturing in one statement the list of growing concerns shared by parts of the U.S. government and oppositionists in Panama.[152] Christian Democratic party leader Ricardo Arias Calderón offered a shorter, but equally apt description. He said Panama was experiencing a process of "reverse democratization" in which military intervention in politics and public life was increasing, rather than declining, as the Torrijos plan had proposed.[153] During the next three years, 1986–1989, these characterizations proved to be increasingly accurate descriptions of the situation in Panama and the policy dilemma facing the United States.

Notes

1. Rumors persist that the United States tried to overthrow Torrijos in 1969 because of his leftist tendencies. A coup was attempted in December during Torrijos's first trip abroad since taking power. While Torrijos was in Mexico City enjoying the horse races, Col. Amado Sanjur, with the aid of David Samudio, announced a coup. As soon as Torrijos found out, he frantically searched for an airplane and called on his loyal subordinate, Colonel Noriega, for help. Noriega, then in command of the Chiriquí military region, provided a landing strip and loyal troops to accompany Torrijos to Panama City. William Jorden provides a detailed account of the coup attempt and Torrijos's reactions in *Panama Odyssey*

pp. 143–146. Seymour Hersh presents the strongest evidence of U.S. complicity in the coup attempt in "The Creation of a Thug," pp. 81–87. Whether the CIA instigated the coup, and whether a bureaucratic struggle between the CIA and the Army 470th Military Intelligence Group was the U.S. motive, Torrijos apparently believed the United States was involved.

However, the United States also facilitated Torrijos's resumption of power. A State Department official working on Panama policy at the time said that the United States actually assisted Torrijos's successful return by allowing him access, through U.S. territory, to Panama City via the Bridge of the Americas (confidential interview, Little Rock, Arkansas, February 1990).

2. A copy of the agreement is reprinted in Correa, *La gran rebelion blanca* Vol. I, pp. 19–20.

3. Juan O. Tamayo, "Panama Eyes 1984 Elections, Threat of Power Shift," *Miami Herald*, November 2, 1982.

4. Citations in this account are direct quotes reported by confidential sources to a military officer in U.S. Department of Defense, Confidential [excised], "Panama: Significant Changes," March 4, 1982.

5. U.S. Department of Defense, Confidential [excised], "Comments by a National Guard of Panama (GN) official on the recent changes and future of the GN," March 19, 1982.

6. U.S. Department of Defense, "Panama: Significant Changes."

7. U.S. Department of State, Confidential Panama 07932, Sec. 01, p. 1.

8. Numerous sections of the law were later declared unconstitutional by the Supreme Court.

9. Ropp, "Panama," p. 170.

10. U.S. Department of State, Confidential Panama 07932, Sec. 01, p. 1.

11. Ibid., Sec. 02, p. 1.

12. An indication of U.S. concerns at this time is contained in a congratulatory letter to Paredes upon his retirement from the chairman of the Joint Chiefs of Staff, General John Vessey. Although such letters usually include laudatory comments, this one also refers to the Caribbean Basin perspective that was slanting U.S. views of the region at this time and affecting relations between the U.S. military and the PDF. The letter states, "As a result of your personal leadership that relationship has matured to one of full partnership and mutual trust and respect. Indeed, you have advanced the cause of liberty, peace, and democracy in Panama and for the entire Caribbean basin" (U.S. Department of Defense, Confidential [excised], "Letter for Gen. Paredes," August 12, 1983).

13. Tamayo, "Panama Eyes 1984 Elections."

14. Ibid.

15. U.S. Department of State, Confidential Panama 08658. Richard Millett reports that Paredes also got into a clash with U.S. Ambassador Briggs that undermined Paredes's image and credibility—a clash probably engineered by Noriega for that purpose (Millett, "Looking Beyond Noriega," p. 50).

16. The embassy reported in 1981 that Paredes had been "shopping around for support" that year, along with President Royo and Aquilino Boyd, in an attempt to form a coalition of center-right groups (U.S. Department of State, Confidential Panama 10412). At this time, the PRD was badly factionalized and disorganized. Since its creation, the party had both left and right "wings"; Torrijos apparently modeled the PRD on Mexico's ruling party, the PRI (Institutional Revolutionary party).

17. U.S. Department of State, Confidential Panama 8658.

18. Ibid., p. 2.

19. Tamayo, "Panama Eyes 1984 Elections."

20. U.S. Department of Defense, Confidential [excised], "US visit of BG Ruben Paredes Rios," date excised [estimate June 1982].

21. Ibid.

22. Conte-Porras, *Requiem por la Revolución*, p. 518.

23. Tamayo, "Panama Eyes 1984 Elections."

24. U.S. Congress, *Country Reports*, 1982, p. 595.

25. Tamayo, "Panama Eyes 1984 Elections."

26. Ironically, de la Espriella himself had been accused of using government funds for the PRD only six months earlier. In late July 1983, Rafael Rodriguez, the attorney general, was forced to resign after he charged de la Espriella, General Paredes, and top PRD leaders with "usurping public funds to benefit the PRD" (U.S. Department of State, Confidential Panama 07308, August 1, 1983).

27. This and the next Arias quote are from U.S. Department of State, Confidential Panama 00739, pp. 1, 2.

28. U.S. Department of State, Confidential Panama 01628.

29. The new acting vice-president was Carlos Ozores.

30. U.S. Department of State, Confidential Panama 01722, pp. 1–2.

31. Miller, "Panama and U.S. Policy," p. 132. Miller served in the U.S. embassy in Panama, 1985–1987.

32. Tamayo, "Panama Eyes 1984 Elections."

33. CONDECA functioned from 1963 to 1969 as a loose organization of Central American militaries that was organized by SOUTHCOM; it focused initially on opposition to Castro but never became a strong organization. Honduras's General Gustavo Alvaraz Martínez attempted to reactivate CONDECA in late 1983 and early 1984, to support his plan to aid the Contras by setting them up in a liberated zone as a rival government, and using CONDECA to invite the U.S. to use military force to defend them. This plan was supported by NSC staff aide Oliver North and the CIA field agent Dewey (also known as Duane) Clarridge; Assistant Secretary of State Langhorne Motley said, however, that the plan was floated several times but never received a high-level review or approval. See Gutman, *Banana Diplomacy*, pp. 176–180. President Illueca was not alone in criticizing CONDECA and Alvaraz's plan; so did political leaders in Guatemala and El Salvador.

34. Elsewhere I have argued that Noriega used Barletta's candidacy as an irresistible lure offered to the United States to comply with repeated calls for elections without really relinquishing control or disrupting the military regime (Scranton, "Elections as U.S. Policy Option").

35. *Newsweek*, February 27, 1984, p. 63.

36. Both quotes are from Georgie Anne Geyer, "Panama Canal: Reason Wins," *Dallas Morning News*, January 20, 1984.

37. Vote tallies and projections are taken from U.S. Department of State, Information Memorandum, To: The Secretary, Fm: ARA - Tony Motley, "Panama Election Update," May 9, 1984.

38. U.S. Department of State, Information Memorandum, To: The Secretary, Fm: ARA - Tony Motley, "Panama's Election," May 12, 1984.

39. Col. Díaz Herrera later explained the techniques Noriega used to steal the election, including the names of those on the Electoral Tribunal who accepted and refused bribes. The best analysis of the election, particularly of the counting process and the significance of vote challenges and valid and invalid votes, was written by the embassy's political officer, John Cason. See U.S. Department of State, Confidential Airgram 002005.

40. The May 7 and May 30 incidents were reported by AP in "Alleged Vote

Fraud Causes Riot; Dozens Arrested in Panama," *Tulsa World*, October 11, 1984, p. C15.

41. *US News and World Report*, May 8, 1984, p. 40.

42. *Time*, May 21, 1984, p. 61.

43. U.S. Department of State, Information Memorandum, To: The Secretary, Fm: ARA - Tony Motley, "Panama-Barletta's Proposal for a Joint Action Agenda," September 25, 1984, p. 1.

44. Ibid.

45. U.S. Department of State, Confidential Briefing Memorandum, To: The Secretary, Fm: ARA - Tony Motley, "Your meeting with President-elect Barletta," October 3, 1984, p. 1.

46. Ibid., pp. 1–2.

47. Ibid., p. 5.

48. "Alleged Vote Fraud," p. C15.

49. Ibid.

50. Ibid.

51. *Time*, October 22, 1984, p. 59.

52. U.S. Congress, *Country Reports*, 1985, p. 649.

53. Guillermo A. Cochez, "Panama: A Strategic Ally on the Brink of Chaos," *The Wall Street Journal*, December 6, 1985, p. 27.

54. Zhu Manting, "Panama," p. 14.

55. Ibid., p. 41.

56. John M. Goshko, "Austerity Campaign Fuels Panamanian Unrest," *The Washington Post*, September 1, 1985.

57. Quoted in ibid.

58. Cochez, "Panama."

59. *Newsweek*, January 15, 1990, p. 17.

60. Detailed accounts are provided in Kohn and Monks, "Dirty Secrets of George Bush"; and Emerson, *Secret Warriors*.

61. Details of these activities have been widely presented, beginning with the Iran-Contra investigation. One of the first reports of interagency rivalry based on Noriega's services appeared in *Newsweek* on July 13, 1987. Stephen Engelberg wrote a long article, "Alliance with US Military and Agencies Helped Noriega Resist Pressure," about Noriega's alliances with U.S. agencies, describing him as "a master at developing relationships in the American military and intelligence agencies that forestalled diplomatic and legal pressure against him" in *The New York Times*, February 7, 1988. Much of the documentation on drugs and money laundering issues, along with Noriega's relations with DEA, comes from congressional hearings on those issues during 1987 and 1988.

62. These citations are from U.S. Department of Defense, Confidential [excised], "193d Infantry Brigade Weekly Intelligence Summary for 28 Feb–8 Mar 1985," March 8, 1985. [Hereafter cited as WIS, March 1985.]

63. U.S. Congress, *Issues in U.S.-Panamanian Anti-Narcotics Control*, p. 51.

64. WIS, March 1985.

65. Geyer, "Panama Canal."

66. Ibid.

67. Two recent books provide detailed accounts of all three of these incidents, particularly the Darién operation, as well as additional facets of the drug trade in Panama. See Dinges, *Our Man in Panama*, chap. 1; and Kempe, *Divorcing the Dictator*, chap. 12.

68. José Blandón, who was then a close confidant and personal emissary of Noriega, provided the account of Castro's involvement in these events, which

Blandón witnessed; see U.S. Congress, *Drugs*, Part 2. Hearings before the Subcommittee on Terrorism, Narcotics and International Communications, 100th Congress, 2nd session, February 8, 9, 10, and 11, 1988 (Washington, D.C.: GPO, 1988), especially, pp. 105–108. Dinges tried to verify Blandón's account and concluded that portions could not be substantiated (*Our Man in Panama*, p. 25).

69. Kempe discusses the Melo affair in *Divorcing the Dictator*, pp. 187–188, 195; Dinges discusses the affair in *Our Man in Panama* in several contexts, especially pp. 16–24 and 185.

70. Kempe, *Divorcing the Dictator*, p. 186.

71. Dinges (*Our Man in Pamana*) cites this figure in a note for p. 185 at p. 363.

72. Richard Millett's testimony before Congress; see U.S. Congress, *Human Rights and Political Developments*, p. 76.

73. Ibid.

74. U.S. Congress, *Human Rights and Political Developments*, pp. 3–4.

75. Ibid., p. 4.

76. Ibid., p. 34.

77. Seymour M. Hersh, "Panama Strongman Said to Trade In Drugs, Arms and Illicit Money," *The New York Times*, June 12, 1986, p. 6.

78. Ibid.

79. *Human Rights and Political Developments*, p. 76.

80. Cochez, "Panama" p. 27.

81. Sánchez-Borbon, Kempe, and Dinges give differing accounts of Spadafora's killing and torture. In 1985, the fact that his beheaded body was found in a U.S. mailbag thrown just across the Costa Rican border was sufficient for most reports to describe the incident as the worst yet on Noriega's political record. See Sánchez-Borbon, "Panama Fallen Among Thieves," pp. 62–63.

82. U.S. Department of Defense, Confidential [excised], "[subject excised, subtitle "C. (U) Spadafora vs. Noriega"]," January 14, 1982, Sec. 03.

83. Ibid.

84. U.S. Department of State, Confidential Panama 10680, p. 2.

85. Quoted in *The New York Times*, January 12, 1986.

86. Sánchez-Borbon, "Panama Fallen," p. 58.

87. U.S. Department of State, Secret Panama 10515, Sec. 01, p. 1.

88. Ibid.

89. U.S. Department of State, Confidential San José 08180, p. 1.

90. U.S. Congress, *Drugs*, Part 2, p. 206.

91. Editorial, *The Washington Post*, December 6, 1985, p. A26.

92. Reports at the time merely mentioned that Barletta was forced out; Dinges and Kempe provide detailed accounts, based on interviews with Barletta and others, of the pressure brought to bear on Barletta and Noriega's role in the process.

93. U.S. Department of State, Confidential Panama 10680, Sec. 01, p. 3.

94. Ibid.

95. U.S. Department of State, Confidential Panama 10752.

96. Ibid.

97. U.S. Department of State, Confidential Panama 10680, Sec. 01, p. 3.

98. U.S. Department of State, Confidential Panama 10803, Sec. 01, p. 2.

99. U.S. Department of State, Secret Panama 11589.

100. Stephen Kinzer, "Panama Military: Too Deep in Political Trenches," *The New York Times*, February 17, 1986.

101. The United States was concerned not just with press freedom; the

embassy was receiving considerable anti-U.S. comment based on its close relations with the PDF; see U.S. Department of State, Secret Panama 10986.

102. According to the Panamanian constitution, a president could separate himself from office for a period of ninety days without penalty of losing office. Thus, Barletta's statement was addressed to the people of Panama, rather than the National Assembly, to which a resignation would be submitted. Although a separation differs legally from a resignation, an incumbent may lack the political power to resume office. Barletta may have hoped that U.S. pressure would force Noriega to back off so that he could resume the presidency; if so, he was disappointed.

103. *Springdale News*, September 29, 1985.

104. U.S. Congress, *Human Rights and Political Developments*, p. 76. Millett also reported that the attempt at influence created a disruption in relations between the U.S. embassy and the government of Panama. Norman A. Bailey described Briggs's protests as vigorous in "Panama Coup: Dangerous Reversal of Latin American Democracy," *Tulsa World*, November 10, 1985.

105. Moss, Report on Panama, p. 9.

106. James LeMoyne, "The Opposition Takes Cover in Panama," *The New York Times*, October 13, 1985.

107. Sánchez-Borbon, "Panama Fallen," p. 57.

108. Ibid.; James LeMoyne, "Elements in Ouster of Panama Chief: Beheading and a Power Duel," *The New York Times*, October 2, 1985; Miller, "Panama and U.S. Policy," p. 133; and Bailey, "Panama Coup," p. 4. John Dinges (in *Our Man in Panama*) gives a slightly different interpretation, suggesting that Díaz Herrera was trying to divert Noriega's attention from the coup that he had just attempted.

109. "Attorney's Office Takes Díaz Herrera's Deposition" FBIS-LAT 87-150, August 5, 1987, p. J2.

110. Ibid., p. J3.

111. Miller, "Panama and U.S. Policy," p. 133.

112. Bailey, "Charges and Counter-Charges," p. 65.

113. Ibid., p. 68.

114. These austerity measures did, in time, have an effect. Public sector debt as a percent of GDP fell from 11 percent in 1982 to 1.9 percent in 1985; the estimate for 1986 was 1.3 percent. See Koenig, "Hard Choices," p. 41.

115. U.S. Congress, *Human Rights and Political Developments*, p. 5.

116. Ibid., pp. 5, 30. One such decision that Abrams mentioned was whether Marcos should be allowed to reside in Panama as an exile; Delvalle refused, according to Abrams, over strong objections from the PDF.

117. Cochez, "Panama," p. 27.

118. Kinzer, "Panama Military."

119. *US News and World Report*, October 21, 1985, p. 46.

120. Bailey, "Charges and Counter-Charges," p. 68.

121. U.S. Department of State, Panama 11058, pp. 1–2.

122. Kinzer, "Panama Military."

123. U.S. Congress, *Human Rights and Political Developments*, p. 76.

124. AP report by Richard Cole, "Noriega's CIA Links Worry US," *Arkansas Democrat*, January 6, 1990, p. 8A.

125. The phrase comes from a report in *Time*, February 24, 1984, p. 63.

126. Spadafora's murder was also the subject of an investigation by the OAS Inter-American Human Rights Commission, which gave its report to the Panamanian government in early 1988. This investigation shed further light on the details of the case and PDF complicity, but it had no apparent effect on the

PDF or Panamanian government. The Commission issued its findings in Case #2726 on January 14, 1988, condemning the government of Panama for the brutal homicide of Hugo Spadafora.

127. Seymour Hersh, *The New York Times*, June 12, 1986, pp. 1, 6; and June 13, 1986, pp. 1, 8. A similar report in *US News and World Report* a month later asked, "Is Panama Run by a Military 'Mafia'?"

128. Hersh, "Panama Strongman," pp. 1, 6.

129. Knut Royce, "Panama a Haven for Traffickers," *San Antonio Light*, June 10, 1985. Other reports in Royce's series were "Panama's Powerful Figure in Drug Money Laundering [Noriega]," June 11; "Gunrunning Plays Part in Panama's Complexity," June 13; and "Drug Money Snowballing in Panamanian Banks," June 14; all are reprinted in U.S. Congress, *Panama*, pp. 45–53.

130. *Newsweek*, June 6, 1983.

131. Ambassador Moss, for one, could see no apparent "news 'peg'" that would explain why so many reporters focused on the Noriega story at the same time (Moss, "The U.S.-Panamanian Relationship," p. 12). A year later, *Newsweek* reported that NSC Adviser Poindexter authorized the leaks for Hersh's story; this would confirm the administration's intent to generate negative coverage about Noriega, but not the timing of the release of Hersh's series. Steve Ropp, however, said that competition from *The Washington Post* accounted for the *Times* decision to publish. Ropp found out that earlier in the year CIA Director Casey had told the editor of the *Post* to lay off his investigative reporting of CIA involvement in Central America. When the editor of the *Post* related the incident to the editor of the *Times*, he was so insulted that he had not also been contacted by Casey that he told Hersh to "go dig up some dirt" on Central America policy. Serendipitously, he picked Panama.

132. All of the citations in this paragraph are from Hersh, "Panama Strongman."

133. This was old information. A cable from the U.S. embassy on November 9, 1981, five years earlier, had reported that

> a small group of senior Government of Panama (GOP) and Panama National Guard (GN) officers are involved in facilitating, if not outright assisting, the 19 April Movement (M-19) [in Colombia] . . . the predominant motivation is personal profit. The master hand behind this involvement they [sources] believe is GN G-2 Ltc. Manuel Noriega. Others they suspect are GN G-2 Maj. Julean [Julián] Melo [who was later charged and dismissed for drug trafficking], Carlos (Pérez) Herrera who manages the Panama-Kadafy Liaison, and Leonardo Kam who manages the Panama M-19 Liaison.

See U.S. Department of Defense, Panama 10110.

134. U.S. Congress, *Panama*; and U.S. Congress, *Issues in U.S.-Panamanian Anti-Narcotics Control*.

135. This was the second day of the hearings in U.S. Congress, *Human Rights and Political Developments*.

136. U.S. Congress, *Panama*, pp. 38–43.

137. Ibid., p. 44. Foreign Minister Abadía's statement is also printed in this hearing on pp. 43–44. Dr. Abadía stressed what Panama perceived as "mixed signals" coming from official and unofficial sources. On the positive side, he cited and released the text of DEA administrator Lawn's letter to Noriega, thanking him for cooperating in enforcement efforts.

138. U.S. Congress, *Panama*, p. 37.

139. This delicate approach to Panama was in marked contrast to U.S. official statements on Mexico. Department of State spokesman Charles Redman had publicly said that high officials in the Mexican government were corrupt (U.S. Congress, *Panama*, p. 5.)

140. U.S. Congress, *Panama*, p. 22.

141. Ibid.

142. Charles R. Babcock and Bob Woodward, "Report on Panama General Poses Predicament for US," *The Washington Post*, June 13, 1986. The study, compiled by the CIA, documented Noriega's involvement in smuggling drugs and arms, his involvement in money laundering, and his contacts with Cuban intelligence.

143. Moss, "The U.S.-Panamanian Relationship," p. 11.

144. All of Noriega's citations in this paragraph are from his interview with James LeMoyne, "Panamanian, Denying Charges Says He Won't Quit," *The New York Times*, June 18, 1986.

145. Quoted in U.S. Department of State, Confidential Panama 08978, Sec. 01, p. 1.

146. Ibid.

147. AP report in *Arkansas Democrat*, June 15, 1986.

148. U.S. Department of State, Confidential Panama 08978, Sec. 01, p. 1.

149. LeMoyne, "Panamanian Denying Charges"; quotes in the rest of this paragraph are from this interview.

150. Kempe, *Divorcing the Dictator*, p. 177.

151. "Is Panama Run by a Military 'Mafia'?" p. 37.

152. Eisenmann, "Unanswered Questions," p. 53.

153. Arias Calderón, "The Challenge to Democracy," p. 77. Arias provides several examples of military intervention, ranging from pressure by Col. Díaz Herrera, to recommendations by legislators to change personnel, to naming military officers to head agencies formerly run by civilians. Also see Arias Calderón's article "Panama: Disaster or Democracy?"

6

Noriega Must Go . . . But How?

From late 1986 until the abortive October 1989 coup, the objective of U.S. Panama policy was deceptively simple: Noriega must go. Changes in Panama and the United States made the policy of working with Noriega less and less tenable. Noriega faced an opposition movement that could be temporarily cowed but not eliminated. The regime was becoming increasingly unpopular and repressive. This alone, however, was not sufficient to cause the United States to discontinue its "play ball" strategy. Important changes in other priority policies, namely aid to the Contras and the drug war, were the main sources of the U.S. decision that Noriega must go.

When the policy of providing covert support for the Contras was undermined by the Iran-Contra scandal, Noriega's value as an ally was damaged. Previously, Noriega's support for the Contras had been a convenient service; the Central Intelligence Agency and the National Security Council appreciated this covert help in their "off the shelf" endeavors.[1] After the story of the Iran-Contra scandal broke in November 1986, Noriega was a liability to an administration attempting to refurbish its image. Concurrently, Noriega lost two allies, CIA Director Casey and NSC staff aide Lt. Col. Oliver North, who had previously argued on his behalf; their departure shifted the bureaucratic balance of power toward the Department of State. Casey was suffering from cancer; he was hospitalized in December 1986 and died in June 1987; North was dismissed from the NSC, questioned by Congress, and tried in federal court for his part in the Iran-Contra affair.

The second change in U.S. priorities that affected Panama policy was the drug war. As an issue, international narcotics trafficking accelerated during 1986 and 1987 and became a full-blown, salient national priority in 1988. Noriega was not just on the wrong side of this issue, he was in the enemy camp. The more salient the drug issue became, the more the Reagan administration was motivated to sever connections with Noriega and seek his removal from power. When indictments naming Noriega were about to be

105

unsealed in early 1988, the CIA finally stopped paying the general. Changes in the status of drug policy also deprived Noriega of a bureaucratic advocate, namely the Drug Enforcement Administration. Thus, by 1988, only two players at interagency deliberations continued to assert that the United States gained tangible benefits from working with Noriega. But the DEA stopped making this claim once Noriega was indicted, and during 1989, the other player—the Department of Defense (DOD)—was increasingly drawn toward the position that Noriega must go. Different components of the DOD had different views of Noriega. Those in Panama, at U.S. SOUTHCOM headquarters, advised that Noriega must go as early as June 1987; during December 1987 the office of the assistant secretary of defense took this stance. Several defense advisers, notably Nestor Sanchez, disagreed; nonetheless, during 1988, the DOD became increasingly opposed to Noriega.

From late 1986 through late 1989, the Reagan and Bush administrations shared the objective that Noriega must go. Both administrations took the position that U.S. military force should not be used to achieve this objective. Until October 1989, the military option was deliberately taken off the table. Various alternatives to force—diplomatic, economic, and legal measures— were applied to remove Noriega, but none achieved that goal.

The year 1986 ended with U.S.-Panamanian relations deceptively calm. Secretary of State George Shultz held a meeting with President Eric Arturo Delvalle on September 23, 1986. Neither of the two issues that would dominate U.S.-Panamanian relations for the next five years—removing Noriega and restoring democracy—was on the agenda. Instead, their talk focused on older, hold-over issues: continuing Panamanian suspicions that the United States would fail to honor the Panama Canal treaty, "poor atmospherics" lingering over Hersh's exposé about Noriega, U.S. dissatisfaction with Panama's lack of progress on the Mutual Legal Assistance Treaty and Panama's complaints about Canal treaty implementation and contingency payments.[2] The appearance of calm was deceiving; in a matter of months, Noriega would become *the* issue between the United States and Panama.

Díaz Herrera Unleashes a Storm

In Panama, tensions were building between Noriega and the chief of staff and deputy commander of the PDF, Col. Roberto Díaz Herrera. Díaz Herrera had graduated from the Peruvian military academy a year behind Noriega; both men then moved steadily up the command hierarchy. Díaz Herrera was supposed to succeed Noriega as commandant, but between September 1985 and late 1986, Noriega decided that his long-time rival would have to go. During the first few months of 1987, Noriega froze Díaz Herrera out of his inner circle; Díaz Herrera responded by participating less and less in PDF routines and functions. Finally, a deal seemed to be arranged for Díaz Herrera to retire in exchange for a lucrative ambassadorial appointment. On May 27, 1987, word leaked to the press that Díaz Herrera had been granted an "indefinite vacation" due to "some health problems," and that his retirement was "forthcoming."[3] The retirement order was issued on June 1. The next day, Televisora Nacional announced that Díaz Herrera had been retired "with all the rights to which he is entitled" as chief of the general staff, and that Col. Marcos Justines would replace him.[4] Everything seemed to be going according to Noriega's plan.

Confessions and Accusations

Díaz Herrera soon told a different story: Noriega forced him out, and he feared for his life. The colonel said, "They [not further identified] have already ordered my assassination . . . on Wednesday, 3 June."[5] Alluding to Spadafora's beheading, he said he hoped "his entire body will be found."[6] Díaz Herrera went public, with confessions and accusations against Noriega, partly out of anger and partly to gain protection. When his first interviews failed to bring sufficient attention, he called a late night press conference on June 6 to make a more dramatic presentation. His revelations were so explosive, and the press and popular reaction so enthusiastic, that Díaz Herrera's dialogue with the media continued for several days.

The press conference was a catalyst for a new round of opposition activity both in Panama and in the United States, and for a reconsideration of U.S. objectives. Díaz Herrera's accusations sparked three full days of violence and protests, unleashing popular resentment that had been building for years. The colonel thus became an unlikely source of momentum for the opposition movement.

Who was Díaz Herrera? Like Noriega, he attracted some bizarre associates, including an Indian guru.[7] As a political figure, he acquired a different reputation in different camps. A U.S. Senate report described him this way:

> Among Panamanian supporters of Torrijos, Díaz Herrera was known as "the keeper of the flame" and "the guardian of orthodox torrijismo." Among U.S. diplomatic personnel, Díaz Herrera was known, prior to his departure from the PDF in 1987, as sinister and unprincipled, as a frustrated opportunist, "probably a leftist," as the man who most frequently did Noriega's dirty work.[8]

Just as Torrijos had used Noriega for his dirty work, Noriega used Díaz Herrera. Díaz Herrera might therefore fairly be characterized as Noriega's Noriega. In this capacity, the colonel built a reputation for toughness. One U.S. diplomat went so far as to say, "If you think Noriega is bad, you don't know Díaz Herrera."[9] Consequently, when Díaz Herrera broke with Noriega, it was not easy for opposition leaders to incorporate him into their movement. Díaz Herrera had been a salient instrument of their repression, but even oppositionists flocked to his house during these extraordinary weeks.[10]

As a long-time member of the PDF inner circle, Díaz Herrera had grown so rich from corruption profits and shady business dealings that his denunciations were described as "the second most corrupt man in Panama" taking on the first.[11] Díaz Herrera began his press conference by confessing how he bought his $500,000 house, a "garish . . . mansion"[12] in the affluent neighborhood Altos de Golf: "[My house was] half stolen because it was built with the money of the people who came from Cuba, from the visas."[13] He was not exaggerating; the going rate for bribes from selling visas to Cubans who were using Panama as a staging point for emigration ranged from $3,500 to $10,000 each.

These confessions sparked reporters' interests, but what really transformed the press conference into a political landmark were his accusations against Noriega and the PDF. Some of these were true and some were not; some were later recanted. Díaz Herrera's charges spanned numerous cases of bribery, missing government funds, electoral fraud, Spadafora's murder, and even a plot to kill Torrijos. He confessed to his own role in rigging the 1984 election, to tapping telephones, and to other forms of corruption. Excerpts from his long, rambling interview were published in *La Prensa* on June 7 under the headline "Fraud Finalized at My House, Díaz Herrera Confesses."[14] *La Prensa* carried the full text the next day, June 8, and Channel 13 televised a lengthy segment that night.[15]

Political Repercussions

Díaz Herrera's outburst was a sensational event. People flocked to his house, including Hugo Spadafora's brother Winston, Archbishop Marcos McGrath, and traditional opposition party leaders. Mayín Correa conducted a live radio broadcast from a nearby corner, where reactions in the streets were as much of the story as Díaz Herrera's ongoing interviews.[16]

The substance of the colonel's charges was not new at all. What was unprecedented was a public split in Noriega's inner circle, a defection from the highest ranks of the PDF. Moreover, because Díaz Herrera was known as a voice of *Torrijismo*, his removal indicated programmatic changes in the PDF. Díaz Herrera's decision to fight back created the most serious political crisis the regime had experienced since the military took over in 1968.[17]

The Catholic church described Díaz Herrera's charges as a detonator; many observers commented on the amount of latent hostility that had built up, waiting to be ignited. On June 8, 1987, some 100,000 people—one-fourth the population of Panama City—spontaneously took to the streets at noon.[18] Some wore T-shirts saying "I Love Sedition"; others said "Down with the Pineapple," a reference to Noriega's visage. Díaz Herrera unleashed more mass protests than the Spadafora crisis had ignited in September 1985; the 1987 demonstrations sparked the worst street violence in recent history. In June 1987, more people responded; they also had higher expectations that the dictator could be dislodged. The issues were the same in 1987 as they had been in 1985: PDF brutality and corruption, narco-military dictatorship, and opposition to Noriega.

New opposition leaders joined the fray. An umbrella organization of twenty-six civic, business, labor, professional, women's, and students' groups was formed on June 7, 1987. It was initially called the National Civilianization Crusade (NCC), referring to the civilianization process that the 1984 election had derailed. The name was later shortened to National Civic Crusade.[19] Calling themselves "civilistas," these new leaders, along with traditional political party oppositionists, began to ride the biggest wave of antigovernment protests the country had ever seen. People and organizations previously on the sidelines were politicized. The groups most heavily involved in the NCC were the Panamanian Chamber of Commerce, Industries and Agriculture; medical and lawyers' associations; and business executives' groups. Some of the less-publicized members were: Lions, Rotary, and Kiwanis clubs; the Children's Welfare Association; the Association of Panamanian Life Insurance Brokers; the Association of Automobile Spare Parts Distributors; the Association of Professors of the Republic of Panama; and the Association of Travel Agencies and Tourism.[20]

Thousands turned out for three solid days of demonstrations. Many engaged in traditional *pailas* at noon and 6:00 P.M., banging pots and pans as a sign of opposition. Some demonstrations turned violent. At one, "thousands of angry youths constructed barricades of burning rubbish and tires, and fought pitched battles with squads of riot police."[21] Various organizations demanded Noriega's removal, immediate national elections, and an end to military dominance of Panamanian politics.

Noriega's retaliation was also the worst yet: special riot police, the newly created Dobermans, bashed demonstrators in a brutal crackdown. Dozens were injured, hundreds were arrested, and many were detained overnight. The government declared a state of emergency that lasted nineteen days. Julia Preston noted another first: for the first time Noriega was on the defensive and acting in an "uncharacteristically reckless" manner.[22] He had underestimated Díaz Herrera, and he was surprised by the amount and intensity of the opposition that erupted.

The political situation was fluid. Rumors flourished. One report suggested a schism had developed between the PDF and the military's political party, the PRD. The PRD president, Rómulo Escobar Bethancourt, denied the report and asserted that "any leftist movement within the party has not been weakened."[23] To bolster public perceptions of PDF solidarity and loyalty, Noriega arranged for a "manifesto" to be issued by majors and captains on June 8. They confirmed their "unyielding loyalty to the

institution and to our commander in chief" and, in a thinly veiled reference to
Díaz Herrera, they rejected "the paranoiac treason and conspiracy against our
institution." The document ended with a proclamation: "General Manuel
Antonio Noriega: We are loyal to the principles of professionalism, loyalty,
and the fatherland that you have taught the institution. Once more, we say:
Present! Not a step backwards! Give us your orders, Commander!"[24]

Events were harder to decipher on the opposition side. At the Legislative
Assembly, the visitors' area was packed with government workers who had
been brought in by legislators representing the government coalition
(UNADE) to deny space to opposition supporters. The government workers
booed opposition legislators any time they tried to speak about Díaz Herrera
or the current situation. On June 8, all of the opposition legislators staged a
"walk out."[25]

Then, an unexpected development occurred: Arnulfo Arias stepped
forward to claim the presidential sash denied him when the PDF stole
the 1984 election. Members of the Authentic Panameñista party met with
Díaz Herrera to discuss a plan for Arnulfo Arias to achieve power. For
an entire week discussions were held about electoral fraud, Arias's views
on the military, Díaz Herrera's demands that the basic structure and hierarchy
of the PDF be respected, and possible reforms of the PDF, particularly
retirement of senior officers on schedule, according to Law 20, the military
organic law. For a brief moment, it appeared that enough significant political
players could piece together a reform plan that would be acceptable to
the opposition, the PDF, and the PRD. Through his denunciation, Díaz
Herrera moved into an entirely different leadership role: he tried to guide a
dialogue to reshape the PDF and reform the regime. However, the political
dynamics bringing together oppositionists and PRD/PDF reformers were not
strong enough to cement a mutually acceptable solution, and the moment
passed.

While the civilistas were organizing, politicians were maneuvering, and
people were demonstrating, Díaz Herrera was reconsidering. Whether he had
planned to create a popular uprising that might lead to Noriega's overthrow,
or whether he simply lashed out as a last resort will never be known.[26]
Several days after his confession, he claimed a political motive, saying,
"This is an illegitimate government that has created an institutionalized
crisis. . . . I knew that the only way to change the system is to get rid of
Noriega."[27] Once he became the focus of a rapidly growing movement, Díaz
Herrera had an even bigger problem: sooner or later Noriega would come after
him with a vengeance. While protests raged in the streets and supporters
gathered outside his house, Díaz Herrera tried to recant and reverse the course
events were taking. Flanked by his own family, the Spadafora family, and
others, Díaz Herrera made another statement to the press: "I don't think that
anyone is to blame, not even the specific persons I have blamed and not even
General Noriega himself."[28] The words were conciliatory but the setting,

particularly with the Spadaforas present, invoked his initial accusatory message. As time passed and the crisis continued, Díaz Herrera's personal struggle with Noriega receded in importance. As government and opposition leaders stepped forward to respond to fast-breaking events, Díaz Herrera's role diminished. He had unleashed a storm, but he could neither guide it nor arrange a denouement—it had developed a momentum of its own.

The Senate Chastises Noriega

The Reagan administration perceived events in Panama as serious, but it was divided over how to proceed. While the administration deliberated, the Senate mustered a majority to take a strong rhetorical stance. Several senators—Jesse Helms, John Kerry, Edward Kennedy, and Alphonse D'Amato—had become actively interested in the issues of drugs and human rights in Panama. They were eager to seize the opportunity Díaz Herrera provided to make a strong statement and pressure the White House into a similar stand.

The senators were encouraged by a vigorous lobbying campaign by Gabriel Lewis Galindo, a Panamanian businessman who had served as Panama's ambassador during ratification of the Panama Canal treaties in 1978. Lewis, who had been having his own difficulties with Noriega, went into exile on June 13, 1987, after failing to mediate between the general and the opposition. He set up headquarters in Washington and began working against Noriega. While providing funds for the NCC to oppose Noriega back home, Lewis coordinated U.S. pressure against the military regime from the Congress, the administration, and the courts.

Lewis's first success came on June 26, 1987, when the Senate passed S. Res. 239 by an overwhelming 84 to 2 vote, calling on Noriega and other officers to step down pending an investigation of Díaz Herrera's charges. The resolution also expressed U.S. support for human rights and the evolution of genuine democracy in Panama. The wide support this resolution gained, under the leadership of an unlikely but effective alliance between the conservative Helms and liberal Kennedy, showed how few friends Noriega had in Congress. As a "sense of the Senate" resolution, S. Res. 239 had no binding effect, but its message was clear and hostile. The resolution gained little attention in Washington, but it was well publicized in Panama.

One of the two senators who voted against the resolution was Christopher Dodd, one of the Senate's leading experts on Central America. He went to Panama soon after the crisis began and met with more than 150 individuals, including General Noriega. Dodd concluded that harsh public condemnation was not the most effective way to achieve Noriega's removal, but his attempts to amend the resolution were rejected.

Noriega Takes the Offensive

U.S.-Panamanian relations edged closer to open confrontation. To the government of Panama, S. Res. 239 was blatant U.S. intervention. The Legislative Assembly voted unanimously, but with only the thirty-nine progovernment legislators present, on a resolution of its own. This called on President Delvalle to declare U.S. Ambassador Arthur Davis persona non grata and accused the United States of meddling in Panama's internal affairs.[29]

The situation in Panama was chaotic. All sides were pushing, push was coming to shove, and Noriega shoved first. He selected several targets: the opposition press, the Civic Crusade, the Christian Democratic party, and U.S. government buildings, including the embassy itself. His first move was to lift the state of siege, a legal step that allowed "pro-regime vandals" to take to the streets and attack opposition political headquarters and a department store owned by *La Prensa*'s Roberto Eisenmann. On June 30, some 5,000 supporters were led by three cabinet members on a march along Avenida Balboa toward the U.S. embassy. Some in the crowd began overturning cars and hurling paint and rocks at buildings, causing considerable damage.[30] Most of the demonstrators were government workers who had been given the day off and told that their paychecks would be handed out at a progovernment rally. Twenty-eight Doberman riot police, in full riot gear, had been stationed near the embassy; they were removed at about 11:00 A.M. and replaced by thirty policemen.[31] None of the police interfered with the hundred or so activists who were throwing rocks, inciting the crowd, and "trying to stir up trouble," indicating that the violence was a message from Noriega.[32] These were the first attacks on U.S. government facilities in more than ten years.

The crisis continued to simmer. The opposition press resumed publishing on July 1, 1987, printing several days' backlog of material. Political opponents organized daily demonstrations against Noriega. One reporter noted a symbolic first: there were as many anti-Noriega slogans on walls in Panama City as anti-U.S. graffiti.[33] The mood among protesters and bystanders at demonstrations in June and early July was often gay and carefree. People carried signs ridiculing Noriega and sang protest songs. It was widely rumored that armed plainclothes agents were infiltrating the crowds, and people noticed when someone seemed to be observing instead of participating. To allay suspicions and make light of the situation, protesters created a chant they accompanied with jumps: "¡ *El que no brinca es sapo!*" ("The one not jumping is a snitch"). Even if it was unrealistic, because armed agents could jump without dislodging their concealed weapons, the chant was fun. Some would sing the words and others would beep its rhythm on their horns.[34]

Government supporters were active, too. On July 2, 1987, a group attacked and burned down the Dante Commercial Center in Panama City. On

July 4, a date selected for its symbolic association, a statue of Franklin D. Roosevelt, which had stood for forty years, was torn down and smashed.[35] In a deliberate slight to the United States, no Panamanian officials attended any of the embassy's Fourth of July events.[36] Reports characterized the situation as reaching a "permanent boil."[37]

Both sides were testing each other's resolve. Noriega appeared to be playing for time. On July 7, 1987, the Panamanian government banned all public protests and rallies, but this had no effect, as three days later thousands turned out for a demonstration in Panama City. Drivers honked horns, and people waved flags and white handkerchiefs and beat pots and pans. Thousands of people poured out of their offices and apartments to join the procession.

However, events were anything but gay on July 10, the day soon known as *Viernes Negro*, Black Friday. Noriega retaliated with the worst violence against civilians in recent history. The opposition was defying a clear ban on protests, and the military responded with unusual force: hundreds of helmeted riot police, carrying shields and nightsticks and armed with tear gas and bird shot, streamed onto the streets to control the crowds.[38] An angry mayor of Panama City told police and judges to begin "imposing jail terms of up to two years for such infractions as spreading leaflets, painting graffiti and 'the unnecessary use of horns.'"[39]

The government also set new rules to constrain the opposition press. The government announced that it would allow the press to reopen after the Legislative Assembly passed a new press law. New rules prohibited "printing any text that 'offends the dignity' of Noriega or anyone in government"; barred "'adulterated' economic news and any story that is 'an apology for foreign intervention'"; forbade the use of unidentified sources; and prohibited "references to 'physical defects' of government leaders" (e.g., Noriega's "pineapple face").[40]

Deliberations in Washington

The severity of these developments caused the Reagan administration to announce retaliatory measures even though a consensus on how to respond to the crisis of regime had not yet been reached. To signal U.S. displeasure and concern, consular offices and the U.S. Information Agency library were closed; officials hinted that U.S. aid might be withheld until Panama paid for property damage. Panama paid $106,000 for damage to the U.S. embassy on July 29, but Ambassador Davis refused to repaint the building, preferring to leave the large splotches of bright red paint on the white walls as a reminder of the incident. The Panamanian government retaliated by having its radio stations broadcast commentaries denouncing the United States, and playing the Nicaraguan national anthem and selections from the writings of the Libyan leader Muammar Quadhafi.[41]

Meanwhile in Washington, high-level executive advisers continued to debate alternative responses. Press reports cited U.S. analysts as "now openly saying that Noriega must go," but also admitting that only the PDF could remove him, and prospects for a PDF coup were deemed extremely unlikely. Other officers had not followed Díaz Herrera's example. Civilians had flocked to Díaz Herrera—Crusade leaders, party leaders, Archbishop McGrath—but not one of the six colonels, thirteen lieutenant colonels, and sixty-five majors who comprised the senior officer corps followed him. The crisis had created an opportunity for dialogue between some elements in the government and the opposition, but the PDF appeared to remain solidly behind Noriega. The administration's objective could not be attained by Panamanians at this time because the military appeared unwilling and the civilians, although stronger than before, were not in a position to overthrow the regime.

Although its rhetoric was relatively mild, the Reagan administration took quiet, unannounced steps to distance itself from Noriega in early July. The CIA was directed to stop making payments to Noriega's personal account. The administration suspended military assistance and economic aid going directly to the Panamanian government (humanitarian aid was exempted) and rejected a pending request to buy tear gas. Additional measures were taken in mid-July. Daily military contacts, including training and exercises, were downgraded "to the lowest level of contact possible," and the aid suspension was extended to include a ban on normal spare parts and equipment.[42] Soon the only U.S. military contact with any PDF counterpart was channeled through Brig. Gen. Marc Cisneros, several levels down SOUTHCOM's chain of command; all informal contact was severed. A similar signal was sent by the Department of State. When Deputy Assistant Secretary for Inter-American Affairs William Walker conducted a fact-finding trip on July 14, he pointedly avoided contact with Noriega; in a deliberately marked contrast, his meetings with civilistas were well publicized. All of these signals and steps were designed to reinforce one message: the PDF would be better off without Noriega.

Paredes Attacks and Noriega Counters

In Panama, General Rubén Paredes, who had retired in 1983 to run for president in 1984, sent the same message to the PDF. On July 21, 1987, he urged the PDF "to toss him [Noriega] out for the good of the institution."[43] Paredes's message was published in an open letter to *La Prensa* on July 24. Later that day Paredes was interviewed on television. He said Noriega was directly responsible for "the conflict for not permitting the implementation of a democratic accord and for 'sacrificing' the FDP [PDF] by not abiding by Law 20."[44] Paredes was referring to Noriega's failure to support his bid for the presidency and the failure of Noriega and other senior officers to retire after twenty-five years of service. Opposition leader Arias Calderón welcomed Paredes's statement, saying that "Paredes has people who were or are beholden to him in the military. . . . There could be an alliance drainage. A significant number of officers in the mid and upper ranks and a significant number of troops are already asking where is this man [Noriega] leading us?"[45] Arias Calderón hoped that reformist officers would heed Paredes's appeal and oust General Noriega. The time was not yet ripe for a coup, however. Paredes had supporters in the PDF, but Noriega was actively working to neutralize opposition within the officer corps.

Noriega sent his own message to the PDF, partly to snuff growing opposition activity at Díaz Herrera's residence, and partly to counter Paredes's statement. Noriega began by closing down the press, which had just published Paredes's open letter. On July 26, 1987, upon an order from the attorney general, officials from the Ministry of Government and Justice ordered employees to leave the premises and sealed the doors of all of Panama's independent presses: *La Prensa*, *El Siglo*, *Extra*, *Quiubo*, and *Gaceta Financiera*. Radio K.W. Continente and Radio Mundial were also closed and their frequencies were canceled.

Noriega then moved against Díaz Herrera, whose home had become a haven for increasing numbers of opposition leaders and groups. On July 27, he ordered a military raid to capture Díaz Herrera and his followers. At 5:30 A.M., a truck brought thirty armed members of UESAT, an Israeli-trained special forces unit specializing in antiterrorist operations, to Díaz Herrara's house. With several Huey helicopter gunships hovering overhead, UESAT forces attacked an hour later. Díaz Herrera's guards returned fire.[46] An officer called to Díaz Herrera over a megaphone, ordering him to surrender. He replied: "Tell Noriega to come and get me."[47] Bravado could not prevail, however, and after only an hour, Díaz Herrera and forty-five others were arrested.

Charged with sedition, Díaz Herrera faced a fifteen-year prison term. Several days later he appeared before the assistant district attorney for Panama City to "clarify" the charges he had made on June 7, 1987.[48] Again and again he denied personal knowledge of the events and charges he had related seven weeks earlier. Most observers considered these depositions withdrawing his accusations to have been the price Díaz Herrera had to pay for his exile.[49]

U.S. Policy Shift: Nudge Noriega Out

Prior to June 1987, the U.S. strategy was to play ball with Noriega and the military regime. During 1986 and early 1987, as negative reports about the regime increased, the Reagan administration downplayed Noriega's liabilities compared to the contributions he had made to U.S. objectives. The Díaz Herrera episode caused the administration to reconsider Noriega's value and adopt a new objective: nudge Noriega out of power. The United States was not ready to force Noriega out, and the situation in Panama, although unexpectedly unsettling, did not seem to require drastic action. The administration decided to suggest that it was time for some changes in Panama.

During these deliberations, Panama policy was treated at a higher level than usual in a series of restricted interagency group meetings (RIGs) held during July and August. Administration officials were reported, through leaks to the press, to be "fed up with Noriega's flagrant corruption" and "sharply critical of his leadership."[50] These leaks referred to a speech given by Assistant Secretary of State Elliott Abrams to the Washington World Affairs Council on June 30, 1987, was quoted in *The Washington Post.* His sharpest comment was that "military leaders must remove their institution from politics, end any appearance of corruption and modernize their forces to carry out" their mission to defend the Canal.[51]

Other comments for the media were more subtle, reflecting the consensus that a nudge was more appropriate than a push. Assistant Secretary of Defense Richard Armitage articulated this position: "We want the continued development of democracy in Panama. Manny Noriega can be part of the solution, and if he is the man who brings this democratic aspect to the fore, good. If he doesn't, then perhaps somebody else will."[52] The State Department's official comment called for "free and untarnished elections and the full development of an apolitical professional military institution."[53] The statement endorsed democratization and extrication of the military from politics, but remained silent about the major obstacle to achieving these goals, namely Noriega's control over the PDF.

During July and August, different U.S. agencies had different views and preferences about what to do if Noriega could not be nudged out of power. The Department of State wanted the White House to adopt a two-part strategy: making increasingly harsh public denunciations of Noriega while discretely approaching the PDF's inner circle. State wanted the PDF to select a moderate military man to serve as caretaker until presidential elections could be held, taking the position that an alternative to Noriega could be secured, and a transition government that would hold elections—as messy as that process might become—would be preferable to Noriega's continuance. The Defense Intelligence Agency was reported to be trying to identify a potential successor.[54] The NSC staff was leaning toward a similar conclusion; by October 1987 they, too, agreed that any alternative would be better than Noriega.

The CIA and the Pentagon took a different view, emphasizing that the United States could not be sure what would happen next in Panama. Part of that uncertainty concerned what Noriega would do next, and part concerned who could replace him as commander. This perspective was articulated by an "anxious former U.S. official" who said, "Noriega is bad, but he keeps the lid on. Don't corner him. He will fight and he holds the trump. We've got a catastrophe in Nicaragua. Do we need another one in Panama of our own making?" As an example of "what could happen," this official cited a recent incident, in which several U.S. servicemen and a U.S. employee of the Panama Canal Commission were picked up by police and held overnight along with a group of Panamanian protesters.[55] His point was that Noriega could make Panama a very difficult environment. Noriega's particularly tough crackdown following the demonstration on Black Friday, July 10, 1987, provided confirming evidence for this position. The Pentagon emphasized the risk of having some 50,000 U.S. citizens in Panama who could become targets of PDF violence or even become hostages.

In Panama, SOUTHCOM was in transition. By coincidence, Gen. Frederick Woerner replaced Gen. John Galvin on July 5, just two days before Díaz Herrera's confession. General Woerner's change of command speech had been planned well in advance; his text, which took a hard line on democracy, had additional significance in the changed Panamanian context. Woerner delivered his remarks in Spanish, saying that the United States "will continue supporting democratic processes."[56] As Panama's rumor mill digested the events of this extraordinary week and tried to predict the impact the new SOUTHCOM commander would have, Woerner's words were interpreted as stinging criticism of Noriega and the PDF.

Meanwhile, investigations of Noriega on drug charges were proceeding. The Department of Justice was not included in the Panama policy review July and August 1987, but the participants involved were aware of cases before two Florida grand juries. In early August, *The New York Times*, the *Miami Herald*, and the *Los Angeles Times* reported that a Miami grand jury had turned up large amounts of evidence about Noriega. Congressional committees were continuing their investigations, too. Congress passed S. 1614, which suspended all U.S. assistance to Panama pending the establishment of a civilian government and restoration of human rights. That suspension was endorsed again by the Senate on September 24, 1987, in an amendment to the DOD authorization bill. Noriega was the focus of yet another round of negative publicity.

Given these divergent agency views, the administration implemented a low key but more critical stance toward Noriega during late 1987. The situation in Panama was seen as worsening, but not yet nearing crisis proportions; apparently the administration hoped to avert a crisis by using quiet diplomacy and private pressure to persuade Noriega to leave. The nudge policy was initially implemented as an offer the Reagan administration hoped Noriega would not be able to refuse.

The U.S. Offers a Golden Parachute

The administration had begun in July to explore contingency plans for Noriega's departure, including places where he might be welcome as an exile. Spain and the Dominican Republic were the most likely sites. At that time, there was no consensus, however, on how he would be removed, by whom, or when his departure might occur. The scenario several officials had in mind was based on the ouster of Ferdinand Marcos in 1986. Those events created a "Philippines model" for removing dictators: a combination of vast popular mobilization—"peoples' power"—on the streets, reformist colonels willing to challenge the dictator, plus U.S. pressure on the dictator. Several administration officials hoped that the Philippines model could be applied in Panama, causing Noriega to "bow to the inevitable and seek asylum."[57] But Panama was not like Marcos's Philippines, Somoza's Nicaragua, or Duvalier's Haiti. Unlike the Philippines and Nicaragua, Panama currently lacked a pivotal opposition figure, like Corazon Aquino, or group like the Sandinistas. And, unlike Duvalier, Noriega did not seem willing to accept a "golden parachute," exiting with his wealth intact. Plus, as one analyst pointed out, the United States had far less leverage over Noriega than over Marcos.[58] Unlike Marcos or Duvalier, Noriega was the general in charge of the military; the fact that he held direct command made it much harder to instigate a military coup. Nonetheless, each of the other three dictators was eventually persuaded that he must retire. Thus, the administration hoped, as conditions worsened and as the United States withdrew support, that the PDF would take the initiative to oust Noriega and reform itself. Were that to occur, the administration was ready to facilitate an exit to exile.

The Parachute: The Blandón Plan

Although is fierce crackdown in July made him appear determined to stay in power, Noriega was also extending feelers to see if a golden parachute would be offered and how favorable a deal he could get. This was the opening that those in the administration who advocated an exile option had been waiting to seize. Panama's consul general in New York, José I. Blandón, made the approach. Blandón was a long-time PRD leader and a close associate of Noriega, so he was considered as representing a serious initiative. Blandón later explained how the negotiations began; he said Noriega had asked him "to devise a contingency plan for a transition government that would allow Noriega to step down gracefully."[59]

Throughout August, Blandón met with opposition figures (Gabriel Lewis, Roberto Eisenmann, and Ricardo Arias Calderón) and U.S. representatives. The degree to which he consulted with Noriega remains unclear.[60] By late October, Blandón had prepared a detailed plan, "Thoughts on a Panamanian Political Solution," sometimes referred to as the Blandón plan, which provided for the following:

> —Noriega would set his own date for stepping down, but this would be no later than the first week of April 1988;
> —before retiring, Noriega would remove his inner circle from power, retiring all PDF officers with more than twenty-five years of service (this would leave only two officers from the inner circle in place);
> —a transition regime would take office for a one year interim, from May 1988–1989; Noriega would be succeeded by the next ranking officer, Col. Elías Castillo; and President Delvalle would continue as president;
> —presidential elections would take place, as scheduled, in May 1989; during the interim year, an independent electoral tribunal, selected with the agreement of the opposition, would prepare for the campaign and election.[61]

Gabriel Lewis described the plan as "the only serious blueprint to emerge in the whole crisis." "Its value," he emphasized, "was that it was developed by someone in the government."[62] Lewis, like many others, was convinced that only a Panamanian solution would be viable; the shape of the "deal," he believed, had to be set by the Panamanians who would implement the transition. As these, and other discussions progressed, however, a power struggle erupted in Panama between the regime and its opponents and among rival factions.

Power Struggle in Panama

Early in Blandón's discussions during the first two weeks of August 1987, the situation heated up in Panama. About 10,000 people were demonstrating on a daily basis. On August 6, a crowd estimated at 300,000 gathered for a rally near El Carmen Church. According to a Gallup poll taken during the first week of August, 75 percent of the population in Panama City and Colón favored Noriega's resignation. President Delvalle's approval rating was not much better. When asked who makes the government's decisions, 79 percent said Noriega; 8 percent picked Delvalle. Not only was Delvalle seen as relatively powerless, 59 percent agreed that he should step down if Noriega does.[63]

President Delvalle described his situation in a interview in August. "There is no doubt the president of the Republic has command," he said, "but he has to negotiate with that party [PRD] which has ties with and was formed by the Defense Forces."[64] When asked about his relations with the PDF, Delvalle explained how old habits were impeding the transition to civilian rule. He began by noting that the PDF "used to rule the entire government," creating the "habit of going to them to resolve problems." He continued,

I have received great cooperation from Gen Noriega. [I tell him:] Whoever goes to you, send him to me. Receive him, hear his story, and then send him to wherever he should go. There has been great understanding. On some occasions, he has made decisions or recommendations that another president might feel jealous about but that have not bothered me. I know he does so for the common good and to overcome some problem with individuals with whom he thinks he, rather than I, can better handle. He has been dealing with them for so many years.

One of Delvalle's problems, in fact "the biggest problem" he mentioned, arose from trying to dislodge the role of head of government from the commander of the PDF. Torrijos had begun the practice of visiting towns to inaugurate projects and oversee programs;[65] Noriega continued it. Delvalle explained that it was "very hard" for Noriega to say "no, I am not going to go" because a welcome with "300, 500, or 1,000 people" would be planned. Delvalle then made his point:

They make him [Noriega] the guest of honor at all the affairs that flatter us politicians. Therefore I have always said that because of this lack of will power on his part [to decline invitations] it creates the appearance that he is the one who is jumping all over the place, meeting and talking with all the sectors of the country.

Noriega, in short, was acting as if he were the president. In fact, several times he happily upstaged Delvalle at such functions. In his interview, Delvalle admitted, wittingly or not, his own lack of power: "However, he cannot be prohibited from doing so." As a solution, Delvalle proposed "a formula" whereby "he would say: I don't touch those problems; those are the president's problems. Then, if we find ourselves in the same place, there will be no problem."

In normal times, such habits might have been broken. During the summer of 1987, however, Panama was anything but normal. A U.S. Senate report described the deterioration of human rights since June 1987 as "tragic and unprecedented" and documented the use of excessive violence in breaking up demonstrations, particularly "point blank shotgun shootings using bird shot even against women and children."[66] Between June and September there were more than 1,500 arrests; 500 suffered bullet and bird shot wounds, including 60 cases of damage to eyes; and three people were killed.[67] In one protest, a twenty-four-year-old student was shot and killed in El Valle for shouting, "¡*Abajo Noriega!*" (Down with Noriega!).[68]

As the crisis continued, prominent civilians resigned from key political positions in the government. As a result, Noriega became more, not less, involved in running the government. When the general manager of the National Bank of Panama and one of his chief deputies resigned in July, their friends told reporters that they left because "of disgust over manipulation of the financial system for the short-term benefit of the military."[69] Even Vice-President Roderick Esquivel began to criticize the government. He described government calls for dialogue with oppositionists as "insincere . . . if press outlets are closed and if leaders are fearful of persecution."[70] Esquivel finally broke with President Delvalle in October, over the government's increasingly repressive handling of the crisis. When the vice-president criticized those measures while on a trip abroad, Delvalle responded by having Esquivel's office locked and his allies fired. This caused the "Esquivel wing" of the Liberal party to leave UNADE, the government coalition. Esquivel then called, publicly, for Noriega's resignation.[71]

Esquivel's defection exemplified a shift in the orientation and power base of the regime. As the government lost supporters holding moderate and rightist views, the PDF-PRD coalition became relatively more leftist. In July 1987, Noriega dispatched Aquilino Boyd—a former ambassador, seasoned diplomat, and well-known member of the government coalition—to Washington to deliver precisely that message. Boyd warned the Reagan administration that further pressure on Noriega could drive the PRD "into the arms of the radical left."[72] Noriega further increased this shift, and reinforced his message to the United States, by reaching out to more radical and leftist groups at home and by playing his "leftist card" in foreign policy, reaching out to Nicaragua, the Soviet Union, and Cuba. In July, for example, just two days before the attack on the U.S. embassy, Noriega invited Daniel Ortega for a state visit. In November 1987, he extended landing rights to the Soviet airline, Aeroflot, and in January 1988, he arranged a surprise visit by the Cuban foreign minister. Playing the leftist card not only appealed to the new "center" of Noriega's power base at home, it also reminded the Reagan administration that Noriega had options the United States preferred him not to exercise.

Admiral Murphy: Back Channel or Private Initiative?

While Noriega was solidifying his power base and pressuring the Reagan administration, he was also pressured by the United States. A former U.S. official made two unofficial visits, one in August and another in November. This private initiative was undertaken by Adm. Daniel J. Murphy, retired, in his capacity as a business consultant and risk analyst. Murphy conveyed the same message to Noriega that he had been hearing from the Reagan administration and from Blandón: it was time for a change. Given Murphy's past positions in government—chief of staff to Vice-President George Bush, operational chief of the South Florida Task Force Working Group and chairman of the National Narcotics Border Interdiction System (1982–1985), deputy under secretary of defense for policy under Harold Brown, and deputy director of intelligence while Bush was CIA director—Murphy could speak credibly and authoritatively with Noriega.[73]

When Murphy met Noriega in August, he "described the ill feeling about him in the United States [and] explored with him what it might take to improve the atmosphere." Murphy told Noriega:

—Get the military out of politics in Panama;
—Turn government functions over to civilians;
—Firmly establish an election date for the next president;
—Announce steps to ensure no military interference in the elections;
—Ensure honest elections by having international observers;
—Bring in computers so that people will feel that it's an honest election;
—Provide for adequate campaigning; and
—Meet with the opposition.
—I thought it was maybe possible to move up the elections. I suggested that that should be looked at.
—And set a date for stepping down as the head of the military forces, and take steps to prove that you are serious.[74]

Thus, despite subsequent congressional suspicions and criticism of these unofficial missions, Murphy did not tell Noriega anything at variance with U.S. policy. Instead, Murphy conveyed his best professional assessment of how bad the situation was and how much change was needed. Murphy later said, "I didn't see myself sending a conflicting message. I thought maybe I was sending a corroborating message."[75]

Murphy found Noriega's response to contain "very little maneuvering room." Noriega said,

The military is not involved in politics at all, so there is nothing to turn over to the civilians.
The constitution establishes the election date. That's already known, so that's not a very important point.
All of my speeches assure free elections. So, what more do you want?
We can't move up the election because it's set by the constitution, and I'll leave office when a new president is elected and he elects a new head of the military in 1989.[76]

If Murphy had been trying to gauge, privately and informally, the amount of give in Noriega's bargaining position, he certainly got a clear, direct answer. The term Murphy used to characterize Noriega's stance was "in deep cement."[77]

To make matters worse from a bargaining perspective, Murphy found the opposition to be equally obdurate. Murphy described Noriega's position to them. "Their reaction was vehement. They wanted Noriega out now—no negotiation, no room for compromise."[78]

When he returned to Washington, Murphy debriefed Armitage; Abrams; National Security Adviser Frank Carlucci; Vice-President Bush's chief of staff, Donald Gregg; and Kerr of the CIA. Murphy heard nothing from the administration or Panama until November, when he "was told" that Noriega "was interested in talking to me again, and there were hints now that there might be some more maneuvering room than there was in August."[79]

At the November meeting with Noriega, Murphy presented a four-step plan, similar to the process he had outlined in August and similar to steps being demanded by the opposition, which had begun to compromise. These steps were holding free elections, opening the media, granting a general amnesty, and reinstating civil rights. Murphy found Noriega's response to be limited, but more positive than before. As reported by Murphy in Senate hearings:

> One was elections. I said you have to have free elections, they have to be observed, computerized, on time—May 1989, and you have to encourage all of the trappings of a free election—that's TV, advertising, rallies, active political parties. And his answer was OK.
>
> The second point was you have to relax the restrictions on the freedoms of your people, and it would be nice that the President of Panama announced this at, say, like a speech at OAS, where he would get some coverage. And I'm talking about free TV, radio, newspapers, freedom of assembly, releasing political prisoners, and even suggested that there ought to be some way to be as kind as possible to Colonel [Díaz] Herrera, who was the one who had blown the whistle in the first place.
>
> His answer to that was OK, timing to be worked out.
>
> The third point was meet with the opposition. What's needed is a Panamanian solution. The United States is not trying to force a U.S. solution. It's a Panamanian solution that's being sought.
>
> He said OK, we'll meet with the opposition.
>
> And then we get to the sticky one, and I said General Noriega, you're just going to have to get out, you've got to retire from this job.
>
> Now, granted, timing is something that has to be worked out and the date will depend on things like political impact, stability and what's best for Panama. But, make no mistake, you've got to get out before the election in May 1989.
>
> And his answer to that was interesting. He said, "I agree in principle, but must think through carefully. I am not inflexible."[80]

Under Murphy's plan, Noriega would remain in power for some time, perhaps as late as February 1989, and he could remain in Panama after stepping down as PDF commander. This deal would have been more advantageous to Noriega than offers by oppositionists and the Blandón plan, and it would have left the PDF/PRD power structure intact.

Noriega was articulating a much more forthcoming position than he had in August, but his motives were not clear. Did he intend to negotiate an exit? Or was he only probing, sounding more reasonable just to see how much the opposition and the United States were willing to concede? Or was he just playing for time? Only Noriega can give a definitive answer, but the latter two motives are more likely than the first.

Murphy also met with the opposition during his November visit. They, naturally, were pleased with Noriega's responses to points one, two, and three; on the subject of the general's departure, they were willing to suggest a date and said, "July 1988 . . . would be a reasonable time."[81]

Murphy returned to Washington in an encouraged, enthusiastic frame of mind, and he was surprised to have no further contact with Noriega or the opposition during December or January. In February, once Noriega was indicted, "it became quite evident," Murphy said, "that this was an area that I didn't want to be operating in."[82]

Who was Murphy representing? Not the Department of State, although Noriega told his staff, according to Blandón, that Murphy was speaking on behalf of Secretary Shultz and National Security Adviser Colin Powell. The Department of State did provide a briefing on current U.S. policy for Murphy before he went to Panama, but so did other agencies. And the same departments and agencies debriefed Murphy upon his return. Although confirmation is not now available, the Murphy missions may well have been commissioned, however informally, by Vice-President Bush. Murphy claims that he was simply trying to speak plainly to Noriega in order to end the political crisis as soon as possible.

Murphy was accompanied on his trips by South Korean businessman and financier Tongsun Park, who provided transportation and funding for the visits. Murphy suggested that the motive shared by Park and the U.S. businessmen he was encouraging Murphy to represent was to resolve the political crisis in order to return economic stability and business confidence to Panama. Park's apparent purpose on the two visits was to provide the financial incentive to get Noriega to accept the deal. According to Blandón, whose account is based on what Noriega told him, Park said he would arrange for Japanese economic assistance for Panama to replace suspended U.S. funds. The incentive Murphy offered, again according to what Blandón reports about Noriega's version of events, was that the United States would agree to resume joint military maneuvers with the PDF in January 1988 if Noriega would accept the plan.[83]

The Crisis Continues

While Murphy's missions were under way, a political power struggle continued in Panama. On August 5, 1987, opposition headquarters were raided and a "10-point plan" was seized. This was reported to provide for the overthrow of Delvalle and for democratization through a series of legislative and judicial elections. This plan could have been an early version of the Blandón plan or one of several plans opposition leaders were considering at the time. The government attempted to use the document to discredit the opposition, perhaps as a bargaining tactic to influence discussions with Blandón or Admiral Murphy.

Announcing that he had discovered a plot to overthrow the government, Attorney General Carlos Villalaz held a dramatic midnight news conference to display the seized documents.[84] Arrest warrants were issued on August 6, 1987, for six NCC leaders on charges of conspiracy to overthrow the government. In September, five NCC leaders went into exile to avoid arrest. In response to the raid on its headquarters, the NCC called for a general strike, which closed 80–90 percent of the businesses in Panama.

The Reagan administration had mixed reactions. Admiral Murphy's August debriefing conveyed a negative assessment about prospects for compromise. One report said that Washington is "now considering in earnest ways to pry him [Noriega] from power."[85] Other reports described an interagency split, with the Pentagon and CIA still hoping to "patch things up" with Noriega, whereas the Department of State was insisting that Noriega must go as soon as possible. One source reported that U.S. officials were evaluating the political opposition more positively, because of the strike's success, as having "staying power," a necessary ingredient for a Philippines scenario. Another report said that Washington now evaluated the costs of not moving against Noriega as starting to outweigh the dangers of doing so. Administration officials characterized Noriega, whom they had considered as such a shrewd bargainer, as making mistakes "all the time."[86] *Time* reported that U.S. officials were sounding "more and more as if they believe Panama can quickly follow the Philippines and South Korea on the march toward democracy. 'Noriega's days are numbered,' says one official. 'He just doesn't know it.'"[87]

These reports may have reflected unrealistically optimistic attempts to take credit for Noriega's imminent fall, or they may have been strong bargaining signals directed at opposing factions in the interagency debate in Washington or in Panama. If they were deliberate overstatements designed to pressure Noriega, they failed to have the desired effect.

In Panama, however, Noriega was so bothered by protesters' graffiti that public workers were dispatched, night after night, to paint over the demonstrators' slogans. Noriega claimed that only 5,000 Panamanians actively opposed his rule. Soon thereafter, this question was written on a wall in Panama City: "If there are only 5,000 of us, why are you erasing this?" A few days later that question, too, was covered with black paint.[88]

Noriega also ordered a severe crackdown on demonstrations. For weeks, Panamanian workers and passersby had gathered in the financial district twice a day, at noon and 6:00 P.M., to march along Calle 50 (50th Street) with white handkerchiefs waving and pots and pans clanging. But on October 10, 1987, *Newsweek* reported "not a hanky in sight."[89] For the moment, Noriega won "the Battle for 50th Street."[90] The crackdown continued; a report in

November described the government as "slowly but firmly tightening its grip to quell continuing ferment."[91]

U.S. citizens were also targeted. On September 13, 1987, a U.S. embassy official was arrested and held incommunicado for more than eight hours because he had observed Panamanians, dressed in civilian clothes, fire on an antigovernment demonstration where one person was killed and five were wounded. And on October 7, nine off-duty servicemen were "arrested arbitrarily and falsely charged with participating in an anti-government protest."[92]

While Noriega faced an opposition movement at home that could be temporarily quashed but not eliminated, press reports began to surface in the United States about a new adversary, the drug war, which would not go away either. Noriega and several of his associates were under investigation by two federal grand juries in Florida. Concurrently, the *Miami Herald* ran a series about Panama as a drug and money laundering capital and how the international drug market worked.[93] A reporter in Washington observed "growing sentiment in the administration and Congress that Noriega's departure [would be] essential to restoring Panama's political stability," and that the new "chill in official relations" facilitated legal action against Noriega.[94] Congress, for its part, passed legislation (P.L. 100-202) on December 22, 1987, that suspended U.S. assistance, prohibited funding of joint military exercises, suspended Panama's sugar quota, and instructed U.S. representatives to multilateral banks to vote against Panamanian loan applications.

Armitage Mission

In the interim between Noriega's apparent acceptance of the Blandón plan just before Christmas 1987 and his rejection of it in January 1988, the United States made an official, but secret, overture to Noriega. The mission was conducted by Assistant Secretary of Defense for International Security Affairs Richard Armitage. This may have been a follow-up to Murphy's November mission, a coordinated move to support the Blandón plan, or an unrelated initiative. Armitage, along with another Pentagon official, went to Panama on December 30, 1987, to suggest a timetable for Noriega's departure and that the "U.S. would prefer him to be part of the solution instead of the problem."[95] The message he delivered was that it was time for Noriega to "step back." According to his instructions, Armitage was "representing all agencies of the U.S. Government," and his purpose was not to issue an ultimatum but rather to "reiterate our position on events in Panama and prospects for democratization."[96] This was a clear signal that the administration had closed ranks, reached an interagency consensus, and was ready to maintain a unified front. This unified position was supposed to convince Noriega that he had no bureaucratic allies left to espouse his cause, and that the United States was unalterably and irrevocably opposed to his continuance in power.[97] Thus, Armitage was making an official statement confirming what Murphy told Noriega. Noriega, however, did not respond with a bland "OK" this time.

Noriega heard Armitage's message, but he made sure that his closest advisers did not. Noriega met Armitage alone; no Panamanian officers heard their exchange. Afterwards, however, Noriega deliberately set the scene so that it appeared that he and Armitage were exchanging friendly toasts. He told his officers that relations with the United States would soon be business as usual.

In Washington, Secretary of State Shultz reiterated the "step back" message. Senior officials were speaking clearly and with one voice, but Noriega rejected the message. He countered by portraying himself as a victim of U.S. intervention, claiming that Armitage had arrogantly issued an ultimatum. Whatever his intent about a negotiated retirement had been in November, by late December Noriega had decided to reject a deal with the United States. In retrospect, November may have been the last opportunity for Noriega and the Reagan administration to cut a deal. Thereafter, Panama policy became so salient that domestic politics in the United States foreclosed offering a golden parachute; Noriega's calculations also appeared to change.

Noriega Rejects the Blandón Plan and Blandón

It was in this worsening climate, on December 21, 1987, that Blandón presented the final version of his plan to Noriega. According to Blandón, Noriega had been positively disposed toward a negotiated solution as late as December 9, when Noriega told him the plan was "valuable." To Blandón's surprise, however, Noriega telephoned him in New York on December 21, and told him to break off the talks. The plan was opposed by senior officers who were worried about their status, wealth, and security once General Noriega left office. More importantly, Noriega was concerned about grand jury investigations and probable indictments on drug trafficking charges. When the Reagan administration refused to agree to grant Noriega immunity from prosecution, the Blandón plan looked much less attractive. Noriega fired Blandón on January 14, 1988.

The 1988 new year began with Noriega "facing unprecedented political isolation in Panama"[98]—unprecedented because Blandón's firing opened the first public split in the political leadership of the PRD. In fact, top party leaders openly rejected Noriega's demand that they expel Blandón from the PRD. The party had been a solid base of support for Noriega, and by January 1988 it was the only influential civilian organization that still supported him, but at that point it, too, was starting to split.

Blandón had been one of Noriega's closest advisers. He soon became one of Noriega's most visible opponents in the United States, testifying before congressional committees, and being interviewed on news programs and in the press. In the process, Blandón provided so many details of sordid operations and corrupt practices that the series by Seymour Hersh in 1986 seemed bland in comparison. Just as Díaz Herrera, the ultimate military insider, could reveal how the PDF's regime had functioned, so could Blandón, a PRD insider, document government wrongdoing. Blandón had conducted secret diplomatic and business ventures for Noriega; he revealed the inside story of Noriega's involvement in international drug trafficking, terrorism, and supplying embargoed goods to Cuba. And, just as Esquivel's resignation had been a harbinger, Blandón's defection also signaled changes in the government's power base. Blandón's departure marked the exodus of another prominent civilian and the defection of a loyal senior adviser.

Noriega Is Indicted

Noriega was indicted on February 4, 1988; on February 5, the two federal indictments were unsealed. One was the result of a fourteen-month investigation by the Drug Enforcement Administration and the U.S. attorney's office in Miami headed by Leon Kellner. This charged Noriega and twelve others on twelve counts of racketeering, conspiracy, and cocaine trafficking. The Miami indictment asserted that Noriega made at least $4.6 million from the Medellín cartel for ensuring the safe shipment of at least 4,400 pounds of cocaine to the United States between 1981 and 1986. The thirty-page indictment also covered charges of money laundering, receiving payoffs for sheltering drug cartel leaders, and supplying precursor chemicals for processing cocaine.[99] The maximum charges associated with this indictment were 145 years in prison and more than $1.1 million in fines. Among those named in the Miami indictment were Capt. Luis del Cid, a close adviser to Noriega and reported liaison to the cartel, and Colombian drug lord Pablo Escobar Gaviria.

The other indictment resulted from an investigation by the U.S. attorney's office in Tampa, in conjunction with the FBI and the U.S. Customs Service. It charged Noriega, Enrique Pretelt, and a prominent businessman with importing (one count) and trying to import (two counts) 1.4 million pounds of marijuana into the United States and with accepting a $1.1 million bribe to do so. If also convicted of these charges, Noriega's total sentence could reach 165 years in prison and $1.65 million in fines.

When the indictments were unsealed, Noriega scoffed at the charges. He also asked three of Miami's top defense attorneys to fly to Panama. During the next two years, attorneys Raymond Takiff, Neal Sonnett, and Frank A. Rubino worked closely and regularly with Noriega; Rubino stayed with the case after Noriega's surrender.

The indictments had an enormous political effect in the United States, pushing the White House toward calls for Noriega to resign and reinforcing the image, already set in Congress and the media, that Noriega was a drug-dealing dictator. In fact, news coverage and official comment became increasingly laden with villainous imagery. A long report appeared in the February 15, 1988, issue of *Newsweek* with the title: "Drugs, Money and Death: The Sordid Story of How Panama's Outlaw Dictator Sold His Country to the Highest Bidders." At the same time that the Reagan administration was calling on Noriega to resign, however, it was also trying to appeal to the PDF. On the day the indictments were announced, a State Department spokeswoman said they did not reflect on the Panamanian government or the PDF.[100]

The White House called on Noriega to resign, but opponents in Panama and some officials in Washington wondered if the legal strategy might backfire. They argued that the indictments removed the one incentive to leave that might be meaningful to Noriega, namely the prospect of a legally safe exile. With the indictments came the threat of extradition to the United States for prosecution. One report argued that this cut off the escape route Noriega and his allies needed; now they could only stand and fight. An opposition leader predicted that things would now get worse because Noriega would radicalize the crisis in order to gain a better bargaining position.[101] Unsealing the indictments appeared, at least for a while, to remove the golden parachute from the bargaining table.

Noriega's determination to resist did seem to increase. He again closed down *La Prensa*, which had begun publishing in January; he also shut down two radio stations. A public relations offensive was launched in Washington. The Panamanian embassy produced a 306-page book, "Panama, 16 Years of Struggle Against Drug Traffic," replete with "attaboy" letters from U.S. officials praising Panamanian cooperation in drug enforcement.[102] In Panama, Noriega staged a display of unity within the officer corps by having a group of captains and majors pledge allegiance to him in a televised ceremony.[103]

Delvalle Turns Against Noriega

At this point, President Delvalle began to drift toward the opposition. Heretofore, Delvalle had been dismissively characterized by some U.S. officials and numerous reporters as a loyal lackey. Once Noriega was indicted, however, Delvalle was subjected to considerable pressure from opposition leaders and U.S. officials. He reevaluated Panama's prospects if Noriega were to remain in control and decided to take the drastic step of ordering the general to step down. A close friend later explained that Delvalle "didn't want to go into history as a Panamanian who lacked the guts to do what his country needed."[104] Details of this episode are not yet clear; various reports give partial and conflicting accounts, along with plenty of criticism of Delvalle and U.S. policy.

Assistant Secretary of State Abrams met with Delvalle secretly in Miami on February 17, 1988. Some reports assert that Abrams suggested that Delvalle fire Noriega—not because he was likely to comply but to create a constitutional crisis. This would be the catalyst that would set a Philippines-style ouster in motion, bringing people onto the streets, sapping officers' loyalty, and weakening Noriega's international support. A Pentagon correspondent, C. Robert Zelnick, confirmed this scenario and added that it was planned by Abrams in conjunction with the private sector lawyers who engineered the financial squeeze plan. Zelnick's sources, who clearly reflected an anti-Abrams viewpoint, asserted that Abrams pulled a fast bureaucratic maneuver. They said Abrams did not inform Secretary of State Shultz, who was then in Europe, about the plan until the "eleventh hour," bypassing NSC Adviser Powell, who was with Shultz, and cutting Secretary of Defense Frank Carlucci "totally out of the loop."[105] The implication in Zelnick's report was that the Department of Defense would have squelched Abrams's plan.

After meeting with opposition leaders and Assistant Secretary Abrams, Delvalle explored the possibility of exchanging Noriega's resignation for dropping the indictments. Word of this leaked to the press, however, and the option was quickly dropped. Abrams's public response was "no deal."[106]

Delvalle Fires Noriega

Delvalle made extensive preparations before he approached the moment of firing Noriega. First, he took the preliminary step of suggesting, several days in advance, that Noriega should step down voluntarily in order for an investigation to proceed. Noriega refused, allowing Delvalle to claim that he had no alternative but to remove Noriega. To actually fire Noriega, Delvalle videotaped an announcement of his order to be broadcast on television and radio. He did not need a face-to-face meeting to fire Noriega; Noriega would get the message. To protect the safety of his children and grandchildren, Delvalle arranged for them to be taken, before the tape was aired, to the U.S. ambassador's residence. He consulted various opposition leaders in Panama, coordinating particularly with Arias Calderón, who planned to return to Panama City just after the tape aired. Finally, he asked Noriega to meet him at the Papal Nunciature, where Delvalle planned to tell him he was "separated" from his office as commandant. Noriega failed to show, and Delvalle released the tape to the media and went home.[107]

The video was broadcast nationwide at 5:30 P.M., just before the evening news, on Thursday, February 25, 1988. Whether anyone had really expected Noriega to comply, he did not; further, the legality of such a separation order was questioned.[108] Defensive actions followed in quick succession. Moments later police blocked the streets leading to Delvalle's home and cut his telephone lines; ten riot police stood guard outside. The PDF ordered Channel 5, owned in part by Delvalle, closed for security reasons. *La Prensa* was closed by military order at 7:30 P.M. Arias Calderón was detained at the airport for forty-five minutes, refused entry into the country, and put on a plane for Costa Rica. "I refused to go," he said, but "then they started shoving me and eventually had to carry me onto the plane."[109]

In his taped speech, Delvalle said he was encharging the leadership of the PDF to the chief of staff, Col. Marcos Justines, but Justines responded with a succinct public comment: "I reject that order." The chief of police, Col. Leonidas Macías, made the PDF's position even more clear. He appeared on television, flanked by colonels and lieutenant colonels, to announce, "None of us want the (Panamanian military) command, the commander stays and we all stay. The president goes."[110] Ironically, Macías later participated in a barracks coup against Noriega.

Noriega Ousts Delvalle

Several hours later, at 1:15 A.M. Friday, thirty-eight of the sixty-seven members of the Legislative Assembly voted to replace Delvalle with then Minister of Education Manuel Solís Palma.[111] This rump session lasted only ten minutes. The opposition cried foul, charging that a quorum was not present and that PRD legislators used forged proxy vote authorizations to dump Delvalle. Solís Palma was sworn in as minister in charge of the presidency at 3:30 A.M.

President Delvalle was under an undeclared house arrest. In a show of U.S. support, Ambassador Davis tried to visit on Friday, but he was turned away by the police. The Department of State urged the presidents of neighboring states to support Delvalle and his assertion of civilian control over the PDF.[112] Alerted that he was about to be arrested, Delvalle escaped on foot through the back of his house, wearing a disguise. Panama now had governments under two leaders: Solís Palma in office and Delvalle in hiding. The United States continued to recognize Delvalle.

Reactions

International reactions were mixed. Within hours, the foreign ministers of Brazil, Argentina, Uruguay, Peru, Colombia, Venezuela, and Mexico suspended Panama from the Group of Eight; only Cuba and Nicaragua continued to support the PDF regime. Beyond this initial show of support, however, Delvalle received little international help. Some states recalled their ambassadors, but none recognized Delvalle's government.

Popular reactions in Panama were much slower. Only scattered demonstrations occurred after Delvalle's speech Thursday evening. The lack of thousands of demonstrators flooding the streets occasioned much critical comment.[113] A senior Pentagon official commented, "No one is happy that we are virtually powerless to do anything and that there is no strong, viable opposition in Panama."[114] Noriega was still able to mobilize a crowd, however; on Friday, he addressed a rally attended by 10,000 supporters. Meanwhile, Panama's streets were calm and business proceeded as usual. PDF units surrounded and closed the Chamber of Commerce building—the headquarters of the NCC—and the offices of the Christian Democratic party. The opposition was, nevertheless, planning to act on two fronts: it called for a four-day general strike in Panama to begin the first week of March, and oppositionists in Washington developed a legal strategy to deprive Noriega's government of funds.

In Washington, the situation was treated as a minor crisis. President Reagan canceled plans to go to Camp David for the weekend, the NSC prepared regular briefings for the president as the situation unfolded, and, at the working level, cables flew as experts tried to keep up with events and keep track of which Panamanian officials were going with Delvalle or staying with Noriega. Assistant Secretary Abrams met with Panamanian Ambassador Juan Sosa, who declared for Delvalle.[115] At SOUTHCOM, one official said, "We're literally not dealing with anybody at the moment."[116] U.S.-Panamanian relations were characterized as reaching their worst level in twenty years.[117] Noriega was featured on the cover of the March 7, 1988, issue of *Time*; the caption read, "The Drug Thugs: Panama's Noriega Proves They're a Law unto Themselves."

Economic Pressure Strategies

A strategy of using financial pressure to force Noriega to leave office was initiated in March 1988 by a coalition of oppositionists in exile, Delvalle supporters, and U.S. lawyers. These pressures and additional economic sanctions were implemented during 1988 and 1989; they had an increasingly devastating impact on the people and the economy, but they did not dislodge Noriega.

This coalition had developed a financial squeeze plan before Delvalle tried to fire Noriega on February 25, 1988.[118] They hoped that the combination of a constitutional crisis and a severe financial squeeze would bring Noriega down in a matter of weeks. A U.S. official explained the plan this way: because Panama's economy was so closely tied to the U.S. economy, through trade and use of the dollar as Panama's currency, Panama would be "so susceptible to U.S. pressure that it would be relatively easy to force Noriega out. The theory was that the Panamanian political, business, and military leadership would come together and decide that, for the collective good of everyone, Noriega should go."[119] It was thought that if a severe enough cash shortage could be created, Noriega would be unable to meet the payrolls of his two strongest constituencies, the PDF and government employees, and their discontent would provide the irresistible pressure to make Noriega go. As one member of Congress put it, "what the Administration was looking for, was a quick hit, a week, two weeks, a month."[120]

Initially, the financial squeeze plan seemed to have a good chance of succeeding. The Panamanian economy was already in serious trouble. Oppositionists had adopted a deliberate strategy of denying revenues to the government, advocating such measures as refusing to pay taxes and fees and abstaining from the national lottery. They had also removed their own money from Panamanian banks—between June 1987 and January 1988, local deposits had declined by 13 percent,[121] and, more significantly, Panamanians had shipped $500 million abroad since February 1987.[122] In addition, a DEA money-laundering sting operation, Operation Pisces, had a chilling effect on the volume of cash flowing into Panama's banks. At the beginning of 1987, bank deposits amounted to $40 billion; as of February 1988, deposits had dropped to $8 billion.[123] Moreover, banks were closing.—First Chicago, the largest and oldest offshore bank in the country, closed its offices; other banks were said to be assessing their options.

The government was already in financial trouble before the financial squeeze and sanctions were applied. In June 1987, it had defaulted on the principal of its $4 billion debt.[124] In October, President Delvalle had announced that Panama would not be able to pay government salaries on time or meet its debt or interest payments. Noriega raided government reserves to get through the next few months. Then, in February 1988, the government announced it would have trouble making its March interest payments.[125] Noriega had hoped to use government spending as an incentive to maintain support among his constituencies, but he ended up cutting the budget. The crux of his problem was that because Panama used the U.S. dollar as its paper currency, the government could not finance its deficit by printing more money; furthermore, Panama could not borrow dollars because it had defaulted on existing loans, and multilateral banks would not make new ones.

In this context, following Delvalle's February 25 attempt to fire Noriega, the opposition called a four-day strike to begin on March 1, 1988. Banks stayed open during the strike, but by Friday, March 4, fearing the start of a "run," they closed their doors. International banks closed first; Panamanian banks followed.[126] The squeeze had begun.

The Financial Squeeze

The squeeze play was planned and orchestrated by a three-part coalition: Gabriel Lewis, a businessman in exile since June 1987, who operated in

Washington and coordinated with the NCC in Panama; a team of twenty lawyers at the firm of Arnold & Porter, headed by William D. Rogers, who represented the Delvalle government; and officials of the Delvalle government in Washington, principally Ambassador Juan Sosa. As the financial squeeze strategy was implemented, this group coordinated closely with the Department of State.

The idea of using financial pressure to bring Noriega down originated with Rogers and Lewis. Rogers had been involved in behind-the-scenes negotiations on Panama policy before, having served as the intermediary who arranged for the Baker-Byrd amendment (also known as the leadership amendment) to be accepted by Panama and added to the Panama Canal treaty. Rogers's good offices had saved the 1978 canal treaties at a crucial moment.[127] Rogers also knew the region and economic issues, having served as President Ford's assistant secretary of state for inter-American affairs, as under secretary of state for economic affairs, and before that, as the director of the Alliance for Progress for President Kennedy.[128] Rogers explained his involvement in the squeeze strategy, which he referred to as a "revolution by litigation" this way: "When the Noriega regime began to deteriorate a couple of years ago, I became quite persuaded that if he stayed around until the year 2000, Panama would not be the kind of country that ought to have fiduciary responsibility for managing that terribly important asset [the canal]." In early 1988, he continued, "my friends called me up."[129] That call, from Gabriel Lewis, was made on February 28, three days after Delvalle's removal.

Rogers and Kenneth Juster, a member of the legal team, spent the last weekend in February doing legal research and considering possibilities. Lewis then dropped by to see Rogers and Juster. His purpose was to retain the firm to represent the Delvalle government and secure resources to fund its operation and to bring maximum financial pressure to bear on Noriega. Rogers described the "conscious plan" that was developed "to tighten the financial noose around the neck of the Noriega regime: . . . starve the banking system of cash, force the banks to close, and thus cause—not to put too fine a point on it—very considerable economic, financial distress in Panama."[130]

During the first week of March, the lawyers identified the location of Panamanian assets. Despite his mounting financial problems, Noriega had left the bulk of the Panamanian government's money, amounting to about $60 million, in four New York banks: Republic National, Chase Manhattan, Irving Trust, and City Bank.[131] The initial tactic the lawyers tried was to send letters to the chairmen of these banks asserting the Delvalle government's claim to those assets.[132] These were sent on Tuesday, March 1, but they did not have the desired effect. That evening, the lawyers received an "intelligence report" that Republic National Bank had been asked to transfer $10 million to Panama and planned to comply the next day.

An emergency meeting was held in the "war room" (Bill Rogers's office and conference room) at 6:00 P.M. The group—lawyers, Ambassador Sosa, and Gabriel Lewis—decided to seek a temporary restraining order to block the transfer. Lynda Clarizio prepared an affidavit for Ambassador Sosa, who would be designated the legitimate Panamanian official with authority over the funds. Stewart Griffiths and Dan Resneck drafted the complaint in consultation with a senior litigator in New York. Griffiths took the 5:30 A.M. shuttle to New York on March 2 and met Ken Handle at the Federal Court House for the Southern District for a quick review of the documents. The two lawyers then appeared before Judge Lloyd F. MacMahon. Handle's argument was quite simple: (1) the Panamanian government has funds in the United States, (2) President Delvalle and Ambassador Sosa are recognized as the lawful government of Panama, (3) the United States does not recognize Noriega's government, and (4) therefore the court should enjoin Republic National from transferring funds to Noriega's government. Judge MacMahon agreed and issued the temporary restraining order.

Within a day, the Arnold & Porter team reached a settlement with Republic National Bank. The $10 million was transferred into Account No. 1 at the Federal Reserve Bank of New York, which became the working account for the Delvalle government. On Wednesday and Thursday, the three other banks holding substantial Panamanian government assets determined that they also needed a court order directing to whom these assets could be legally released. The legal team readily complied, beating another emergency deadline to submit court documents before tens of millions of dollars were transferred to Noriega. At this point Noriega's government was deprived of some $50 million.

The entire "revolution by litigation" strategy was premised on two crucial points: a legal precedent and State Department coordination. The Edge Act of 1941 specified that, concerning the assets of a foreign government, the U.S. government must designate a person who has the authority to dispose of or control the transfer of those funds, and any federal reserve bank or insured member bank must comply with that designation. This law, and its application on behalf of governments forced by Hitler into exile during World War II, provided the precedent Delvalle's lawyers needed. But they also needed the Department of State to designate, in a timely fashion, the Delvalle government as the lawful government of Panama and Ambassador Sosa as its representative.

U.S. officials "soon coalesced" behind the Rogers-Lewis team.[133] The Department of State was eager to do so; previously, it had wanted to implement a tougher economic strategy, invoking the International Emergency Economic Powers Act (IEEPA) against Panama. This act had been invoked against Iran, South Africa, Libya, and Nicaragua, and would require the president to declare the situation in Panama to be a threat to the national security, foreign policy, and economy of the United States. The Department of the Treasury and the Federal Reserve blocked this idea, opposing IEEPA's application to Panama as too heavy handed a step to take against a "friendly" country.[134] Secretary of Defense Carlucci argued that such severe pressure would be counterproductive, strengthening Noriega's resolve to stay; White House Chief of Staff Howard Baker and NSC Adviser Powell argued in favor of a more moderate course.[135] The administration had previously split over using severe economic pressure against Noriega, but the Lewis-Rogers initiative broke this stalemate.

U.S. Economic Measures

Thus the Department of State was eager to comply, right on time, with a diplomatic note drafted by the Arnold & Porter lawyers (who were acting as a foreign office as well as legal representatives), stating that the Delvalle government designated Ambassador Sosa to control its financial assets in the United States.[136] The appropriate official statement was read at the department's regular noontime press briefing. That afternoon, March 2, 1988, the assistant secretary signed the certification making Ambassador Sosa the official designee, and he became the custodian of Account No. 1. The same day, the chairman of the House Merchant Marine and Fisheries Committee called on the administration to put U.S. government payments to Panama in escrow.[137]

The impact in Panama was immediate. On Thursday, March 3, the National Bank of Panama issued a communiqué advising local banks that it could not meet their requests for money because U.S. authorities had prevented the shipment of $10 million from Republic National Bank. In an attempt to conserve cash, private banks then limited the amount patrons could withdraw. The next day, the government ordered banks to close. Within days, financial transactions came to a halt. Merchants refused to accept checks from customers, fearing that they could never be cashed. People hoarded dollars, and the more they hoarded the less money circulated. Bartering began.

Some in Congress favored tougher measures. On March 3, when Delvalle and Sosa called for a trade embargo, twenty-four senators did too. Senators D'Amato, Kerry, and Kennedy introduced a bill (S 2134) to impose harsher sanctions in the form of a total trade embargo. In calling for the move, D'Amato said, "If we can't take on this petty dictator, what hope do we have in taking on bigger dictators?"[138]

On March 4, the Senate Foreign Relations Committee unanimously approved S. J. Res. 267, which called for economic sanctions and urged the Reagan administration to cut all ties with Noriega.[139] The anti-Noriega coalition, which Senators Helms and Kerry had started building in 1986, had expanded. During 1988 and 1989, coalitions in both the House and Senate frequently urged the White House to take stronger action, including military force, against Noriega. Their resolutions, however, seldom gained majority votes on the floor.

Although the Reagan administration opposed an embargo, it was ready to apply economic pressure. On March 1, the administration de-certified Panama (along with Afghanistan, Iran, and Syria) under the Anti-Drug Abuse Act as failing to cooperate in drug enforcement. This made mandatory the suspension of U.S. economic and military aid that was already in effect and required the United States to oppose any future Panamanian loan requests to intergovernmental banks. *Congressional Quarterly* characterized this decision as a "dramatic shift in policy" compared to previously close working relations between the DEA and PDF.[140] Other economic moves followed.

On March 11, President Reagan ordered that all payments to Panama from U.S. government agencies be placed in escrow Account No. 2, denying direct payments to the Panamanian government. This would deny another $6.5 million per month from the Panama Canal Commission (PCC), as well as receipts from the oil pipeline in Panama.[141] Reagan also ordered increased attention on drug transactions involving Panama by U.S. immigration and customs agencies.[142] Presidential Proclamation 5579 was issued on March 23, 1988, rescinding Panama's preferential status under the Generalized System of Preferences and the Caribbean Basin Initiative. This affected some $96 million worth of goods on a yearly basis. The Senate urged the administration to go even further, passing a resolution by an overwhelming ninety-two to zero vote on March 25, 1988, calling for additional pressure and the extradition of Noriega, additional U.S. support for President Delvalle, and economic assistance for a post-Noriega government.

Effects in Panama

As Rogers and Lewis had hoped, Noriega was having trouble meeting his semi-monthly payroll of $54–65 million.[143] The government needed $9 million for the PDF, $8 million for teachers, and $7 million for civil service retirees. For the March 15 pay period, the entire PDF received full pay in cash, but teachers and other government employees got $75 in cash and the balance in a check. Teachers, telephone workers, longshoremen, and employees of the Ministry of Treasury and Finance went on strike. For the March 31 pay period, only high-ranking PDF officers were paid, not the entire force. Teachers and other civilians were not paid.[144] The government arranged for partial payment of social security checks, but the checks could not be cashed. Thousands of angry retirees marched on the Ministry of Public Health, brandishing their checks. The government made another partial payroll just before Easter, and announced that government checks could be used as legal tender for payments for government utilities and other fees. Noriega also took direct action to provide goods to his constituents. The PDF raided two flour mills that had closed and took away more than 13,000 bags of flour to be sold on the open market.[145]

One foreign banker characterized the situation in late April: "What this country had going for it was an excellent location . . . political stability, financial confidence and the U.S. dollar. Now all Panama has going for it is geographic position."[146] After six weeks, the various economic measures had taken a severe toll. Panamanian economist Guillermo Chapman reported the following indicators as of late April:

- Industrial production is down 40%
- Gasoline sales are down 50%
- Supermarket sales are down 30%
- Business for the tax free zone . . . is down 50%
- More than 75,000 Panamanians have been laid off
- More than 150,000 government employees have received only a fraction of their pay
- Sales of consumer goods have virtually halted
- Hundreds of businesses have been forced to close[147]

Noriega, however, was scraping enough money together to endure the pressure, and having made it through the first crucial weeks, the longer he lasted the more his chances improved for outlasting the squeeze. The nationwide general strike began to lose momentum on April 4, when many retail stores opened for the first time since March 18. The embassy reported that "commercial activity in Panama is nowhere near normal,"[148] but it no longer appeared that the economic squeeze could topple the government.

During March, additional "clean up" lawsuits were filed, concerning additional funds at smaller banks and the assets of Panamanian businesses in the United States. The Delvalle government and Gabriel Lewis hoped that the Reagan administration would immediately follow up on their legal actions with IEEPA measures and sanctions tough enough to break the Noriega government. They, and the legal team, grew increasingly frustrated as the opportunity created during the first few weeks of their revolution by litigation began to evaporate. The lawyers considered their actions as a stop-gap measure, "plugging the dike"; they had to proceed bank by bank as assets were discovered. This allowed Noriega's government to utilize undiscovered assets and, once it realized what was happening, to move assets beyond the control of U.S. courts. The Rogers team argued that the administration, if it so desired, could set up a wall. Panamanians were also frustrated. Eduardo Vallarino, a leader of the NCC, described the sanctions as "too few and far between" to force Noriega out. He also voiced a widely articulated criticism: "The dosage will almost kill the patient before it cures the sickness."[149]

Applying IEEPA

The Department of State had been unable to get support for IEEPA before, and it was not until the first week of April that an interdepartmental consensus was reached on IEEPA. The way was prepared on March 25, 1988, when President Delvalle issued a decree suspending payment of fiscal obligations to the Panamanian (Noriega's government) treasury. On March 31, the Senate passed S Res. 403, calling for sanctions, by a vote of ninety-two to one. President Reagan signed Executive Order 12635 declaring a national emergency and invoking IEEPA on April 8, 1988. This prohibited all U.S. payments to the Noriega government and froze its assets in the United States. The intent was to deprive Noriega of cash from approximately 45,000 U.S. residents and 100 U.S. businesses in Panama, and from an additional 450 U.S. companies doing business in Panama. A wide range of payments were affected by this move: income and social security taxes; direct taxes, excise taxes, and user fees; export fees and import duties; and rental fees.

Implementation of IEEPA was deliberately delayed, however, during discussions with Noriega "seeking his voluntary removal from power," which were conducted by Deputy Assistant Secretary of State Michael Kozak during April and May.[150] Some in the administration considered the prospect of IEEPA sanctions as enhancing the U.S. bargaining position—the threat of implementation should encourage Noriega to depart, and if the talks failed sanctions could then be applied. Critics, on the other hand, argued that this rationale was faulty on two grounds: Noriega was not likely to be impressed with the threat, and delayed implementation damaged the effectiveness of the broader financial squeeze strategy. Delayed implementation would still damage the Panamanian economy but was not likely to deliver the knockout punch the squeeze play required. Once the discussions were broken off on May 25, 1988, regulations implementing the sanctions were prepared.

In the interim, a press release providing guidance to U.S. companies about prohibited and permissible payments was issued on April 30. That document and the regulations themselves were prepared by the Office of Foreign Assets Control (OFAC) of the Department of the Treasury, in consultation with representatives of affected companies, businessmen, and professional groups. Panamanian Transaction Regulations (31 CFR Part 565) were issued on June 3, 1988.[151]

This delay in implementing IEEPA created a period of uncertainty for those in Panama who were supposed to comply, and, more importantly, it diluted the sanction's impact. Congressman Gejdenson was particularly critical of the first delay, arguing that invoking IEEPA on March 31 or April 1, rather than April 8, would have deprived Noriega of some $250 million in quarterly tax payments.[152] As a result of this delay, the impact of tax payment prohibitions did not occur for another three months. Some in the administration were more critical of the second delay, arguing that Noriega was more likely to take negotiations with the Department of State seriously if those were supported by tough economic sanctions. General Woerner, for example, believed that the deliberate negotiating strategy of demonstrating U.S. good faith by withholding implementation of the sanctions was not likely to have the desired effect on Noriega.[153] The IEEPA sanctions were likely to have a severe impact on U.S. businesses in Panama and on U.S. personnel and Panamanians working for the PCC. Consequently, the April 30 press release and the June 3 regulations specified a number of exemptions to IEEPA: utilities (electricity, water, garbage); postal, telephone, and telegraph payments; travel-related payments (departure fees, ticket taxes, landing fees, and fuel taxes); indirect (sales and excise) taxes; and administrative fees for basic business activities. These exemptions were criticized as weakening the symbolic value and the strong message IEEPA was supposed to represent, but the OFAC defended them as necessary and reasonable. The target of sanctions was Noriega, not U.S. residents and businesses, and the Department of the Treasury was trying to achieve a "delicate balancing act" between denying cash to Noriega and, in the long term, preserving "the American presence in Panama so that economic conditions favorable to the return of stable democratic rule are not destroyed." The OFAC calculated that IEEPA sanctions deprived the Noriega government of approximately $296 million as of late July 1989.[154]

Despite the relief these exemptions were designed to provide, U.S. residents, Department of Defense personnel, and Panamanians employed by the PCC suffered increasingly harassing treatment.[155] The Panamanian government retaliated by denying services and stepping up enforcement for violations, for example, against drivers who lacked license plates because they could not pay the fee. Much later, on June 23 and August 24, the Department of the Treasury allowed retroactive payments of social security taxes tied to health-care benefits and of import duties and port fees.

Meanwhile, in Panama the financial crisis was beginning to ease. The government ordered banks, which had closed in mid-March, to reopen. On April 18, banks partially reopened only to accept deposits. This move and the additional liquidity it provided allowed the government to make it through one more payday. The banking system, however, had been almost destroyed by the crisis. By mid-April, 60 of the 120-odd banks in Panama had either shut down or would do so as soon as they could transfer their assets abroad.[156] The 1988 Annual Report of the Inter-American Development Bank listed Panama's annual rate of growth in its gross domestic product at 2.4 percent; estimates of the relative decline in the economy ranged from 17 to 25 percent.[157] Assistant Secretary of State Abrams claimed jubilantly that Noriega was holding onto power "by his fingertips."[158] A report from the scene presented a different perspective; a journalist described the sanctions policy as of late May 1988 as "a fiasco feeding upon itself."[159]

Political Dialogue in Panama

Although Admiral Murphy's discussions and Blandón's negotiations failed to coax Noriega out of office, they had provided opportunities for a complicated array of government supporters and opponents to begin to communicate. Discussions in autumn 1987 about a timetable for Noriega's exit, composition of a transition government, national elections, and steps toward restoring democracy provided a foundation for talks, once Delvalle was ousted, about forming a new government of national reconciliation.

Delvalle's insistence that he was the president of Panama, and U.S. recognition of that legal fact, created a new bargaining opportunity: rival governments, headed by Delvalle and Solís Palma, could be merged into a government of national unity or reconciliation. Renewed dialogue began with representatives of all sides taking intransigent positions. The NCC took the strongest stance, refusing to negotiate with government representatives until Noriega stepped down. Two of its constituents, medical and educational groups, were the most resistant to supporting a transition under Delvalle.[160] Party leaders were more willing to talk, but their long-standing opposition to Delvalle made them reluctant to consider him as their president. The dominant political opposition group, based on electoral performance, was Arnulfo Arias's party, the Authentic Panameñista party (PPA), but it was split into factions with competing representatives. Arias was aged and ailing, and his party was undergoing a succession struggle. Guillermo Endara soon emerged as the Arnulfistas's lead negotiator.

To some oppositionists, Delvalle had two strikes against him: he had headed a puppet government, serving Noriega's interests, and once deposed he seemed too amenable to the United States. Professor Miguel Bernal characterized the idea of a joint provisional government headed by Delvalle and Solís Palma as "*Norieguismo* without Noriega."[161] A headline in *La Prensa Digest* called this option "Kiss the Pineapple" because Noriega would retire with full military and civic honors and continue to live in Panama. Although Noriega would hold no office under the provisional government, oppositionists feared that as a billionaire he could easily buy the 1989 election.[162] In addition to the difficulty of building a coalition around a former enemy, secrecy concerns, arising from the fact that Delvalle was in hiding, hampered the dialogue.

Nonetheless, a declaration of objectives was signed on March 6, 1988, by Arnulfo Arias and Carlos F. Rodríguez for the PPA; Ricardo Arias Calderón for the Christian Democrats; Gilbert Mallol for the NCC; Gilberto Arias for MOLIRENA; José Blandón for the PRD; and two independent oppositionists, Roberto Eisenmann and Gabriel Lewis. Their "principal objective" was "to establish jointly a Government of national reconciliation capable of providing justice, due process of law, liberty, reconstruction of democratic institutions, fiscal order and economic development."

Participating in the new government would be representatives of political parties and "other forces dedicated to the reestablishment of democratic order." Concerning the PDF, the joint statement said the new government would "seek an understanding with the Defense Forces, so as to define the legitimate role that the professional institution of the armed forces will play in accordance with the Constitution."[163] While these direct talks were under way during March and April, presidents of neighboring states were attempting to encourage the talks and mediate with Noriega.

Regional Initiatives

From March 7 to March 15, 1988, just after Delvalle's ouster, a regional initiative was undertaken by three former presidents: Carlos Andrés Pérez of Venezuela, Daniel Oduber of Costa Rica, and Alfonso López Michelson of Colombia. They met with officials in the Department of State on March 7. Pérez then met with Noriega several times and believed that he had secured Noriega's agreement to depart.[164] Two other foreign leaders joined this effort, Costa Rican President Oscar Arias and Spanish Prime Minister Felipe González. This was a positive sign because Spain was often mentioned as an exile site. However, a military coup by a reformist faction of the PDF on March 16 interrupted the mediation and probably altered Noriega's bargaining calculus. President Solís Palma announced that Noriega was willing to resign before the 1989 elections "provided that opposition groups agree to an unspecified national dialogue."[165] The mediation process resumed, but it soon failed.

On March 25, delegations representing the government and opposition parties went separately to Costa Rica to meet with President Arias.[166] Two days later, Oscar Arias met with the former presidents and other mediators to discuss how best to get Noriega to leave.[167] When Pérez returned to Venezuela on March 29, he said "Noriega will retire in May," and claimed credit for having persuaded Noriega to accept mediation by Archbishop McGrath to develop a timetable for restoring democratic rule to Panama.[168] Either Pérez misread Noriega's intentions or Noriega misled Pérez, because the very next day Noriega rejected the regional mediation effort. Noriega said, "I do not accept what they [Arias/González] have proposed. . . . Carlos Andrés Pérez is trying to help his own political campaign . . . I do not agree with Pérez' work."[169]

The March 1988 Coup Attempt

Rumors about disaffected majors and colonels who were ready to take matters into their own hands had begun circulating in March. This was also the time that unpaid public workers were joining oppositionists on the streets. Behind the scenes, negotiations were under way to form a new government that would alter the role of the PDF. Noriega had not made a public appearance in ten days. Shocking events had occurred in rapid succession:

- February 25: Delvalle tried to fire Noriega and was ousted instead
- March 3: U.S. lawyers blocked transfers of Panamanian funds from New York
- March 6: Opposition parties, the Crusade, and the PRD, represented by Blandón, unified
- March 11: President Reagan announced sanctions

In this context of accelerating crisis, on March 16 several officers launched a barracks revolt.

The leaders of the coup were the chief of police, Col. Leonidas Macías; Maj. Fernando Quezada, head of operations and training; Maj. Augusto Villalaz, Noriega's pilot; Maj. Jaime Benítez; Maj. Aristides Valdonedo, head of intelligence; and Capt. Humberto Macea, a former executive assistant to Col. Díaz Herrera.[170] Villalaz, who escaped and defected to the United States, later said that planning for the coup began about three weeks in advance, which would have been the last week of February, when Noriega ousted Delvalle. Villalaz said disaffection with Noriega had been building since the Spadafora crisis in 1985; he added that Blandón's defection was one of the events that precipitated the coup. "For us," said Villalaz, "it was hard to believe that a man who was so involved with so many important situations was changing his attitude toward Gen. Noriega." More importantly, Villalaz continued, "We felt that General Noriega would throw away the institution . . . to further his personal interests."[171] A fairly large group, estimated to include twenty-four men, plotted a barracks rebellion. Three colonels on the general staff, about twelve other officers, and between thirty and a hundred other PDF personnel were involved in the March 16 coup.

Although one reporter said that the United States was forewarned by the plotters, there was no suggestion of U.S. involvement in the coup itself.[172] Noriega claimed, however, that the officers involved had ties to the CIA. His suspicions were aroused by the fact that the ringleaders had recently been on training missions in the United States where, he asserted, the coup was planned.

Some of the officers made contact with the opposition. Quezada said the majors were in contact with two oppositionists; Guillermo Cochez was reported to be one of Quezada's connections; and Valdonedo was in touch with someone in the Christian Democratic party. Quezada said the officers realized that changes had to be made, and they contacted the opposition with a plan to promote a more professional PDF. Major Valdonedo prepared a speech, to be broadcast after the coup, describing the officers' goals and plans. When the plotters were attacked during the coup, Valdonedo ate the document to prevent the incriminating evidence from falling into Noriega's hands.[173]

One reporter described this coup as "hastily planned" and "a study in failure."[174] Reports at the time denigrated both the execution of the coup and the motivation of its leaders. Major Quezada later said, "Coordination among the majors, especially at headquarters," was the problem most responsible for the coup's failure.[175] The original timetable for the coup was advanced two times. The first change resulted from the majors' concern about arms that Noriega was stockpiling. In three missions to Cuba, the latest being completed on March 14, Villalaz brought back forty-seven tons of arms. Included were AK-47 rifles, RPG-7 grenade launchers, and mortar rounds. Villalaz and Maj. Raoul Anel Adames, who also defected, both claimed that the coup plotters were alarmed by the nature and amount of these arms and the fact that thirteen more flights were planned. They were particularly concerned that these weapons were "stockpiled outside regular Defense Forces channels" at Tocumen, near the Costa Rican border, and near Río Hato. Alarm about these weapons caused the organizers to advance the timing of the coup, apparently by several days.[176] Reports to the U.S. embassy at the time confirmed this concern, citing "a delivery of Cuban arms for distribution to Noriega supporters apparently prematurely triggered action by Macías."[177]

The coup's timetable was advanced a second time, from Wednesday night to Wednesday morning. Because the officers planned to arrest Noriega at the Comandancía, the headquarters of the PDF, they had to strike while he was there. Whether because of inaccurate intelligence, betrayal, bad luck, or Noriega's good fortune, the general was elsewhere when the rebel officers arrived at 7:00 A.M. on March 16. Although the entire story is not yet clear, one source accused Colonel Macías of falsely telling the plotters that Noriega had gone to the Comandancía on Tuesday night. Macías had been included in the plot because he, in contrast to the majors, had armed men under his direct command. Macías may have betrayed the coup or been misinformed about Noriega's whereabouts; Noriega may have sent a decoy to the Comandancía or he may have departed during the night.

As the coup was initiated, Major Quezada prepared to address a company of troops inside the Comandancía. This was the point, according to Villalaz and Adames, when the general staff was supposed to withdraw its support for Noriega and have him arrested. Instead, an officer who was supposedly part of the coup shouted, "This man [Quezada] wants to overthrow Commandante Noriega. Arrest him!" The plotters were betrayed. A loyal officer, Moisés Giroldi, fired shots into the air to bring additional troops to the scene. Loyal troops, from the Urraca Company headquartered at the Comandancía and commanded by Giroldi, put down the coup.

Noriega drove up to the Comandancía in his bullet-proof Mercedes at 8:15 A.M. The coup attempt was finished by 9:00. At 9:30 Noriega appeared, dressed in a white *guayabera*, to pose on the steps with his senior officers and take reporters' questions. Noriega was in high spirits, exhilarated by his victory. One reporter asked when government workers were going to get paid. Noriega replied, "Tell the gringos to give back the money they stole from us."[178] Another asked about shots that had been heard earlier from inside the Comandancía; Noriega's answer: "Just kisses, kisses for journalists."[179]

Meanwhile, reports of the coup sparked street violence, cheering in government offices, and disruptions of services. Public sector workers went on strike, and electrical workers cut power to the oil pipeline, causing a shutdown affecting the flow of 600,000 barrels per day.[180] When opposition leaders called for a general strike, Noriega declared a "state of urgency" (emergency) and dispatched Doberman riot police to quell demonstrations. The next day, March 17, people in Panama City "awoke to the heaviest military presence ever seen."[181] Government workers remaining on the job were sent home by mid-afternoon, and the city seemed to shut down. *La Prensa Digest* reported, "Nearly all businesses were closed, taxis and buses stopped running, banks remained closed, and some industries were forced to close in the wake of street violence and the cut-off of electricity."[182] Burning barricades were set throughout Panama City, and sporadic gunfire was heard.

Colonel Macías, the four majors, and some thirty other coup participants were arrested, beaten, and imprisoned. Some of the majors were tortured and then imprisoned at regional command centers, as punishment and to intimidate prospective plotters. Three of the nineteen members of the general staff were forced to retire; the number of colonels was reduced from six to four. As many as 100 officers, mostly from police and military intelligence units, were subsequently investigated for aiding or abetting the coup.[183] Noriega took steps to strengthen his position and prevent another coup, firing his chief of intelligence, Col. Bernardo Barrera, and four other officers. Barrera was replaced by Lt. Col. Guillermo Wong; Colonel Macías was replaced by Lt. Col. Eros Ramiro Cal, a long-standing Noriega associate. When asked about the PDF after the coup, Villalaz suggested that although most officers still thought Noriega had to go, Noriega had put enough loyalists in place to feel secure.[184] Villalaz predicted that Noriega would "never relinquish power voluntarily." As evidence, Villalaz recalled a statement Noriega had made: the regime, said Noriega, was "one ship, and it if sinks, it will sink with everybody on it."[185]

Nonetheless, the coup attempt shattered the myth of total PDF loyalty. Noriega quickly moved to solidify his power base, searching for enemies and advancing his friends. Personal loyalty rather than professional advancement characterized the PDF promotions announced on March 21, 1988. As these changes took effect, the relative proportion of "thugs" at higher ranks increased. Noriega created an advisory group to rival the general staff—a Strategic Military Council (CEM), which met once a week and also informally. The CEM included one of the five colonels, three of the twelve lieutenant colonels, ten of the fifty-five majors, and six captains; they constituted a "shadow" general staff, one more loyal to Noriega. However, although creating the CEM and promoting loyalists enhanced Noriega's power base in the short run, these steps eroded the integrity of the PDF as an institution and made the U.S. policy of encouraging reform from within increasingly less tenable.

Nonetheless, the Reagan administration continued to signal the PDF that it wanted to work with a reformed military. A White House spokesman stated the official policy on March 22, 1988: "The United States favors the integrity of the Panamanian Defense Forces as a professional military institution, and we look forward to the PDF playing an important and constructive role under a civilian regime." The meaning of "important and constructive" was clarified through press leaks and diplomatic channels. A White House official told reporters "the statement was meant to send a 'strong signal' to the PDF to oust Noriega and restore civilian rule."[186] Thus, the United States was relying on the PDF to "put its house in order."[187] To encourage reform from within, opposition leaders were urged by U.S. officials to promise that no officers would be tried for human rights or other abuses under a new government. The objectives of U.S. policy remained unchanged; the Reagan administration continued to rely on a Panamanian solution shaped by the PDF. Although U.S. rhetoric included references to a professional military under a civilian government, reform guided by the PDF was guaranteed to yield a substantial role for the military rather than a new regime.

Noriega also engineered changes in civilian positions following the March coup attempt. The Assembly rejected two new Supreme Court replacements who had been appointed by Delvalle. The government fired and replaced diplomatic personnel who remained loyal to Delvalle; some of these continued to represent the Delvalle government.[188] During the next few months, Noriega took additional steps to keep the population under control. He called in a "Cuban crisis group" of about fifteen advisers who helped the PDF organize neighborhood watch committees, allegedly to resist a U.S. invasion. These committees were renamed Dignity Batallions.[189] Initially, they recruited released criminals and other civilian "volunteers"; later, children as young as thirteen participated in some units. The Dignity Batallions expanded and soon were dominated by youths and adults who constituted a paramilitary force more loyal to Noriega than the PDF.

In this context, during the spring of 1988, the press began reporting for the first time that Panamanians were calling for U.S. military intervention. On the nightly news in the United States, viewers could see hand-lettered signs that read: "US: You Created the Monster, You Get Rid of Him."[190] A middle-class protester told a *Time* reporter, "The Americans put Noriega here. Now they have to get him out."[191] At the same time, however, reporters unanimously judged the likelihood of U.S. military action to be remote. One concluded, "Since any resurrection of the big stick appears remote at the moment, Panamanians may realize that ousting Noriega is up to them."[192]

Status of the Military Option

At the same time that he took stiffer economic measures, President Reagan ruled out U.S. military intervention except to protect the Panama Canal from attack or to protect U.S. lives. These two caveats were a constant element in U.S. declarations about the use of force. During early 1988, however, extreme threats to the canal were not considered as imminent as threats arising from street violence. As Noriega beefed up the PDF presence on the streets and developed his Dignity Batallions, the Reagan administration dispatched additional U.S. forces to Panama. Between 500 and 700 Military Police (MPs) were sent in March; during April 6–8, an additional 1,300 U.S. troops were deployed.

Thus far, the United States had consistently declined options that would use U.S. military force to remove Noriega. Throughout February and March, various officials had asserted that the military option was not being considered. A week after Delvalle went into hiding, Speaker of the House Jim Wright said, "Obviously we don't want to go there with the force of military arms—that's ridiculous."[193] In late April, an administration official commented on the sanctions policy: "There are other things that you can do," he said, "but they all involve putting our military assets into play, and we're not going to do that."[194] The U.S. objective was still to rely on events in Panama, combined with external economic and diplomatic pressure, to remove Noriega.

A Deal to Coax Noriega Out

A Panamanian who "knows Noriega well" assessed the postcoup situation: "The general is willing to go, but he's not going to be dragged out like a dog."[195] Noriega began to explore a deal that would maximize his power after exile or retirement. Noriega requested a direct meeting with U.S. officials; he also tried to involve the Papal Nuncio on his behalf in discussions with Aurelio Barría, the president of the NCC.

The Walker Mission

When Noriega requested a meeting with a representative of the Department of State right after the coup, Deputy Assistant Secretary of State William Walker and the department's legal advisor for Latin American affairs, Michael Kozak, were immediately sent to Panama. They met with Noriega, Colonel

Justines and Rómulo Escobar Bethancourt late in the evening on March 18, just two days after the attempted coup; they met again on Saturday morning.

Walker's objective was to arrange a deal for Noriega's exit in which the United States would agree to refrain from seeking his extradition for prosecution if he would seek asylum in another country.[196] This offer was consistent with previous official and unofficial missions: the time had come for Noriega to step aside, and to accomplish this the United States was willing "to guarantee the integrity" of the PDF under a new government.[197] The Department of State described the talks as "unproductive"; the PDF described the U.S. position as "unacceptable and un-Panamanian."[198] The brief Walker mission ended unsatisfactorily for both sides.

An Uneasy Interim

The Reagan administration decided to observe the effect of financial pressure and other mediation efforts before making another approach to Noriega. The opposition took a second step toward unity on March 25, when the NCC and opposition parties issued a "blueprint for progress." This document endorsed a government of national reconciliation under President Delvalle, Noriega's removal, and the restoration of constitutional order.[199] The proposed "national dialogue" did not, however, produce an agreement between the opposition and Noriega's government.

By mid-April, it became clear that neither the economic squeeze and sanctions nor dialogue with the opposition would remove Noriega. Frustrations rose in Washington as the situation in Panama seemed increasingly unstable and unmanageable: multiple and confusing negotiating and mediation initiatives were under way, street violence and repression continued, changes were occurring in the PDF, and a new paramilitary force was expanding. In addition, the Cuban presence in the country was increasing and posing more direct threats to U.S. interests. On April 12, a Marine unit in the canal area engaged in a two-hour fire fight with unknown, supposedly Cuban, intruders. This was one of several unusual skirmishes rumored to involve Cuban troops that occurred during the year. These were interpreted in Washington as pressure tactics by Noriega. A U.S. military official confirmed that these incidents occurred and that U.S. forces took deliberate steps to alter perimeters at the facilities involved in order to minimize direct conflict with the attackers.

As the situation continued to deteriorate, some in the Department of State suggested using U.S. military force to end the crisis. Two ideas were advocated by Shultz and Abrams: a military strike against Noriega and a plan to install a headquarters for Delvalle's government at a U.S. facility to be surrounded and defended with U.S. troops. The NSC and DOD took opposing stands, and both ideas were vigorously criticized by Crowe, Carlucci, and Powell.[200] A senior Army officer summarized the critique: "State always talks about a 'surgical' military operation. . . . There is no such thing."[201]

The administration wished that the PDF would oust Noriega and reform itself, but after the March coup another attempt seemed unlikely, at least for a while. The administration needed an option; the only one that was bureaucratically acceptable in April 1988 was to return to the bargaining table.

The Kozak Mission

Deputy Assistant Secretary of State Kozak conducted three sessions in Panama: April 15–17, April 28–mid-May, and May 22–25, 1988. The United States had two principal objectives: to remove Noriega and to restore civilian government. Noriega's objectives were to step down and to leave the system intact. Ultimately, the two proved to be irreconcilable. When faced with a deadline for accepting the deal on May 25, Noriega could not say yes.

Evolving over a six-week period, the deal had different provisions at different times. The final package offered to Noriega on May 25 involved a sequence of seven steps, each of which had to be fulfilled prior to implementation of subsequent steps.[202]

Step 1. As a sign of good faith and as a face-saving device for Noriega, the United States would announce the suspension of economic sanctions it imposed in April. This would allow Noriega to claim, once U.S. pressure was withdrawn, that he was doing what he had always wanted to achieve, namely, to democratize the country.

Step 2. Noriega would then take the second step within an hour of the U.S. sanctions announcement. Noriega would announce his forthcoming retirement, on August 12, 1988, the fifth anniversary of his command. He would call on the National Assembly to pass a law limiting the term of PDF commander to a maximum of five years, retroactive to August 12, 1983, the date his tenure began. This would legally end Noriega's term on August 12, 1988, and provide another face-saving device for the general. In addition, Noriega could choose his successor as PDF commander, a move designed to reassure officers who might fear retribution after Noriega's departure. In his speech, Noriega would call for the National Assembly to pass legislation, within three to ten days, restoring civil and political rights and granting pardons and amnesty for oppositionists in jail, hiding, or exile. He would also call for a conclave of national reconciliation to develop a transitional government.

Step 3. Then, Noriega was supposed to answer a question planned in advance and posed by a friendly member of the press: "General, what are you going to do after you step down?" Noriega's answer was to constitute the third step; he would say that he was going to take a vacation abroad with his family. He would not run as a presidential candidate in 1989, a step he had hinted at and not ruled out. Instead, he would leave Panama after retiring for the nine months preceding the presidential election, although he could return briefly for holiday visits. His postelection status was left up to the new government.

Step 4. This step was to be taken by Noriega on or before August 12, 1988: he was supposed to retire and depart.

Step 5. Once Noreiga stepped down, the Reagan administration would agree to a motion by Noriega's attorneys that the indictments against him be dismissed. The U.S.'s affirmative response would be conveyed to Noriega through the Papal Nuncio.

Step 6. This step concerned Panama's two governments. The United States would continue to recognize Delvalle as president, and Solís Palma would remain as acting president in Panama. The United States would work with both governments and the opposition as they conducted a dialogue of national reconciliation and prepared for elections.

Step 7. Elections would be held in May 1989. If the resulting government were sufficiently broadly based and constitutionally justifiable, the United States would recognize it and release the funds placed in escrow since March.

As details about various steps appeared in the press, opposition to the deal emerged in Congress. The Senate passed a resolution on May 17, while negotiations were still under way, criticizing the idea of dismissing the indictments.[203] The resolution, sponsored by the usually supportive Robert Dole, passed by a vote of eighty-six to ten, indicating a bipartisan consensus against such a deal.[204] Even Vice-President Bush spoke out publicly against a deal for Noriega, saying he would not negotiate with drug dealers. Most significantly, the presiding judge for the U.S. district court in Miami, William Hoeveler, issued a strong public statement against a deal. Judge Hoeveler said, "[I am] not obliged to dismiss the indictments upon a request from the administration, and may not do so if asked."[205] This may have been the deciding factor that turned Noriega against the deal.

When the negotiations bogged down in mid-May, Kozak returned to Washington for high-level consultations. Kozak, Treasury Secretary James Baker, Shultz, Carlucci, Powell, and Attorney General Ed Meese met at the White House for two and a half hours on Saturday, May 21. The group decided that May 25, the day Reagan and Shultz were due to depart for a summit meeting in Moscow, would be Noriega's final deadline. Kozak returned to Panama to make a final offer. Four days later, the deadline passed and Secretary Shultz announced the failure of the talks. On Wednesday afternoon, May 25, Secretary Shultz told reporters, "Noriega wouldn't carry through with the arrangements his representatives have negotiated."[206]

Reports at the time laid blame for the failure squarely on Noriega.[207] He, in turn, said that his officers rejected the deal "because they found no security to the continuity of the constitutional mandate of President Manuel Solís Palma."[208] Noriega denounced the Kozak mission in what was described as a "rambling 75-minute monologue" to the National Assembly.[209] Others suggested that Noriega rejected the deal because the Reagan administration really did not sign on to Step 6, which would, in effect, quash the indictments. Critics suggested that either Kozak did not convince Noriega that the administration could drop the indictments or that Noriega doubted that the United States would keep its commitment after he left Panama.

The deal was not popular with the U.S. Congress, either. One reason was that its terms were more advantageous to Noriega than earlier offers. Congressional critics asserted that the administration had retreated from its position that Noriega had to relinquish power and go into permanent exile. Previously, the United States had insisted that Noriega leave power and Panama; now, the United States was asking him to leave office, but not relinquish all of his power, allowing him to appoint a successor, and requiring him to leave Panama only temporarily.

The administration tried to minimize the fact that it was offering Noriega a better deal; spokesmen denied that U.S. objectives had changed. However, two months earlier, when President Reagan had been asked by a reporter if he would be satisfied if Noriega stepped down but did not leave Panama, Reagan had replied, "We feel Noriega should leave Panama."[210] The administration tried to arrange an exile option, but Noriega had rejected that deal. Marlin Fitzwater, the White House spokesman, tried to justify the terms produced by the Kozak mission: "Our policy is that General Noriega must go, which means leave power. We've talked about that a number of times. We have said we prefer him to leave Panama, but the policy issue is to leave power."[211] Fitzwater was trying to argue, with little success, that the essential objective of U.S. policy had not changed.

The administration also tried to convince Congress of the merits of negotiating Noriega's removal, even if the price were a deal more to his advantage than previous offers. After all, Noriega had rejected those. Kozak argued that Noriega would not bow to pressures alone; instead, terms specifying his situation and a transition in Panama had to be clarified. Kozak asserted that the United States needed clarifications, too. He told a House committee:

> The effect of the measures arrayed against General Noriega by the United
> States, by the international community and, most importantly, by his
> own people, is substantial indeed. But pressure alone is not a policy. A
> mechanism for translating the pressures into a concrete result
> compatible with our policy goals is essential. That is the purpose of
> negotiations.[212]

Pressures could bring Noriega to the bargaining table. If the United
States wanted Noriega to depart voluntarily, however, a deal would have to be
sufficiently attractive to gain his acceptance. In May 1988, the Reagan
administration offered the most generous deal it could, but even those terms
were not attractive enough for Noriega.

To one Panamanian oppositionist, it looked as if the United States
preferred "to lose a tool and save the system."[213] This comment, by Gilma
Camargo, typified opposition concerns that the United States was focusing
so much on Noriega that it was overlooking the larger problem, what
oppositionists called the "narco-military" system. Pointing out that the
opposition had been excluded from the negotiations, Roberto Eisenmann said
he felt that the United States was "giving away the store." "Unfortunately,"
he continued, "they were giving away *our* store."[214]

In Panama, the situation was difficult to diagnose. Noriega was in
trouble—the opposition was active, with demonstrations and strikes, and its
leaders were negotiating with government representatives. Economic
sanctions were taking a severe toll. Opposition demonstrators were being
beaten, subjected to psychological pressure and harassment in jail, and
bloodied on the streets. However, neither national dialogue among leaders nor
popular pressures seemed likely to remove Noriega from power.

In fact, Noriega was still able to mobilize his supporters. Huge pro-
Noriega demonstrations were organized, and Noriega took pains to stage
impressive media events to flaunt his defiance of the United States. The most
dramatic of these was reported on May 1, while the Kozak mission was under
way. Addressing a meeting of 300 Latin American labor leaders, Noriega
stood at the podium brandishing a machete. Steel machetes, engraved with
the national seal, were given to conference delegates as they entered the hall
for the closing ceremony. Noriega shouted, "This is the machete of
Panamanian dignity, of Panamanian valor." The audience chanted in reply
"¡Ni un paso atras!" ("Not one step back!"). The scene was replayed on the
nightly news in the United States; Noriega's picture, with raised machete,
appeared on the covers of news magazines and in newspapers. In Panama,
machetes engraved with the Panamanian seal became popular souvenirs.[215]
"Not one step back" accurately conveyed Noriega's bargaining stance.
Noriega's failure to accept the deal also put the Reagan administration in a
position where it could not step back. The collapse of the Kozak mission
marked the end of the coaxing phase of U.S. policy. The administration then
authorized implementation of IEEPA sanctions and initiated covert actions.

Covert Actions

In all, five covert operations, serially named Panama 1 through Panama 5, were authorized by the Reagan and Bush administrations. (Panama 1 through Panama 4 are described below; Panama 5, which occurred during fall 1989, is described in Chapter 7.) Details about Panama 1 and Panama 2 remain murky. One of these involved funding political activity by the opposition: money for printing, advertising, transportation, and communications.[216] The other operation may have involved a plan to encourage dissident officers to overthrow Noriega.

Panama 3

The first covert operation that has been well documented was named Panama 3. President Reagan signed a "finding"—the official mechanism used to authorize a covert operation—for Panama 3 in mid-July 1988. The finding provided $1 million for activities "short of a paramilitary operation to remove General Noriega, such as kidnapping him."[217]

Reagan telephoned President Delvalle on July 15 to inform him about the finding; opposition leaders and Ambassador Sosa were briefed on the project at meetings with Michael Armacost, the under secretary of state for political affairs.[218] Given these discussions and subsequent press leaks, it is difficult to call Panama 3 "covert." A headline, for example, on page one of *The Washington Post* on July 27, 1988, proclaimed: "Covert Action on Noriega Is Cleared." Critics charged that the administration was deliberately using the plan to boost opposition morale and appease its critics rather than as a serious effort to remove Noriega.

The central figure in Panama 3 was Col. Eduardo Herrera Hassan. In 1988, at age forty-six, he had been in the military for twenty years, during which he developed a reputation in Washington for being strong, clean, and professional. These characteristics made him an ideal choice, from a U.S. perspective, to mount a coup and reform the PDF.[219]

Herrera Hassan had been away from Panama while Noriega took command and restructured the PDF. His last assignment in Panama had been in 1982, when he served as executive secretary to the general staff. After clashing with Noriega in 1983, he had taken an assignment as a military attaché in Panama's embassy in Venezuela. Noriega had identified Herrera Hassan as an officer who was likely to oppose him. In August 1985, a month before Spadafora's murder, Noriega moved Herrera Hassan to a more secure post, as Panama's ambassador to Israel. In Israel, one of Noriega's close advisers, a Mossad agent named Michael Harari, was able to keep him under surveillance and report any plotting to Noriega.[220] Noriega brought the colonel back to Panama for a brief stint as chief of police during 1987, a tour that coincided with Díaz Herrera's confessions and the Black Friday crackdown on civilian protesters. Analysts in Panama suggested that Noriega was setting Herrera Hassan up to discredit him; Herrera Hassan managed to get reassigned to Israel.

Herrera Hassan said that he began planning a coup in April 1987. His idea was to gain support for Noriega's removal among exiles and dissident PDF officers.[221] Herrera Hassan may have been planning an operation on his own, before being contacted in 1988, or his plans may have been elicited through Panama 1 or Panama 2. The contact for Panama 3 was made by Deputy Assistant Secretary of State William Walker in March 1988, almost a week prior to the abortive March 16 coup. Herrera Hassan was flown to Washington, supposedly in secret, on March 7, 1988, for a series of meetings with U.S. officials. After a week of meetings, he returned to Israel. Noriega quickly learned of Herrera Hassan's visit; *La Estrella de Panama* reported on April 22, 1988, that Col. Herrera Hassan had been discharged as ambassador to Israel "because he failed to return to Panama as directed" by Noriega.[222] Nonetheless, plans and discussions about Panama 3 continued, and Herrera Hassan shifted his base of operations to Miami.

Herrera Hassan described his activities to Katherine King as: "I developed a plan. It was my plan with my people. It would have operated outside U.S. borders. The CIA people thought it was great."[223] King also reported that Herrera Hassan was being paid $4,500 per month for this work. Another reporter said, based on interviews with U.S. and Panamanian officials, that the "Herrera group" received $1.3 million during 1988 from escrow accounts.[224] Herrera Hassan told Stephen Engelberg more about the plan itself: "What we wanted to do was enter Panama with a force and stage a coup. We would have seized him, arrested him, maybe burned him. . . . We didn't know what would happen."[225]

This was the aspect of the operation that concerned the secretary of defense, the Joint Chiefs of Staff, and the national security adviser. They had two concerns: complying with the executive order banning involvement in assassination and protecting the integrity of U.S. bases overseas. Consequently, two constraints were placed on the operation: no U.S. troops could be involved and no U.S. bases could be used to launch the operation. Even with these caveats, all of these advisers argued the president should not authorize Panama 3.

According to the July 1988 finding, the CIA would coordinate with Herrera Hassan and provide a power transmitter for a radio station to notify the Panamanian people the coup was under way and to mobilize their support.[226] The CIA also authorized support for "Panamanian opposition groups and to promote internal unrest."[227] Administration officials later told a reporter how Panama 3 was supposed to occur.[228] Herrera Hassan and his followers would enter Panama clandestinely, and "from safe houses on American military bases or other U.S.-controlled territory" operate a campaign of increasing pressure on Noriega. Their activities would include sabotage operations and propaganda, which is why the radio transmitter became such a crucial item. The main objective was to incite a counterattack by Noriega against those areas; Noriega's attack thus would allow the United States to intervene for the reason the administration had been stating all along—to protect U.S. lives and property.

This scenario, and similar plans to establish a Panamanian government in exile on a U.S. base, entailed exactly the sort of risks to military base rights that Adm. William J. Crowe, Jr., JCS chairman, was determined to avoid. "Imagine," he later wrote, "how the governments of Greece, Spain, the Philippines and Portugal would react."[229]

Congressional intelligence committee leaders were given a condensed briefing about Panama 3 on July 15, just prior to a recess.[230] When they returned and held a regular committee session to consider the finding on July 26, 1988, their reactions were skeptical and critical. One congressional source, who described the plan as "not a serious, detailed plan," said "it sounds to me that Reagan wanted to have something to tell Delvalle that we are doing."[231] This concern, along with legal and operational criticisms, bore traces of an ongoing bureaucratic battle in which opponents of Panama 3 shifted their ground to the congressional arena. Several committee members expressed serious doubts about the plan's legality. As they understood Panama 3, it appeared to defy the prohibition against U.S. involvement in assassinations that was initiated by President Gerald Ford and extended by Reagan. That executive order was later clarified to allow more flexibility in U.S. support for coups in which a foreign leader might, incidentally, be killed.[232] But on July 26, 1988, the old rules applied, and the Senate Intelligence Committee's unanimous objections were so strong that Panama 3 was abandoned by the Reagan administration after less than two weeks.

Information about the covert operation immediately leaked to the press and was reported in *The Washington Post* on July 27 and 28. Recriminations immediately surfaced. The White House blamed the committees for the leak, and committee leaders accused the administration of leaking the information in retaliation against their objections. Advocates of the plan complained that Congress would not even let the administration provide a radio transmitter. Clearly, the bipartisan consensus that produced such strong and concerted support in April, when the issue was economic sanctions, was torn apart over covert action in late July.

King reported Herrera Hassan's account of these events: "When they [the CIA] came back, their attitude had changed. They said 'Will Noriega die?' I said it was possible. And they said, 'Look, you can't do this. You have to be aware of Noriega's human rights.'"[233] In August, a DIA official told "opposition operatives that they 'should expect nothing, nothing from the military forces of the US.'" Herrera Hassan spoke to a U.S. official in November. He complained, "They made all these promises and then totally left me out in the cold."[234]

Thus, what was supposed to be a tougher U.S. policy, using covert action to remove Noriega rather than extending the most attractive deal possible, failed for lack of consensus within the administration and lack of support in Congress. As the U.S. presidential election approached, observers predicted that Panama policy would drop from the agenda for awhile.

Aftermath of Panama 3

Meanwhile, the now long-running Noriega "ouster crisis" was becoming an embarrassment for both Reagan and Bush. During thirteen months, various strategies had failed to remove Noriega from power. Some even suggested that he was in an even stronger position because of withstanding so much U.S. pressure; he gained prestige by standing up to the superpower "colossus of the North," and he purged the PDF of possible threats. For President Reagan, the ouster policy was characterized as "one of the most embarrassing episodes" of his administration. One White House official admitted, "Whenever Noriega's name comes up, it is a negative for us and will be as long as he remains in power."[235] Vice-President Bush, in the midst of his bid for the presidency, was equally leery of the issue's "negatives" and potential to damage his campaign. Gov. Michael Dukakis, the Democratic nominee, accused Bush of "dealing with drug-running Panamanian dictators" and "defending our relations with Noriega."[236] Bush, for his part, ducked the issue, claiming he had no "direct knowledge," and vowed never to trade away the indictments against Noriega.[237]

Initiatives on Panama policy stopped at the end of July. The hiatus resulted more, however, from exhaustion of options than electoral politics. "Officials" were said to "believe that the status quo will prevail, without any escalation of the crisis," until after the election.[238] Little was heard about Panama during the presidential transition. Delvalle remained in hiding. Although Noriega had not yet moved against him, reports circulated that Noriega would arrest him and seize his family's assets, particularly their sugar business. Reagan and Bush met briefly with Delvalle at the White House on December 22, 1988. Afterwards, Bush's spokesman stated, "There must be no misunderstanding about our policy. . . . Our policy will be that Noriega must go."[239] Soon after taking office, President Bush extended ongoing economic sanctions, but no other activity was reported. Behind the scenes, however, action was progressing on a covert operation to help the opposition win the 1989 election.

Panama 4

For everyone considering the situation in Panama, the next important event was election day, May 7, 1989. At stake would be the Panamanian presidency, two vice-presidential slots, and all sixty-seven seats in the

National Assembly. It was clear that Noriega was determined to win; he believed that a victory for his slate would put him in such a solid bargaining position that the United States would have to compromise with him. The opposition political parties and the NCC also targeted the election as their best opportunity to remove the general. The United States and the opposition agreed on a common goal: to so strengthen the opposition that Noriega could not steal the election or, failing that, to at least make the task of stealing the election so blatant that the fraud would spark sufficient pressure to force Noriega out of power.[240]

President Bush authorized Panama 4, one of his first covert operations, in February 1989.[241] The operation had a dual focus: to get the candidates and their message across to generate votes, and to publicize and minimize opportunities for fraud by the government and PDF. This finding reportedly continued a program authorized by President Reagan in 1988.[242] Bush "personally lobbied" congressional committees and gained their support for $10 million for the opposition campaign, principally for printing, advertising, transportation, and communications.[243]

Subsequent accounts, and occasionally waspish bickering between congressmen and NSC Adviser Brent Scowcroft, confirmed that more conflict occurred behind the scenes than appeared in the press. Robert Pear reported that the administration requested $20 million in covert aid, not $10 million. More importantly, he asserted that Congress rejected the request on the grounds that "the administration lacked a coherent strategy to deal with Noriega."[244] He said members of the Intelligence, Armed Services, and Appropriations committees did not think that $20 million could be spent effectively. Others in Congress judged Panama 4 to be realistic and substantial. One report characterized the plan as "democracy building" by U.S. government and private agencies.[245] Elizabeth Drew reported that the Senate Intelligence Committee approved of the project "but then cut back on some of the funding" because the operation "was threatening to become an embarrassment to the administration" and due to charges that the money was not being well spent.[246]

The administration went ahead with Panama 4, using the $10 million the congressional committees recommended along with money from a contingency fund the president could spend without congressional approval.[247] Malone reported that radio equipment and nonmilitary options were financed "from the interest on Panamanian government assets frozen by the Reagan administration," but in an amount substantially less than $1 million.[248] The National Democratic Institute for International Affairs, a subsidiary of the Democratic party, used funds from the National Endowment for Democracy to help set up election monitoring procedures and personnel. Its aim was to deter fraud and be prepared to expose any irregularities that did occur.

The administration's public position was quasi-neutral; according to *The*

Washington Post, the United States "remains opposed to Noriega" but "does not back any candidates" in Panama's election.[249] Information about Panama 4 soon leaked in Washington and in Panama, confirming the administration's real policy.

The opposition finally received a radio transmitter during Panama 4. Most of the material aired consisted of speeches by opposition leaders. Noriega, with the aid of Cuban technicians, soon traced the source of the broadcasts and used his own transmitter to jam them. Oppositionists complained, "we [could] only get on the air for 30 seconds before jamming starts. We needed better technical equipment, but it didn't come." Then, just a month before the election, on April 4, 1989, the radio transmitter was seized in a well-publicized PDF operation.[250] The radio operator, Kurt Frederick Mase, a U.S. citizen recruited by the CIA, was displayed along with his equipment on Panamanian television.

Even more embarrassing was the arrest two days later, by U.S. authorities, of the central figure in Panama 4, Carlos Eleta Alamarán. His job was to coordinate spending, acting as the "banker" for the operation.[251] Eleta, a former diplomat and presidential candidate, was a natural choice for the job. At age seventy, he knew all the players, and from his position as president of General Mills he had a flexible base of operations. Eleta was arrested on April 6 in Macon, Georgia, on charges of conspiracy to import cocaine and money laundering. The arrest came just a month before the election, and although Eleta pleaded not guilty and two men arrested with him vouched that Eleta was not involved with drugs or money laundering, Noriega used the incident to accuse the opposition of using drug money to fund its campaign.[252] This was the point when congressional committees advised against releasing another $10 million for Panama 4.

The 1989 Election

The United States and Panamanian oppositionists encouraged many outside organizations to send observer missions to the 1989 election. Included among these were a U.S. congressional delegation, OAS observers, and delegates from various political parties and other groups. The Bush administration also supported a nongovernmental international agency, the Council of Freely Elected Heads of Government, which was established and led by former President Jimmy Carter. The Council's aim, in Panama as elsewhere in the hemisphere, was to monitor the electoral process to promote fairness and reduce fraud. Former ambassador to Panama Ambler Moss represented Carter on a Council mission to Panama in the spring to survey and report on prospects for fraud, the status of election machinery, and other political conditions.[253] Evidence gathered by the opposition indicated that extensive preparations had been made to pad the government's tallies, particularly by eliminating known opposition supporters from registration lists and by adding extra names, whom the opposition suspected to be ghost voters.[254] Carter and other members of this group returned in May to observe the election.

The Candidates

The government slate, widely described as "hand-picked" by Noriega, was headed by Carlos Duque, the owner of Transit S.A., a firm described as a front for "military-owned enterprises."[255] Ramon Sieiro, Noriega's brother-in-law and head of the Labor party, and veteran diplomat Aquilino Boyd were the two vice-presidential candidates. They represented an eight-party progovernment Coalition of National Liberation (COLINA). Duque's campaign pledge was that Noriega would continue as PDF commander until the year 2000, when the canal would be turned over to Panama.

This was, in fact, the main issue; the election was widely considered to be a referendum on Noriega. The government slate faced an uphill task. Opinion polls showed Noriega to be "the most unpopular public figure in Panama."[256]

The main opposition comprised four parties joined in a Civil Opposition Democratic Alliance (ADOC). They chose Guillermo Endara as their presidential candidate. Endara, a congenial lawyer well known as Arnulfo Arias's executive secretary, emerged during 1988 as the Arnulfistas's spokesman. Ricardo Arias Calderón, head of the Christian Democrat party and an active opponent of the government since 1964, was the first vice-presidential candidate. Guillermo "Billy" Ford, who represented the smaller National Liberal Republican Movement, ran as second vice-president. The fourth member of ADOC was the Authentic Liberal Party (PLA). Endara promised to fire Noriega if he would not retire.

These three candidates constituted an uneasy coalition that improved with time and experience. Many had doubted that an opposition slate could be created, much less endure the pressures of a campaign. In mid-1988, the opposition political parties were still planning to boycott the election, based on their experience in 1984. They wanted to avoid a "trap" and a "trick to provide legitimacy to the regime."[257] Toward the end of 1988, however, the parties decided to use the elections to bolster the Civic Crusade's campaign and to create an alternative leadership to the increasingly unsustainable Delvalle presidency. They began a long and arduous process of creating an opposition slate.

Without Arnulfo Arias, who died in August 1988, the Authentic Panameñista party (PPA) was in trouble. History dictated that it should have the leading position on the ticket, but the party lacked a salient figure. A minority faction, led by Hildebrando Nicosia, gained control of the PPA label and ran as a second opposition slate. Another faction backed Endara and

ADOC. Endara was known within the party, but he could not automatically assume Arias's mantle. For the Christian Democrats, the best organized of the opposition parties, Arias Calderón was a natural choice, but he was not readily accepted by the other parties as the best man for the presidential slot. Negotiations to form a slate were so difficult that the participants doubted they could succeed. At one point, several leaders approached the Department of State and asked U.S. officials to recommend the strongest candidate. State Department officials sent them back to the bargaining table with no names, but with the advice that the process of selecting a slate would either make or break their prospects. "The strongest candidate will be the one you can agree on," said one U.S. official.[258]

The result—the candidacy of Guillermo Endara—was achieved at the very last minute before the filing deadline passed, a compromise typical of multiparty coalition politics. At the time, Endara and Ford were "widely derided as political neophytes whose only strength was amiability." In Endara's case, "amiability became a potent weapon." Unlike some oppositionists, Endara had not alienated people in the past. As a campaigner, he had "the common touch," taking actions and making statements that resonated with the Panamanian people, if not among commentators in the United States and Latin American sophisticates. Ford, known as the most "macho" of the three, was soon praised as a "spellbinding speaker."[259] Arias Calderón was an experienced organizer, but he seemed an unlikely candidate; he was often described as too austere, cool, cerebral, and intellectual. Events proved that he could campaign, too.

The Context

Conditions during the first half of 1989 were tense and worsening. Economic sanctions were having more and more of an effect: many banks had closed and left the country, and unemployment steadily increased. Clashes between demonstrators and riot police continued sporadically. Incidents between PDF and U.S. forces increased in frequency and provocative intensity. More than 600 incidents of harassment were logged between February 1988 and April 1989, in a "growing campaign of harassment, intimidation and violence by Noriega's regime."[260] Many of these were minor incidents that probably would not have been reported earlier, such as car stops to solicit bribes. But the total also included serious harassment: "forty-two physical assaults, among them one rape and assorted pistol whippings and beatings by Noriega toughs."[261] Military clashes were also included, such as armed intrusions at U.S. military facilities; twenty-five of these incidents involved an exchange of gunfire, and two U.S. soldiers died in these clashes.[262]

In an atmosphere of ongoing harassment and repression, the opposition's electoral activities were also targeted. Despite considerable international attention and media focus on the campaign, the PDF was less than subtle in its intimidation of the opposition. Carla Anne Robbins reported an incident in which PDF police seized a bus carrying seventy people to a rally. The PDF officer told the driver that he "might own the bus, but they [the PDF] own the roads."[263]

As election day approached, polls indicated that the opposition's efforts were paying off: Endara had a two-to-one lead over Duque.[264] Endara proved to be an effective campaigner. Billy Ford was often characterized as a charismatic leader; he was described by one reporter as "a spellbinding orator who brings audiences to a fever pitch with a voice that sounds like a grinding transmission."[265]

Election Day

Long lines formed at polling places throughout the country on Sunday, May 7, 1989, beginning in some areas as early as 5:00 A.M. President Carter had dispatched twenty people from his delegation to polling places in ten different locations. Carter and his aides traveled to many sites during the day and well into the next morning. Some irregularities occurred early, with some precincts opening late, allegedly to discourage voters; in two districts, polls did not open at all. Nonetheless, most observers' early statements, including Carter's, reported no signs of fraud. Carter patiently and courteously questioned election officials about the whereabouts of ballots and tally sheets. He was deliberately giving the government ample time to either comply with proper procedures or, if they were intent on stealing the election, to commit so many abuses that the case against the regime would be devastating.[266]

An exit poll of 1,022 voters gave the opposition an overwhelming victory: 55.1 percent for Endara, but only 39.5 percent for Duque.[267] The margin shocked Noriega, who either was misled by advisers or really believed that the election would be close enough to manipulate with minimal fraud. But as a reporter for *The New York Times* put it, a "pattern of irregularities quickly emerged."[268] Reports of raided voting tables and missing tally sheets began to accumulate, confirming, as Carter had correctly anticipated, "It's the counting that's the problem."[269] In some areas, the PDF seized ballot boxes at gunpoint.

The government had promised that results would be announced within twenty-four hours after the polls closed, which would have been by 6:00 P.M. Monday. Instead, Noriega recalculated his options. He met with close advisers on Sunday night. Some PRD leaders, shocked by the opposition's showing, urged him to declare the election null and void in order to create a space for dialogue with the opposition. They wanted to negotiate a solution from their strongest bargaining position, before the opposition was bolstered by a sizable victory. Noriega then ordered the Electoral Tribunal to stop the count entirely. Several mediation efforts were under way on Sunday night and Monday morning.

Election Aftermath

At noon on Monday, May 8, about 2,000 opposition supporters gathered in the banking district of Panama City to protest. The rest of the city was "practically paralyzed."[270] Endara arrived, after meeting with President Carter, and addressed the crowd. At about 2:30 P.M., the Catholic Bishops Conference announced the results of their exit poll—a "quick count" of 115 voting tables: Endara gained 74.2 percent of the vote, while Duque had only 24.9 percent.[271]

Now fully confident that their overwhelming victory was being denied, the demonstrators proceeded toward the ATLAPA convention center, the headquarters for the Electoral Tribunal. On the way, their progress was blocked by a cordon of police. The protesters shouted, "Not one more day!"[272] This was their rival slogan to the PDF's "not one step back." For more than an hour, Ricardo Arias Calderón talked with officers, trying first to negotiate forward progress, then a withdrawal. The officer in charge asked Endara and his followers to leave; Endara said they would stage a protest and then leave, and the officer agreed. Billy Ford began a speech at about 6:00 P.M. Both demonstrators and police were controlled; Centurion riot police blocked adjacent roads, and a water cannon was visible, but the situation did not escalate.[273] The protesters dispersed.

Meanwhile, behind the scenes, Carter had been trying to mediate. He reached opposition leaders, but Noriega would not respond. The opposition's copies of tally sheets from 80 percent of the *mesas* indicated that the Endara slate had won an overwhelming victory. Carter was convinced that the PDF was stealing the election, and he decided to act. He left his rooms at the Marriott Hotel; carrying the tally sheets, he went across the street to the National Counting Center, which was housed at the ATLAPA Convention Center. The building was surrounded and filled with the PDF. Once inside, Carter walked up to the senior official and demanded: "¿*Está usted honesto o ladrone*?" ("Are you an honest man or a thief?").[274] This was a biting personal affront; the man did not answer.

Carter tried to convince members of the National Counting Board that they must abandon the fraud. When this failed, Carter told them that he would address the press, but the PDF barred him from the ATLAPA's press room. Undeterred, Carter returned to the Marriott Hotel and held his news conference in the lobby. Carter's statement was characterized by one observer as "icily passionate."[275] Carter declared, "The government is taking the election by fraud. . . . It's robbing the people of Panama of their legitimate rights." A member of Carter's delegation said, "I never thought the fraud would be this blatant. These people are absolutely shameless."[276]

The next day, Tuesday, May 9, the first official tallies were posted; these figures put Duque ahead by a 2-to-1 margin. The trend continued the next day, when official totals were posted: ADOC (Endara) had 51,844 votes; COLINA (Duque) had 105,522; and the PPA had almost 6,000.[277]

Expressions of outrage surfaced, but the opposition seemed adrift, "casting about for a way to harness nationwide discontent." A reporter asked Arias Calderón if more demonstrations were planned; he replied, "We are not going to play that game. . . . They expect us to do that. We make a try, they repress it brutally and then everything is over."[278]

Noriega Attacks the Opposition

Nevertheless, the opposition did make another try, and when it was repressed more brutally than ever, the opposition gained unprecedented legitimacy and stature. The images of bloodied candidates and dead protesters defined the opposition and Noriega in new terms, especially to audiences in the United States.

The demonstration began on May 10 with supporters—on foot and in cars—surrounding Endara, Arias Calderón, and Ford. The candidates were riding in a pickup truck and waving at surrounding crowds. When they reached the section of Panama City called Caledonia, they were blocked by police. Then, the paramilitary Dignity Battalions attacked. Dobermen and Centurion units of the PDF riot police, outfitted with helmets and shields, stood by passively; men wearing bright T-shirts, labeling them members of Dignity Batallions, rushed at the demonstrators wielding rubber hoses, metal pipes, nail-studded lumber, baseball bats, and rifles. Uniformed PDF seemed unsurprised; they calmly watched the attack. Some, according to Ambassador Davis, removed their dogtags and joined the attack.

Ford's bodyguard was shot. Ford jumped out of the truck and started arguing with an officer. Angrily shaking his finger, Ford shouted, "Not one more shot, damn it. Not one more shot." Ford was viciously attacked as he walked down the street; then he was arrested. Ford's bloodied image was telecast worldwide, and he was charged with "attacking the armed forces and inciting a riot"; before he was released, he was tried and sentenced to a year without parole.[279]

Within moments, Endara's bodyguard was also dead. Endara was hit on the head with an iron pipe and knocked unconscious. He was attacked again that day, after being released from the hospital, when he went to his office.[280] One of his senior aides, Luis Martíns, was also beaten and kidnapped when he returned to his office.[281] In all, two demonstrators were killed and hundreds were wounded in the hour-long free-for-all.[282] Four soldiers also were reported wounded.[283] A PRD legislative candidate, Mario Rognoni, described the demonstrations from his party's point of view, characterizing the demonstrators' barricades and burning tires as "riots." Rognoni argued that government supporters had been provoked by an incident the day before, on May 9, when five PRD cars en route to the convention center had been attacked by the opposition.[284]

The next day, Endara addressed reporters from the hospital. He sat in a wheelchair, displaying eight stitches in his head. Behind him stood a man holding up a bloody shirt. "I won't back off one inch," Endara said.[285] The setting presented potent symbols: a leader showing his wounds and a bloody shirt. Billy Ford also had a bloody shirt, and his image was captured on television, the front page of *The New York Times*, and the cover of *Time*. Arms outstretched at shoulder level, with his bodyguard's blood covering his light *guayabera*, Ford looked dazed; a PDF soldier in full riot gear stood behind his shield in the background, and a man in a T-shirt holding a long rod stood poised to slash at Ford's ribs.[286] This was the enduring image that redefined the opposition and the situation in Panama.

What had happened? Noriega had been active behind the scenes, meeting with leaders of the PRD and PDF, but he had not been seen in public during the two days following the election. He was stunned, and in shock. President Carter said, "He didn't have a clue that his man might lose."[287] One analyst asserted that Noriega ordered the Dignity Battalions to attack as a "surgical strike" to intimidate the opposition into quiescence.[288] The attack did appear to be a planned, concerted action. Several weeks before the election the Dignity Battalions had been armed, and during the May 10 demonstrations some used pistols to fire on protesters. Some of the people wearing Dignity Battalion T-shirts were members of the PDF; opposition leaders showed photographs to reporters of Transit Police changing from uniforms into freshly unpackaged T-shirts.[289] Ambassador Davis commented that a number of people were wearing [PDF] dogtags under their Dignity Battalion T-shirts.

The elections were also a casualty. At 10:55 P.M. on Wednesday, May 10, the head of the Electoral Tribunal made an announcement on the government television station: "The elections of May 7, 1989, are declared nulled in their entirety."[290] The reasons cited were obstruction by foreigners and lack of tally sheets. Ironically, the announcement was made by Yolanda Pulice de Rodríguez, who had also served as electoral magistrate in 1984. She was the very person Col. Díaz Herrera had accused of falsifying the vote count for Barletta's victory.[291] She played a similar role in 1989.

U.S. Responses

President Bush, who was characterized as becoming "angry" when he watched tapes of these events, condemned the attacks.[292] He met with senior advisers for more than an hour to discuss options. The next day Bush made a public statement: "The United States will not recognize nor accommodate . . . a regime that holds power through force and violence at the expense of the Panamanian people's right to be free."[293] Bush characterized the crisis as a "conflict between Noriega and the Panamanian people" and said the "United States stands with the Panamanian people." Extending a positive signal to the PDF, Bush said the PDF could have an important role to play in Panama's democratic future and that he hoped that the PDF would fulfill their constitutional obligation to defend democracy. Clearly, the president was encouraging the PDF to break with Noriega.

Given the gravity of the crisis in Panama, Bush needed to do more than talk, however, and at his news conference he announced several steps:

1. Hemispheric diplomacy: Bush announced that the United States would cooperate with the OAS, which was planning to debate the crisis and send a mediation delegation.
2. U.S. diplomacy: Bush recalled Ambassador Davis and reduced the embassy staff as a sign of disapproval and to remove potential targets of PDF/Dignity Battalions violence.
3. Preventive measures: Bush ordered U.S. government employees and dependents to be relocated out of Panama or to secure U.S. housing areas in Panama, again removing potential targets; to minimize future targets, he also announced that the Department of State through a travel advisory, would encourage businesspeople in Panama to arrange extended absences for their dependents.
4. Economic measures: Bush announced that sanctions would continue.
5. Reassurance about long-term objectives: Bush announced that the United States would carry out its obligations under the Panama Canal treaties.
6. Strong signal about short-term interests: Bush announced that the United States would enforce its rights under the treaties; later comments clarified that this meant free and unfettered movement of U.S. troops through Panamanian territory.
7. Power capability and intent signal: Bush announced that he was sending a brigade-sized force to Panama to augment U.S. troops and to protect the lives of U.S. citizens.

As a final summation, Bush said that he did not rule out further steps, implying punishment if Noriega endangered the canal or U.S. citizens, but he also stressed that the "way is still open" for an "honorable solution" to the crisis.[294]

The administration's bottom line was that it was trying, through these various signals, to prevent Noriega from doing something foolish. The deployment of U.S. forces was seen as a necessary step, in language Noriega would understand, signaling the PDF and Dignity Battalions to back off and discontinue harassment of U.S. personnel. The forces included a battalion (about 890 soldiers) from the 7th Light Infantry Division at Ft. Ord, California, which would arrive in Panama within forty-eight hours. A battalion (726 soldiers) was also sent from the 5th Division at Ft. Polk, Louisiana, along with eighteen mechanized armored personnel carriers. The third component was a company (165 men) of marines from Camp LeJeune.

The official total of these additional forces was 1,882, which included these three components plus support personnel.[295]

The election and its violent aftermath presented Bush with his first foreign policy crisis as president. Given the saliency of Noriega and Panama policy, U.S. responses in this case were considered as indicators of the new administration's approach to the region. Most commentators gave the president's responses high marks. Bush's speech was tough; he repeatedly called Noriega a dictator. Bush's actions were described as measured and cautious, and they received strong bipartisan backing from Congress. Bush was applauded for consulting with other presidents in the hemisphere and endorsing regional diplomacy.

At this time the military option was still off the table. When Secretary of Defense Cheney was asked how U.S. troops would respond if the PDF did try to overthrow Noriega, he replied that he saw "no role for U.S. troops." "Their purpose," he continued, "is not to be involved with deciding who governs Panama . . . their purpose is to carry out U.S. obligations and rights under the treaty and to safeguard American lives."[296] Some in the Pentagon even opposed this response on the grounds that sending almost 2,000 additional troops into an already volatile context might either tempt or provoke Noriega into a reckless countermove. The Department of State strongly favored a show of military force. The Joint Chiefs of Staff expressed strong concerns about tempting Noriega to take hostages; even with the measures Bush announced, they felt that too many U.S. citizens were still in the line of fire. Their opposition had an effect, at least on implementation of the decision. When Secretary Cheney described the deployment of the additional forces on the evening of May 11, he said that both battalions would be sent immediately, over a period of forty-eight hours. The equipment from Ft. Polk would be sent by sea and take longer to arrive, but the troops would be sent "now." The next day, *The New York Times* reported that those troops would go in slowly, also by sea, over a two to three week period. Deployment by sea, the report noted, also had the advantage of a pull-back: that component "could be turned around if the tension in Panama eased."[297]

At the same time, President Bush escalated his rhetoric, calling on Panamanians to "do everything they can to get Mr. Noriega out of office."[298] Surprised reporters, accustomed to a more cautious tone, called these Bush's strongest remarks yet and asked the president if he wanted to add a word of caution. Bush declined. "I would add no words of caution. The will of the people should be implemented."[299]

The Summer of 1989

Noriega continued to crack down on demonstrators and opposition supporters. By May 15, just five days after the bloody May 10 protest and attack, "hundreds of second rank organizers" had been arrested, and "paramilitary troops" had taken over some rural towns and placed them under "de facto martial law."[300] Concurrently, talks between opposition leaders and government supporters were under way. Some of these were direct and others were mediated by the OAS mission; neither succeeded.

Direct Talks

The day after the election, on Monday, May 8, leaders in both coalitions considered the possibility of forming a power-sharing junta. Given the electoral strength of ADOC, the government's largest backer—the PRD—considered giving the Endara slate junior status in a coalition government. Other PRD leaders disagreed, and it soon became apparent that the PRD was badly split. When the party called a meeting after the election to defend Noriega, Carlos Duque and many other officials were "tellingly absent."[301] Duque was reported to be offended by Noriega's brutal tactics, telling a friend that he "doesn't like to see opposition candidates beat up."[302]

The opposition was willing to negotiate only with the military, not with the government, because they officially recognized Delvalle as the legal government. In addition, the opposition set two conditions for negotiations: (1) any agreement required Noriega's departure, and (2) the idea of power sharing was unacceptable. On the question of power sharing, Arias Calderón made a simple, unequivocal statement: "Nothing doing. No playing with the popular will of the people."[303]

The Labor party took a more moderate stance, endorsing the concept of a national reconciliation junta, which would govern until August 31, when the current presidential term would expire, and then call for new elections. Seeking to compromise, the Labor party called for a three-way dialogue among the government, the opposition, and the PDF. Its effort, however, was premature: too many sides of this triangle were refusing to talk to each other.

Progovernment legislators met behind closed doors at the National Assembly, trying to devise a way to remain in power. Three alternatives were debated: "a junta, possibly headed by the general; some version of a parliamentary system, with General Noriega as permanent Prime Minister; or the creation of a new civilian government, possibly headed by Manuel Solís Palma, the current President."[304] None of these were acceptable to the opposition. Later, a more realistic formula was considered by the government: a junta headed by Endara, and Noriega's retirement within two years.[305] This formula was closer to the opposition's demands, but the two sides were still quite far apart when the first OAS mission arrived. Much of the mission's sessions during the next four months were spent discussing who would refuse to meet with whom, preconditions, and who represented whom. By September one thing was clear: Noriega had succeeded in buying time and remaining in place.

The OAS and Regional Diplomacy

Venezuelan President Pérez had called for an emergency meeting of the OAS on May 11, the day after Dignity Battalions attacked the opposition candidates. Some, including Pérez, hoped that the OAS could take the kind of action on Panama that it had taken in 1979 when its censure of Anastasio Somoza had contributed to his exit from Nicaragua. In that extraordinary instance, the OAS had passed a resolution criticizing Somoza by name and calling for his prompt departure. Panama, however, proved to be more difficult for the OAS to handle. .

The election crisis in Panama presented the OAS with a conflict between two dearly held principles: (1) opposition to intervention and (2) support for free elections and democracy in the region. Many member states had recently joined the hemispheric trend replacing military dictatorships with elected civilian governments; they sympathized with the theft of the Panamanian opposition's victory. They could not overcome, however, their fears that action on Panama would become a precedent for foreign intervention in any of several elections scheduled during 1990–1991, particularly in Nicaragua. Mexico's position illustrated this quandary. The Mexican government issued a communiqué on May 14 that denounced Noriega, by name, in very strong terms: "The Panamanian situation has worsened as a result of the personal stance of General Noriega, whose moral reputation has been discredited."[306] Nonetheless, the statement also affirmed Mexico's support for nonintervention and rejected the idea that the OAS serve as a critic of Latin American electoral processes.

Thus, despite the hopes of the United States and Venezuela for a decisive, united call for Noriega's removal, the OAS reflected the conflicting concerns of many of its members. The resolution on Panama was moderately tough, holding Noriega responsible, by name, for "grave events and abuses" and calling for a peaceful transfer of power from Noriega to a democratically elected government.[307] The vote was twenty to two, with seven abstentions. The OAS also authorized a mediation mission to go to Panama to secure a national accord on mechanisms to accomplish a transfer of power in the shortest period possible.

The OAS delegation was headed by Ecuadoran Foreign Minister Diego Cordovez. Also included were Guatemalan Foreign Minister Mario Palencia, and the foreign minister of Trinidad and Tobago, Bhoendradath Tewarie. OAS Secretary General Joao Baena Soares, accompanied the delegation. They were ordered to report by June 5, 1989.

Had the parties wanted to compromise, the OAS mission could have assisted. Most observers agreed, however, that regional diplomacy was doomed as long as Noriega was interested only in playing for time and trying to outlast the U.S. interest in his removal. The mission's first visit failed; talks, held separately with each side and including an unscheduled four-hour session with the PDF, were described as futile. It took two months for the OAS mission to get the parties to meet together.

A second round of mediated talks was held beginning July 15, 1989. Preliminary assessments were optimistic because the government and PDF agreed to talk "without an agenda, without preconditions and with the commitment that no topic would be excluded."[308] This was a significant departure from their earlier position that Noriega's status could not be discussed and that his position was not negotiable. The PDF, seated as part of the government's delegation, did talk, but hopes soon faded as irreconcilable positions were aired by both sides. The sessions continued into August, but no agreement could be reached.

September 1, 1989, was the date that Acting President Solís Palma's term expired and a new president was supposed to be inaugurated. This was the deadline by which the OAS had hoped to have a solution—either a transitional government or a coalition government—ready to implement. The parties worked until the last moment, holding sessions in Panama on August 1–5, 19–21, and 23–24. Finally, everyone admitted defeat.

In its final report, the OAS delegation blamed "all sides for not making 'full use' of the negotiations."[309] The United States and Panamanian oppositionists blamed Noriega for being unwilling to step down, which was their primary demand. The OAS delegates blamed the United States for executing "inopportune" military exercises, particularly on August 17, which "could have created an incident" that would have thwarted "all efforts to achieve a peaceful solution."[310] Most U.S. officials accused Noriega of negotiating in bad faith and using the talks just to play for time.

The Council of State, at Noriega's direction, selected Francisco Rodríguez to serve as Panama's provisional president. Rodríguez, Noriega's high school classmate, had previously served as comptroller general. Panamanian opposition leaders referred to Rodríguez as "a new facade" for Noriega's dictatorship; U.S. analysts and officials concurred.[311] Rodríguez took office on September 1, 1989.

The OAS Council of Ministers then adopted what was characterized as a "bland statement" expressing its concern about Panama.[312] Disappointed at this outcome, the United States launched a diplomatic initiative to address and expose the issue of Noriega's drug trafficking. Plans were made for Under Secretary of State Lawrence Eagleburger to make a stinging address. The Panamanian government and its OAS representative had called repeatedly for the United States to provide evidence of its allegations against Noriega. Eagleburger did just that in a long, tough speech that was timed for delivery on the day Rodríguez took office.

Eagleburger began by reviewing the charges brought against Noriega in the two Florida indictments and elaborating on the nature of evidence in the U.S. legal system. He continued, "Let us put aside once and for all this contention that General Noriega is a poor, humble, honest man who has been unjustly accused."[313] Then he recited a list of Noriega's properties and other assets; conservative estimates of Noriega's wealth, he asserted, were $200–300 million. Eagleburger offered fifteen pages of evidence in the form of bank records and other financial documents. In one of these, dated February 8, 1988 (four days after he was indicted), Noriega had authorized a London bank to close his account and transfer the $14.9 million balance to a Luxembourg bank. Eagleburger closed with a dramatic finish:

> Colombia and Panama. Barco and Noriega. Could we have a starker comparison of the moral qualities of the best and the worst among us in our hemisphere? Which one deserves our help; which one deserves to be purged, to be driven from our midst? For the United States, at least, the answer is clear.
>   Barco ¡Sí!, Noriega ¡No![314]

Panamanian Ambassador José María Cabrera, called the speech "a pack of lies;" Noriega's lawyer, Frank Rubino, asserted that Eagleburger "failed to provide any evidence of wrongdoing."[315] This war of words reflected growing tensions and frustrations in Washington and Panama City over the continuing crisis. In Panama, words were giving way to an escalating war of nerves.

A War of Nerves in Panama

Beginning on May 25, 1988, when negotiations between Noriega and the Department of State collapsed, restraints on the use of military pressure by U.S. forces in Panama were lifted. Occasionally these were reimposed—such as during the May 1989 presidential election and during the OAS mediation talks—but from mid-1988 onward, a war of nerves was waged between Noriega's forces and the U.S. military in Panama.

An officer on the scene recalled that Noriega was constantly pressuring U.S. forces, partly to demonstrate his own power but also to remind the United States of how much and in how many ways he could threaten U.S. assets, including the canal, other facilities, and U.S. personnel and their dependents. One of the most frequently mentioned incidents involved a U.S. school bus that was detained, after picking up its morning passengers, and taken to PDF traffic headquarters. The children were never threatened or endangered, but the message to their parents, military commanders, and officials in Washington was clear. The officer recalled his interpretation: "Noriega was better able to mess with us than we were with him." In the "war of nerves," he said, "Noriega had distinct advantages, and he used them all."[316]

General Woerner describes the situation: "Imposed upon us were three requirements: to obey U.S. law, Panamanian law, and the treaty. I asked myself, how do I react to a provocation which was also a Panamanian quasi-legal exercise of law and order, like stopping a school bus without a license? How do I react in such a way as to convince Noriega that he should not do that anymore?" Woerner felt that the United States was in a disadvantageous bargaining position.

> The provocations Noriega was giving me were nickel-and-dime things. I told my staff that when I went to that poker table, I had, in essence, about a $20 gold piece to play—intervention—*if* I had support. Noriega had a gunny sack full of nickels that he could play against me. I felt as if I were in a game in which, first of all, I was obeying the Queensberry rules and Noriega was making them up as he was going along. Furthermore, I was playing in his stadium and I had a coach in the United States, a whole bunch of coaches called a committee, back there trying to tell me what to do, where Noriega was the captain and everybody did exactly what he said.[317]

To counter such pressures, SOUTHCOM launched a series of military activities and readiness exercises. These were designed for two audiences: the PDF and U.S. morale. In an official statement, SOUTHCOM described the purpose as "to demonstrate . . . the U.S. commitment and the ability to protect U.S. lives and installations if necessary."[318]

The war of nerves heated up in August 1989 when two U.S. soldiers were arrested by the PDF at Ft. Amador, a joint defense site housing both PDF and U.S. forces. A tense, two-hour confrontation ensued: U.S. MPs were dispatched to the scene, U.S. Army helicopters circled overhead, and Panamanians manned their antiaircraft weapons. To make both sides even, U.S. troops at the front gate arrested two Panamanian MPs. When U.S. armored personnel carriers blockaded the entrance to Ft. Amador, they were surrounded by several Panamanians in civilian clothes carrying a Panamanian flag. However, once each side felt that enough threatening moves had been made, and that a military standoff had been achieved, the situation was diffused. Each side released its arrestees and returned to "normal."[319]

This was one of many confrontations, including some initiated by U.S. forces, that provided a backdrop against which both governments considered their options. Such incidents, along with increasing pressures on U.S. citizens in Panama resulting from the sanctions, continued throughout the summer and into the fall. In this climate of apparently controlled, but increasingly confrontational clashes, escalation of the conflict seemed inevitable. Sooner or later, one side was likely to miscalculate. Tensions were building to the point that one side or the other was likely to perceive one taunt too many, and say "enough is enough." That point came for Noriega during the weekend of December 15, 1989, when he assumed additional powers and taunted the United States with words about a declaration of war. That point came for the United States two days later, after two more incidents against U.S. personnel yielded a casualty, President Bush said "enough is enough."

Several months before this breaking point was reached, however, dissident officers attempted to remove Noriega. Their abortive coup and the U.S. responses provided an opportunity and incentives for the Bush administration to adopt new objectives. These objectives and the escalating war of nerves led to the U.S. decision to invade Panama.

Notes

1. Investigative reporter Steven Emerson provides a detailed account, based on documents and interviews, of the relationship between the CIA's off the shelf (or "off the book") operations and Iran-Contra in *Secret Warriors*.

2. U.S. Department of State, undated Confidential Briefing Memorandum, "Your Meeting with Panamanian Pres. Eric Arturo Delvalle, Tuesday, Sept. 23, 4:00–4:30pm," To the Secretary, From ARA - Richard N. Holwill, Acting, pp. 1–3.

3. "Díaz Herrera Takes 'Indefinite' Vacation," *EXTRA*, June 1, 1987, FBIS-LAT, June 2, 1987, p. J1, J2.

4. "Justines Named New Chief," FBIS-LAT, June 2, 1987, p. J2.

5. "Interview with Retired Col Díaz Herrera," *La Prensa*, June 7, 1987, FBIS-LAT, June 8, 1987, p. J1.

6. Ibid.

7. Frederick Kempe (*Divorcing the Dictator*, chap. 13) provides a detailed account of Díaz Herrera's religious conversion, use of spiritual and occult advisers, and the personal side of this episode.

8. U.S. Congress, *Drugs*, Part 2, p. 297.

9. Comment to Senate staff delegation during a visit to Panama in 1988, cited in U.S. Congress, *Drugs*, Part 2, p. 298.

10. Journalist Mayín Correa provides transcripts of Díaz Herrera's interviews and his handwritten notes in Volume I of her compilation of materials on the events of June 1987, *La gran rebelion blanca*.

11. *Newsweek*, June 22, 1987, p. 18.

12. *Time*, June 22, 1987,-p. 40.

13. "Interview with Díaz Herrera," pp. J1, J3.

14. U.S. Department of State, Confidential Panama 07509. Sec. 01, p. 1. Díaz Herrera's speech is translated in FBIS-LAT. Other media also were present: the opposition paper *Quiubo*; wire services ACAN-EFE, IPS, and Cuba's *Prensa Latina*; and radio station reporters.

15. U.S. Department of State, Confidential Panama 07509, Sec. 02, p. 2.

16. Correa's compilation, *La gran rebelion blanca*, includes transcripts from her broadcasts and photographs of demonstrations.

17. Kempe (*Divorcing the Dictator*, chap. 13) provides a vivid account of Díaz Herrera's decision and related events; John Dinges (*Our Man in Panama*, pp. 259–268) also gives a detailed account and explores the significance of this defection.

18. Tina Rosenberg provides an excellent description of these events in "The Panama Perplex."

19. Crusade leaders described the formation of their organization as a

spontaneous reaction to Díaz Herrera's revelations. They said their disgust and anger over the military's increasingly heavy-handed interference in government and the economy had been building, and that Díaz Herrera's press conference constituted a "last straw." The number of member organizations steadily grew to exceed 150, and the Catholic church served in an advisory capacity. The NCC was governed by a directorate of twelve members representing the different constituent organizations. In her compilation, *La gran rebelion blanca*, Correa collected documents about the Crusade, including internal memoranda, bulletins, statements and press releases, and press reports of NCC activities.

20. "*La Prensa* Publishes List of 'Crusade' Supporters," *La Prensa*, June 11, 1987, FBIS-LAT, June 12, 1987, p. J18.

21. *Time*, June 22, 1987, p. 40. Not all of the fires were authentic; some were reportedly staged to sensationalize the images U.S. reporters would telecast. One Panamanian student who participated in these demonstrations told me that U.S. reporters asked and paid protesters to set several fires.

22. Preston, "Noriega's Grip on Panama Slips Amid Corruption Charges," *Washington Post Weekly Edition*, June 6, 1987, p. 18.

23. "PRD President on Retirement," *Televisora Nacional*, June 5, 1987, FBIS-LAT, June 8, 1987, p. J3.

24. "FDP Officers' Manifesto Supports Gen. Noriega," *Telemetro Television*, June 8, 1987, FBIS-LAT, June 9, 1987, p. J5.

25. "Opposition Legislators Walk Out of Assembly," *Radio Continente*, June 8, 1987, FBIS-LAT, June 9, 1987, p. J6.

26. Kempe reports a Díaz Herrera statement that is, I believe, closest to the truth: "I attacked Noriega with information, disinformation, and misinformation," he said. "When you are being mugged by a gang of hoodlums in a dead-end street, you're not going to count how many punches you're landing or whether all of them are entirely fair" (Kempe, *Divorcing the Dictator*, p. 212).

27. *Time*, June 22, 1987, p. 40.

28. U.S. Department of State, Unclassified Panama 7645, p. 2.

29. U.S. Department of State, Panama City 08671.

30. Accounts of these events can be found in *Newsweek*, July 13, 1987, p. 30; and *US News and World Report*, July 13, 1987, p. 17.

31. U.S. Department of State, Panama City 08671, p. 1.

32. U.S. Department of State, Panama City 08672.

33. *US News and World Report*, July 20, 1987, p. 31.

34. Personal interview in April 1990 with a participant in the demonstrations in August 1987.

35. Stephen Kinzer, "Panama's Government Unleashes Drive to Blame US for Troubles," *The New York Times*, July 5, 1987, p. A1.

36. U.S. Department of State, Confidential Panama 08855, Sec. 01, p. 3.

37. *US News and World Report*, July 20, 1987, p. 31.

38. Ibid., p. 29.

39. Preston, "Protest and Punish, Protest and Punish," *Washington Post Weekly Edition*, November 2, 1987, p. 18.

40. Ibid.

41. *US News and World Report*, July 20, 1987, p. 30.

42. *Washington Post Weekly Edition*, August 3, 1987, p. 19. The amounts of aid scheduled for the year were $6 million in military aid and $20 million in economic aid; officials also considered modifying their $33 million request for the next fiscal year. The tear gas request had been made prior to the attack on the U.S. embassy.

43. Robbins, "Cracking Down," p. 30.

44. U.S. Department of State, Confidential Panama 09899.

45. Quoted in William Branigin, "The Protests in Panama Won't Oust Noriega," *Washington Post Weekly Edition*, August 17, 1987, p. 19.

46. U.S. Department of State, Secret/Sensitive Memorandum, "Panama Situation Report #2," To: ARA - Mr. Wattenberg, From: ARA/CEN Dick Wyrough, July 27, 1987.

47. *Time*, August 10, 1987, p. 21.

48. "Attorney's Office Takes Díaz Herrera's Deposition," *La Estrella de Panama*, August 4, 1987, FBIS-LAT, 87-150, August 5, 1987, pp. J1–J5.

49. Peter Skinfels later reported that Díaz Herrera was sentenced to five years imprisonment, pardoned by Noriega, and sent out of the country ("Spiritualist Practice Common in Panama and the Caribbean," *The New York Times*, December 24, 1989, p. 4). Díaz Herrera's release was facilitated by President Carlos Andrés Pérez, former Costa Rican President Oduber, the head of the Dominican Revolutionary party, and a Peruvian political leader. Díaz Herrera went into exile in Venezuela.

50. *US News and World Report*, June 22, 1987, p. 18.

51. *The Washington Post*, July 2, 1987.

52. *US News and World Report*, July 20, 1987, p. 31.

53. *Time*, June 22, 1987, p. 40.

54. *Time*, August 8, 1987, p. 21. A major problem then, and during the next two years, was that Noriega controlled intelligence information and access to PDF personnel available to the United States. His rivals, or those he suspected of disloyalty, were labeled as leftists and threats to U.S. interests. Senator D'Amato was particularly adamant in arguing, whenever the Pentagon told him that no alternatives to Noriega were readily available, that Noriega had manipulated the DOD, working through Nestor Sanchez, into that perspective (U.S. Congress, *Drugs*, Part 3, pp. 9–13). Sanchez testified before the committee and discussed his contacts, and lack thereof, in July (U.S. Congress, *Drugs*, Part 4, pp. 186–221).

55. Cited by Lally Weymouth in *The Washington Post*, October 11, 1987, p. H2.

56. "Editorial Praises U.S. Southern Command Leaders," *La Republica*, June 8, 1987, FBIS-LAT, June 10, 1987, p. J18.

57. *Time*, July 20, 1987, p. 37.

58. Ibid., p. 38.

59. Julia Preston, "Noriega's Unpopularity Spreads to His Own Ranks," *Washington Post Weekly Edition*, January 25–31, 1988, p. 16. Preston's account of the Blandón plan was based on a draft document, dated October 27, 1987, and memos to and from Blandón, copies of which were given to the *Post* by opposition politicians. That memorandum is reprinted in U.S. Congress, *Drugs*, Part 2, pp. 276–285; that hearing also contained Blandón's testimony. Kempe (*Divorcing the Dictator*) provided an extended account of these negotiations, based largely on Blandón's material. Kempe also detailed the role played by Gabriel Lewis and a U.S. consultant, Joel McCleary. Dinges (*Our Man in Panama*) warned that parts of Blandón's account, particularly his congressional testimony about Noriega and Cuba, cannot be verified and do not correspond with known facts, such as meeting dates. Guillermo Sánchez-Borbon, a political columnist for *La Prensa*, gave more credence to Blandón's role and his portrayal of events.

60. *La Prensa Digest* (February 5, 1988, p. 6) reported that Luis Alberto Arias said "both Noriega and Delvalle knew of the Blandón Plan."

61. Preston, "Noriega's Unpopularity Spreads," pp. 16–17. Blandón was quoted in *The New York Times* (February 7, 1988, p. 6) as adding that no legal reprisals against Noriega would be taken and that he would have amnesty in the

United States. However, those remarks were made the day after the two indictments were issued and make sense in the context of amnesty from criminal prosecution and extradition proceedings. Preston did not report that element of the Blandón plan.

62. Quoted in Preston, "Noriega's Unpopularity Spreads," p. 17.

63. Julia Preston and Kenneth E. John, "Panamanians Want a Change," *Washington Post Weekly Edition*, August 9, 1987. The poll was taken August 1–4 by Carlos Denton's firm CID, the Gallup affiliate for Central America and Panama. The poll also found that 77 percent believed the 1984 election was fraudulent and only 1 percent favored U.S. aid to Panama being used to train armed forces. A group of businessmen paid $16,000 to have the poll taken.

64. This quote and others by Delvalle in this paragraph and the next are from "Interview with President Delvalle," FBIS-LAT, 87-151, August 6, 1987, p. J13.

65. Torrijos took great delight in such visits. Two good accounts of the practice are Greene, *Getting to Know the General*; and Peters, "Panama's Genial Despot."

66. U.S. Congress, *Drugs*, Part 2, p. 306, 307.

67. Ibid., p. 299.

68. Correa, *La gran rebelion blanca*, p. 17.

69. Quoted in Larry Rohter, "Bank Uncertainty in Panama," *The New York Times*, August 10, 1987, p. 26.

70. Quoted in *The New York Times*, September 27, 1987.

71. In a show of support for the opposition, and to preclude Esquivel's arrest when he returned to Panama, Ambassador Davis met him at the airport.

72. Quoted in *US News and World Report*, July 20, 1987, p. 30.

73. U.S. Congress, *Drugs*, Part 2, pp. 224–225.

74. U.S. Congress, *Drugs*, Part 4, p. 246.

75. Ibid., p. 254.

76. Ibid., pp. 246–247.

77. Ibid., p. 247.

78. Ibid.

79. Ibid., pp. 246, 247.

80. Ibid, p. 248.

81. Ibid., p. 249.

82. Ibid.

83. The two exercises scheduled for January and February, named "Kindle Liberty," were later canceled.

84. *Time*, August 17, 1987, p. 42.

85. *US News and World Report*, October 10, 1987, p. 30.

86. Robbins, "Cracking Down," p. 30.

87. *Time*, October 10, 1987, p. 21.

88. Stephen Kinzer, "Noriega's Ouster," *The New York Times*, September 27, 1987.

89. *Newsweek*, October 10, 1987, p. 42.

90. This phrase was the title of a report in *Newsweek*, August 10, 1987, pp. 42–43.

91. *Washington Post Weekly Edition*, November 2, 1987, p. 17.

92. U.S. Congress, *Drugs*, Part 2, p. 301.

93. The Medellín Cartel: A Special Report," *Miami Herald*, November 29, 1987, pp. 1A, 28A.

94. Joe Pichirallo, "Noriega Is Under Suspicion—and Pressure," *Washington Post Weekly Edition*, November 23, 1987, p. 17.

95. *Newsweek*, June 18, 1988, p. 38.

96. U.S. Department of State, Secret State 402455, p. 1. Ambassador Davis was to see Delvalle, prior to Armitage's visit, to make both points clear: it was time for Noriega to go and that this was the position of a unified administration.

97. Whether Noriega perceived this new unity is unknown, partly because of lack of documentation of Noriega's views and because the role and actions of several U.S. officials who had worked with Noriega remain unclear. Nestor Sanchez, for example, was subjected to bitter congressional criticism for his alleged contacts with Noriega and the PDF.

98. Preston, "Noriega's Unpopularity Spreads," p. 16.

99. Stephen Kalish later testified that the organization he formed with Noriega and others had laundered $50–100 million per month in drug money, and that the organization received a 5 percent commission for this service from the Ochoa family (*Arkansas Democrat*, December 9, 1989, p. 4A).

100. *Springdale News*, February 7, 1988, p. 12A.

101. Larry Rohter, "Ouster of Noriega, in Peace, Unlikely, Panamanians Say," *The New York Times*, February 7, 1988, p. 1.

102. Philip Shelton, "U.S. Aides Praised Noriega on Drugs," *The New York Times*, February 9, 1988. The introduction referred to Panama's efforts "to protect the youth of the Americas against that new form of international terrorism that is the drug traffic." The letters were mostly from DEA administrators and dated from the late 1970s through 1987.

103. William Branigin, "Noriega Steps Up the Attack," *The Washington Post*, February 14, 1988. The officers asked Noriega to punish Paredes and to have President Delvalle demand the withdrawal of SOUTHCOM from Panama.

104. Quoted in *Time*, March 7, 1988, p. 27.

105. C. Robert Zelnick, "The Dangers of 'Gringo' Diplomacy in Panama," *Christian Science Monitor*, March 22, 1988, p. 14.

106. Quoted in *Time*, March 7, 1988, p. 27.

107. *Newsweek*, March 17, 1988, p. 53.

108. One source pointed out that if Delvalle had obtained the signature of just one cabinet member, the separation order would have been legal (confidential interview, Panama City, August 1990). Although this would have strengthened Delvalle's position, this technicality may not have altered the PDF's response.

109. Cited in *Time*, March 7, 1988, p. 27.

110. AP report, *Arkansas Democrat*, February 26, 1988, p. 1.

111. The Assembly also removed Vice-President Esquivel, despite the fact that he had already broken ranks with Delvalle and joined the opposition. Fearing for his safety, Esquivel went into hiding on Saturday, February 27.

112. U.S. Department of State, Secret State 058889.

113. One U.S. observer complained, "Everything is going pretty much according to plan. . . . But where are the Panamanian people?" (*Time*, March 7, 1988, p. 27).

114. Quoted in Elaine Sciolino, "U.S. Says It Can Do Little About Noriega," *The New York Times*, February 28, 1988, p. 10.

115. It took several days for Panamanian officials and staff to decide and declare themselves, slowing the tempo of events and making the situation harder to diagnose. At the Panamanian embassy in Washington, for example, three embassy members remained loyal to Noriega, despite Ambassador Sosa's alliance with Delvalle. Similar situations were replayed at the United Nations and OAS missions and embassies overseas.

116. Sciolino, "U.S. Says," p. 10.

117. *Arkansas Democrat*, February 28, 1988, p. 6H.

118. Kempe reported that the overall strategy was developed at a meeting at

Gabriel Lewis's home that included Blandón, Rogers, former U.S. Ambassador Bill Jorden, Joel McCleary, and John Campbell. Kempe (*Divorcing the Dictator*, pp. 265–272) provided detailed accounts of the litigation strategy, including actions against Panamanian businesses as well as the banks.

119. *Washington Post*, May 16, 1988, p. A4.

120. Comment by Rep. Gejdenson; U.S. Congress, *United States Policy Toward Panama*, p. 131.

121. Rosenberg, "The Panama Perplex," p. 22.

122. *Newsweek,*, March 7, 1988, p. 53.

123. *Arkansas Democrat*, February 28, 1988, p. 6H.

124. *Christian Science Monitor*, February 8, 1988, p. 25.

125. *Christian Science Monitor*, February 2, 1988.

126. *Arkansas Democrat*, March 5, 1988, p. A1.

127. Furlong and Scranton, *Dynamics of Foreign Policy Making*, pp. 148–149.

128. Rogers wrote about the Alliance in *The Twilight Struggle*.

129. Both quotes are from Rogers's interview with Marjorie Williams, "The Panama File: A D.C. Attorney's 'Revolution by Litigation'," *The Washington Post*, March 22, 1988, p. D2.

130. Ibid.

131. Press accounts also named Marine Midland Bank and Bankers Trust.

132. The following account, unless otherwise noted, is based on interviews with lawyers involved with the proceedings, Washington, D.C., April 1990.

133. Paul Blustein, "The Shutting Down of Panama," *The Washington Post*, May 1988.

134. Ibid.

135. *Time*, March 21, 1988, p. 35.

136. The legal process inadvertently became a means for pulling various opposition actors together. In addition to the frequent participation of Gabriel Lewis, several other major opposition figures became involved. During the first week, in early March, Ricardo Arias Calderón came to Washington and participated in several meetings at Rogers's office. José Blandón was involved in one long strategy session held on a Saturday. The Panamanian team was headed by Ambassador Sosa.

137. John Felton and Pat Towell, "Panama Crisis: U. S. Embargo Move Slows," *Congressional Quarterly Weekly Report*, March 5, 1988, p. 560.

138. Ibid.

139. Ibid., p. 559.

140. Ibid.

141. As of July 17, 1989, ten agencies made 214 payments to Account No. 2, amounting to $136.4 million; of this amount, the PCC accounted for eighty-seven payments totaling $123.8 million (U.S. Congress, *U.S. Policy Toward Panama*, p. 257). This included the $10 million annual payment to the Panamanian government for services provided prior to 1979 by the Canal Zone government for the new canal area. These funds were not released to the Endara government until late 1990, in part because a complex process had to be developed to implement the release.

142. Kempe provided a detailed account of the supplemental role played by lawyers from the Arnold & Porter firm to aid the Department of State in applying economic pressure (Kempe, *Divorcing the Dictator*, pp. 265–267). Williams also provided a detailed account, based on interviews with participants in 1988, in "The Panama File" pp. D1, D2.

143. *Arkansas Democrat*, March 8, 1988, p. 3A; *Time*, March 14, 1988, p. 19.

144. These figures and those for March 15 are taken from U.S. Department of State, Confidential Panama 03578, p. 2.

145. Brook Larmer, "Noriega Takes on Private Sector in War of Survival," *Christian Science Monitor*, March 28, 1988, p. 8.

146. Larry Jenkins, "A Banking System Lies in Ruins," *Washington Post Weekly Edition*, April 18–24, 1988, p. 8.

147. *USA Today*, April 25, 1988.

148. U.S. Department of State, Confidential Panama 03578, p. 1.

149. Quoted in William Branigin, "Putting the Squeeze on Panama," *Washington Post Weekly Edition*, April 18–24, 1988, p. 7.

150. U.S. Congress, *U.S. Policy Toward Panama*, p. 237.

151. These regulations were amended three times, on June 15 and August 24, 1988, and on January 3, 1989.

152. U.S. Congress, *U.S. Policy Toward Panama*, p. 268.

153. Interview, Washington, D.C., April 1990.

154. U.S. Congress, *U.S. Policy Toward Panama*, p. 236.

155. For this reason, William R. Gianelli, chairman of the PCC, urged the Bush administration in May 1989 to review the sanctions and grant exemptions to alleviate the worst problems PCC employees—85 percent of whom were Panamanian—were experiencing. Gianelli's views were expressed publicly in "Review Panama Sanctions for Canal's Sake," *The Sunday Herald*, May 28, 1989, p. 3B, reprinted in U.S. Congress, *U.S. Policy Toward Panama*, p. 69.

156. Jenkins, "A Banking System," p. 8.

157. U.S. Congress, *U.S. Policy Toward Panama*, p. 155–156.

158. Quoted in *The New York Times*, May 30, 1988.

159. Christopher Madison, "No Easy Way Out of Panama?" *National Journal*, May 21, 1988, p. 1356.

160. U.S. Department of State, Confidential Information Memorandum, "Panamanian Situation, March 9," To the Secretary, From ARA-Elliott Abrams, March 9, 1988; and U.S. Department of State, Confidential Panama 02635.

161. Quoted in Simon, "Noriega Opponent Assails U.S.," p. 28.

162. This point is emphasized by Miguel Bernal in "Diversion in Panama: Make Noise at East, Beat at West," *The Charlotte Observer*, April 27, 1988, p. 15A.

163. "Statement by Panamanian Political Parties and the National Civic Crusade," *La Prensa Digest*, Volume 4/88, March 19, 1988, p. 7.

164. U.S. Department of State, Confidential Caracas 02673.

165. Statement made in a televised speech, cited in *La Prensa Digest*, Volume 5/88, March 26, 1988, p. 4.

166. U.S. Department of State, Secret State 094269.

167. U.S. Department of State, Secret State 096142.

168. U.S. Department of State, Secret State 099809.

169. U.S. Department of State, Secret State 097764.

170. U.S. Department of State, Unclassified Panama 03001.

171. Quoted in Joe Pichirallo, "Noriega Won't Step Down Voluntarily, Defectors Say," *Washington Post*, March 23, 1988, p. A22.

172. Kempe (*Divorcing the Dictator*, p. 276) said that Quezada contacted General Woerner, but received a noncommittal reply; Quezada told me that he had not contacted the United States, nor had he heard that other coup plotters had done so.

173. Interview with Fernando Quezada, Panama City, August 1990.

174. *Time*, March 28, 1988, p. 33.

175. Interview, Panama City, August 1990.

176. Quoted in Pichirallo, "Noriega Won't Step Down," p. A22.

177. U.S. Department of State, Secret State 082820.

178. "Barracks Coup Fails," *La Prensa Digest*, Volume 4/88, March 19, 1988, p. 2.

179. Quoted in *Time*, March 28, 1988, p. 32.

180. U.S. Department of State, Secret State 082820.

181. "Barracks Coup Fails," p. 3.

182. U.S. Department of State, Secret State 083949.

183. Larry Rohter, "Unyielding Panamanian," *The New York Times*, March 21, 1988.

184. Interview with Villalaz, "This Week with David Brinkley," ABC News, March 20, 1988.

185. Pichirallo, "Noriega Won't Step Down," p. A22.

186. *Austin American Statesman*, March 23, 1988, p. A2.

187. U.S. Department of State, Confidential State 088690, "Panama Task Force Situation Report No. 12," March 22, 1988. The Department of State sent a message to all posts in the region saying that they should tell Panamanian military attachés that the United States desired to work closely with the PDF but could not do so while Noriega remained in power.

188. Rohter, "Unyielding Panamanian," p. 7.

189. William Branigin, "Gutter Tactics Destroying Panama," *The Washington Post*, May 5, 1988.

190. Reported by Bernal, "Diversion in Panama," p. 15A.

191. *Time*, March 21, 1988, p. 35.

192. *Newsweek*, March 21, 1988, p. 36.

193. Cited in *Tulsa World*, March 1, 1988.

194. Cited in Peter T. Kilborn, "US Preparing to Relax Panama Curbs," *The New York Times*, April 26, 1988.

195. *Time*, March 21, 1988, p. 36.

196. AP report citing "an anonymous" official, March 18, 1988.

197. U.S. Department of State, "Daily Briefing Report," March 21, 1988, p. 2.

198. U.S. Department of State, Secret State 087336, pp. 5–6.

199. U.S. Department of State, Confidential Information Memorandum, "Panamanian Statement—Blueprint for Progress," To: The Secretary, From: ARA - Elliott Abrams, March 26, 1988. The statement and an NCC press release are attached to this memorandum.

200. John Goshko, "U.S. Aide Visits," *The Washington Post*, April 20, 1988, p. A26.

201. Quoted in *Newsweek*, April 18, 1988, p. 39.

202. The details of the final offer were made public by Under Secretary of State for Political Affairs Michael H. Armacost; John Felton provides an accurate summary in "U.S. Thwarted in Effort to Remove Noriega," *Congressional Quarterly Weekly Report*, May 22, 1988, p. 1463. The seven steps described in the text incorporate congressional testimony, confidential interviews, and additional press reports.

203. *Arkansas Democrat*, May 26, 1988, p. 14A.

204. Two key figures, Christopher Dodd and Lee Hamilton, voted against the resolution on the grounds that getting rid of Noriega was more important that consistency or sending the right signals in the drug war.

205. Ambrose Evans-Prichert, "Pineapple in America's Side," *The Spectator*, June 4, 1988, p. 15.

206. AP report in *Arkansas Democrat*, May 26, 1988, p. 14A.

207. Dinges and Kempe, to an even greater extent, assign responsibility for the failure to the Reagan administration: to the campaign concerns of Vice-President Bush's advisers; to disunity within the executive over objectives, particularly between the Department of Justice and the prosecutors versus the Department of State and others who wanted to drop the indictments; and to unfortunate time pressures caused by the Moscow summit.

208. Cited from *La Republica* in an AP report in the *Arkansas Democrat*, May 26, 1988.

209. "Anatomy of a Fiasco," *Newsweek*, June 6, 1988, p. 36.

210. Reagan's statement was made on March 22, 1988; it was cited in an AP report in the *Arkansas Democrat*, April 29, 1988.

211. Ibid.

212. U.S. Congress, *The Political Situation in Panama*, p. 128.

213. "Reality of the Political Crisis," p. 2.

214. Quoted in "Anatomy of a Fiasco," p. 39 (italics added).

215. AP report in *Arkansas Democrat*, May 1, 1988.

216. Carla Anne Robbins reported that "Reagan set a similar program in motion one year ago," which would have been approximately May 1988 ("Taking Aim against Noriega," *US News and World Report*, May 1, 1989, p. 40).

217. Lou Cannon and Joe Pichirallo, "Covert Action on Noriega Is Cleared," *The Washington Post*, July 27, 1988, p. 1.

218. Cannon and Pichirallo, "Covert Action," p. A11.

219. In August 1989, I asked a U.S. military officer recently stationed at SOUTHCOM if there were any PDF officers with the leadership ability and desire to reform the institution. His answer was immediate: "There is only one: Eduardo Herrera Hassan."

220. Kempe (*Divorcing the Dictator*, p. 290) reported that Harari was playing a double game, keeping tabs on Herrera Hassan for Noriega, but also cultivating him in case Noriega were eventually ousted.

221. Passages about the operation and Herrera Hassan in the few State and Defense Department cables concerning these events that have been released are heavily excised. I provide numerous citations in my account to alert the reader to the sources I am using and the source's source of information because so many details are murky and because conflicting accounts have appeared.

222. A similar radio announcement was made earlier, on April 18, 1988. Much speculation surrounds both Herrera Hassan's plans and how Noriega learned of them. Some asserted that Noriega was informed by Michael Harari. According to this argument, Noriega had not trusted Herrera Hassan for some time and considered him likely to plot a coup; he had assigned Herrera Hassan to Israel precisely so that Harari could keep tabs on him. Others have argued that Noriega was tipped off by a former U.S. official, Nestor Sanchez, a career CIA officer who had worked with and defended Noriega from opponents in the Department of State while Sanchez was deputy assistant secretary of defense for inter-American affairs (1981–1985). Sanchez admits to having seen Herrera Hassan and several other PDF officers leaving a meeting with the deputy assistant secretary of defense on a Saturday in March; when asked directly, he replied "I did not" and he vigorously objected to "the innuendo" that he "was the one who leaked this information to the Panamanian Government" (U.S. Congress, *Drugs*, Part 4, p. 208).

223. King reported her story, "Panama Colonel Recruited by U.S. for Covert

Action, Then Told to Respect Noriega's Human Rights," a Reuters report, in October 1989; it is quoted in Dinges, *Our Man in Panama*, p. 388.

224. William Scott Malone, "The Panama Debacle—Uncle Sam Wimps Out," *The Washington Post*, April 23, 1989, p. C4. Another of Malone's sources said that the amount was "substantially less than $1 million." Malone's report contains many details, but he occasionally mixes information about Panama 3 and Panama 4.

225. Stephen Engelberg provides many details based on his three-hour interview with Herrera Hassan ("Panamanian's Tale: '87 Plan for a Coup," *The New York Times*, October 29, 1989, p. 12). I believe that Engelberg is one year off on his dates; the escrow funds to which he refers were not available until 1988.

226. Malone, "The Panama Debacle," p. C4, citing "one Panamanian source."

227. John Felton, "When a Secret is Not a Secret, Hackles are Raised on the Hill," *Congressional Quarterly Weekly Report*, July 30, 1988, p. 2086.

228. Malone, "The Panama Debacle," p. C4.

229. Letter to the editor by William J. Crowe, Jr., "Elliott Abrams Remains Reckless on Panama," *The New York Times*, October 16, 1989, p. A20.

230. Felton, "When a Secret," p. 2086.

231. Cannon and Pichirallo, "Covert Action," p. A11.

232. The executive order was reinterpreted after the October 3, 1989, coup attempt. William Webster, director of the CIA, said on October 17, 1989, that interpretation of the order had evolved, in the executive and legislative branches, to encompass broader prohibitions than were initially intended. To correct this, Webster worked out clarifications, in conjunction with congressional intelligence committees, on allowable versus unallowable activities to support a coup. See Pat Towell, "Administration Seeks Leeway in Helping Future Coups," *Congressional Quarterly Weekly Report*, October 21, 1989, p. 2812.

233. King, quoted in Dinges, *Our Man in Panama*, p. 388.

234. Malone, "The Panama Debacle," p. C4.

235. Cannon and Pichirallo, "Covert Action," p. A29.

236. AP report, *Arkansas Democrat*, May 10, 1988, p. 10A; "If New Taxes Needed, Dukakis Says..." *National Journal*, June 16, 1988, p. 1855.

237. AP report, *Arkansas Democrat*, May 10, 1988, p. 10A.

238. Madison, "Passing the Torch," p. 1732.

239. Malone, "The Panama Debacle," p. C4.

240. The objective was confirmed in an interview with Endara and other opposition leaders published on election day. When asked whether they expected to actually take power, their response was negative: "Instead, they hope the vote will unify the general's disparate and often-feuding critics and that the fraud will trigger protests. That, they say, could lead the armed forces to revolt and oust their commander" (*The New York Times*, May 8, 1989, p. 6). The reporter judged this outcome to be unlikely; he thought Noriega was still too strong, and the opponents too weak.

241. Robbins, "Taking Aim," p. 40; see also *The Washington Post*, April 23, 1989, p. A30.

242. "Report," *The Washington Post*, April 23, 1989.

243. *The Washington Post*, April 23, 1989.

244. Robert Pear, "Bush Condemns Attack on Panama Opposition," *The New York Times*, May 11, 1989, p. 4.

245. George Black, "Surrender Manny," *The New Republic*, June 5, 1989, p. 10.

246. Drew, "Letter from Washington," p. 101.

247. Pear, "Bush Condemns," p. 4.

248. Malone, "The Panama Debacle," p. C4.

249. "Report," *The Washington Post*, April 23, 1989.

250. Malone, "The Panama Debacle," p. C4.

251. Stephen Engelberg, "Drug Arrest Disrupted CIA Operation in Panama," *Washington Post*, January 14, 1990, p. 11.

252. Ibid. Engelberg reported that the arrest resulted from a sting operation by DEA officials who were unaware of Eleta's role in Panama 4.

253. The Council's detailed report was reprinted in U.S. Congress, *Congressional Record*, April 19, 1989, pp. S4380–S4383.

254. For example, the *Arkansas Gazette* reported on May 7, 1989, p. 6A, that "The names of more than 100,000 voters appear at least twice on the Panamanian government electoral register." Also, "three thousand voters who recently died are still listed on the register, and the swelling list of names on voter rolls outpaced population growth by nearly 2 to 1 since the last election in 1984—adding more than 112,000 'inexplicable' voters."

255. Robbins, "Taking Aim," p. 40.

256. *The New York Times*, May 8, 1989, p. 6A.

257. Lindsey Gruson, "Noriega Gains as Opposition Dithers," *The New York Times*, May 21, 1989, p. 10.

258. Confidential interview, April 1990.

259. Gruson, "Noriega Gains," p. 10.

260. *Washington Post Weekly Edition*, April 17–23, 1989, p. 18.

261. Robbins, "Taking Aim," p. 40.

262. *Washington Post Weekly Edition*, April 17–23, 1989, p. 18. An interview with Col. Pat Corbett, an officer who worked in the office of treaty affairs, confirmed this pattern of incidents and the serious danger they posed for escalating the crisis.

263. Robbins, "Taking Aim," p. 41.

264. AP report, *Arkansas Democrat*, May 8, 1989, p. 5A.

265. Lindsey Gruson, "U.S. Envoy Blames Noriega in an Assault on Opponents," *The New York Times*, May 15, 1989, p. 6.

266. Interview with a member of the delegation, September 1990.

267. AP report, *Arkansas Democrat*, May 8, 1989, p. 1.

268. *The New York Times*, May 8, 1989, p. 1.

269. Ibid., p. 6.

270. Madrid EFE, "Protesters Begin March," FBIS-LAT-89-089, 9 May 1989, p. 44.

271. Both polls were reported in Madrid EFE, "Church Poll on Opposition Victory," FBIS-LAT-89-088, 9 May 1989, p. 45.

272. Madrid EFE, "Riot Police Block March Access," FBIS-LAT-89-088, 9 May 1989, p. 46.

273. San José Radio Impacto, "ADOC's Ford Speaks at Rally," FBIS-LAT-89-088, 9 May 1989, p. 46.

274. Interview with a member of Carter's delegation, Atlanta, September 1989.

275. Hertzberg, "TRB from Washington, p. 4.

276. *The New York Times*, May 9, 1989, p. 1.

277. Tallies were televised on *Nightline*, May 10, 1989.

278. *The New York Times*, May 10, 1989, p. 1.

279. Lindsey Gruson, "Noriega's Foes Say Vote Must Stand," *The New York Times*, May 15, 1989, p. 4.

280. Lindsey Gruson, "Soldiers at Scene," *The New York Times*, May 11, 1989, p. 1.

281. Lindsey Gruson, "Noriega's Foes Say Vote Must Stand," *The New York Times*, May 12, 1989, p. 4.

282. Lindsey Gruson, "Two Top Noriega Opponents Assaulted in a Street Melee," *The New York Times*, May 11, 1989, pp. 1, 4.

283. Ibid., p. 4.

284. Interview televised on *Nightline*, May 10, 1989.

285. *The New York Times*, May 11, 1989, p. 4.

286. *The New York Times*, May 11, 1989, p. 1. The caption on the cover of *Time*, May 22, 1989, was equally pointed: "Politics, Panama-style."

287. Quoted in Richard Herzfelder, "Can General Noriega Survive His Political Mistakes?" *Pine Bluff Commercial*, May 14, 1989, p. 7A.

288. Gruson, "Noriega's Foes," p. 4.

289. Ibid.

290. Ibid.

291. Interview with Retired Col Díaz Herrera," *La Prensa*, June 7, 1987, FBIS-LAT, June 8, 1987, p. J2.

292. Comment by Georgie Anne Geyer, "Washington Week in Review," PBS, May 12, 1989.

293. "Transcript of the President's Statement," *The New York Times*, May 12, 1989, p. 4.

294. Ibid.

295. Interview with Secretary Cheney, "McNeil-Lehrer Newshour," May 11, 1989.

296. Ibid.

297. Richard Halloran, "U.S. Troops to Go Slowly into Panama," *The New York Times*, May 12, 1989, p. 4.

298. Maureen Dowd, "Dropping His Reserve, Bush Urges Overthrow of Noriega and 'Thugs,'" *The New York Times*, May 14, 1989, p. 8.

299. Ibid.

300. Lindsey Gruson, "U.S. Envoy," p. 6.

301. *Wall Street Journal*, May 15, 1989.

302. *Wall Street Journal*, May 17, 1989.

303. Richard Herzfelder, "Panamanians Pray, Protest," *Arkansas Democrat*, May 15, 1989, p. 1.

304. Lindsey Gruson, "Panamanian Leader Spurns Demand by Bush That He Step Down," *The New York Times*, May 18, 1989, p. 4.

305. "Regime Considering Junta Headed by Endara," Paris AFP, May 22, 1989, FBIS-LAT, May 23, 1989, p. J24.

306. Quoted in Robert Pear, "U.S. Seeks Backing on Noriega Policy," *The New York Times*, May 16, 1989, p. 6.

307. This main point of contention concerned naming Noriega. The draft resolution initially omitted a direct reference to Noriega, but the United States insisted that he be named. The official debate began two hours late, due to behind-the-scenes lobbying on this issue, but the United States prevailed.

308. *Arkansas Democrat*, July 16, 1989, p. 8A.

309. John Felton, "OAS Ministers Admit Failure in Effort to Oust Noriega," *Congressional Quarterly Weekly Report*, August 26, 1989, p. 2223.

310. Ibid. General Woerner said that military pressures were withdrawn during the mediation talks, at the request of the OAS.

311. AP report, "Panama Plans Provisional Government," *Atlanta Constitution*, August 30, 1989, p. A14.

312. AP report, "US Heading to Argue Drug Case Against Noriega at OAS Session," *Atlanta Journal and Constitution*, August 31, 1989, p. A19.

313. U.S. Department of State, Press Release, "Address by the Honorable Lawrence Eagleburger, Acting Secretary of State, before the Organization of American States, August 31, 1989," p. 5.

314. Ibid., p. 14.

315. John Felton, "As Noriega Clings to Power," *Congressional Quarterly Weekly Report*, September 2, 1989, p. 2265.

316. Confidential interview, Little Rock, Arkansas, July 1990.

317. Interview with General Woerner, Washington, D.C., April 1990.

318. Quoted in "War of Nerves," *Arkansas Democrat*, July 27, 1989, p. 4A.

319. AP report, "U.S. Forces Blockade Fort," August 10, 1989, p. 7A.

7

Make It Happen:
Military Out, Civilians In

While the war of nerves proceeded in Panama, several younger officers decided to take matters into their own hands. On October 3, 1989, they mounted a barracks coup against General Noriega. The October coup constituted a turning point in the situation in Panama and for U.S. objectives. Previously, both the Panamanian opposition and the administration of George Bush had hoped that a PDF coup could bring to power officers who supported democratization and demilitarization. The United States had been calling for a coup for over two years; the day the March 1988 coup failed, the United States renewed its calls for the PDF to try again and affirmed U.S. willingness to work with a professional PDF after Noriega's departure. The failure of the October coup dashed these expectations.

In Panama, the situation worsened after the coup. Noriega was determined to control the government's own "supporters," many of whom cheered when the coup was first announced, and to subdue the opposition through greater harassment and stricter repression. In Washington, the Bush administration relinquished the objective of reforming Noriega's system in favor of establishing a new regime.

The October Coup

The United States first learned about plans for another coup on Sunday, October 1, when Adela Bonilla de Giroldi, the wife of Maj. Moisés Giroldi Vega, contacted SOUTHCOM to arrange a meeting between U.S. officials and her husband. The message from the Giroldis was that the PDF wanted to conduct its own operation; they wanted only limited U.S. support because they did not want the operation to be tainted with U.S. involvement. Major Giroldi wanted only two things: (1) U.S. forces to block two roads, to prevent troops loyal to Noriega from interfering in the coup, and (2) sanctuary for his wife and children.[1] Both requests were relayed to Secretary of

Defense Richard Cheney. He authorized a positive response on sanctuary but allowed no verbal commitment to be made about blocking roads.

The Plan

Giroldi and his allies prepared a traditional barracks coup. According to the plan, officers and some 200–300 men would take control of the Comandancía and broadcast an announcement proclaiming the coup and the commander's retirement; then they would wait for other officers to declare themselves. The "action" would involve communication among officers, not bloodshed. The process can be compared to a parliamentary vote of no confidence, in which the vote is not attempted until the dissatisfied parties are fairly sure they have a majority. Then upon seeing the size of that majority, the leader steps aside. In a barracks coup, telephone calls to and from regional commanders serve as the equivalent of votes. This is why Giroldi planned to strike while Noriega was away from the Comandancía: he did not want to fight Noriega. He needed to take control of the headquarters as a symbolic action and to secure command, control, and communications links. Giroldi wanted to present Noriega with a fait accompli the general could accept without losing face.

Giroldi and his allies served in the cohort of officers just below the majors who instigated the March 1988 coup. By retiring Noriega and the general staff, Giroldi's group planned to sweep away the commander and the senior officers most loyal to him. Everyone knew that Noriega and his inner circle had stayed in power beyond the twenty-five year retirement deadline specified in Law 20. Focusing on that technicality would allow Giroldi's group (and Noriega) to claim to be acting positively, in accord with institutional regulations, rather than against Noriega.

This coup appeared to be an inside operation by the next generation of officers, who were frustrated by recent changes in the PDF and who wanted to replace Noriega and his generation. The statement they read over the radio described the coup as strictly a military movement and not a political act. The announcer said, "middle ranking officers had forced the entire high command into retirement" because the "high-ranking leaders had exceeded the deadline for mandatory retirements."[2] The statement did not mention Noriega. No one in Giroldi's group had contacted the opposition, and the rebels apparently had no intention of supporting Endara. Instead, they announced that they recognized the recently installed provisional government of Frederico Rodríguez.

These rebel officers were not out to get Noriega. They certainly did not want to be responsible for extraditing him to the United States. Giroldi, at least, was willing to allow him to remain in Panama. During the coup, when Noriega refused to accept retirement, Giroldi got into a serious argument with other officers about what to do next. At that moment, the coup still had some chance of success, but the moment soon passed.

Giroldi's plan ran into trouble at the start. Originally scheduled for Monday morning, October 2, the coup was delayed until the afternoon and then postponed until the next morning. These changes were due to Noriega's unexpected movements, which interfered with the plan's central objective: to take the Comandancía while Noriega was elsewhere. Noriega's increasingly active security precautions made his absence difficult to predict. He habitually used decoy vehicles to disguise his whereabouts, changed locations several times nightly, and varied his daily schedule. This practice paid off for him on October 2 and 3. On Tuesday morning, October 3, Noriega arrived unexpectedly at the Comandancía at about 8:45 A.M., just after the coup had begun.

Changes in the coup schedule on October 2 undermined U.S. officials' already weak faith in Giroldi and his plan. Neither U.S. military nor intelligence agencies had previously considered Giroldi to be a likely prospect for leading a coup. To them, Giroldi's most notable characteristic was his role in putting down the March 1988 coup. Moreover, the newly installed commander in chief of SOUTHCOM, Gen. Maxwell Thurman, suspected that Noriega would stage a false coup or some other provocative action to test the new U.S. commander.[3] Suspecting a trap, Thurman and his advisers were leery of Major Giroldi. Nothing that occurred during October 1–3 allayed their suspicions.

Adela Giroldi later told reporters that the March coup had been the event that finally turned her husband against Noriega. She also explained that he was motivated by disgust "with the corruption of the senior officers and the misery of the enlisted men 'who cannot feed their own families'."[4] These views were not conveyed to the U.S. officials who met Major Giroldi at a brief face-to-face encounter on Sunday night, October 1. Instead, they neither solicited nor gained much information about his motives and intentions. During the coup, Giroldi told Noriega, "You have to retire, because otherwise the people are going to rebel against us."[5] But at the Sunday night meeting, Giroldi said little, and the U.S. officials, under clear and specific guidance, were not inclined to ask questions.

SOUTHCOM's doubts about Giroldi and his motives increased once the coup began. Two rebel officers sent a message asking to talk to Maj. Gen. Marc Cisneros, commander of the U.S. Army component of SOUTHCOM. When he met with them at Ft. Clayton, the Panamanian officers indicated that their group would not turn Noriega over to the United States. The exact message they were trying to communicate remains clouded.[6] They may have been trying to get the United States to volunteer to send U.S. forces into the Comandancía to capture and remove Noriega. They were already under attack from units loyal to Noriega, so they may have been trying to find out how much U.S. support they could get to defend their position. Or, they may simply have been trying to ascertain, from U.S. sources, what was going on beyond the Comandancía.

U.S. officials monitoring events wondered, at this point, whether the rebels actually "had" Noriega. The situation was unclear at the time. Apparently, the rebel officers first had Noriega confined in a truck and later in an office that they controlled. Noriega apparently made a phone call from that office to his mistress, Vicky Amado; he conveyed a coded distress call to her, and she then phoned two loyal commanders. After loyal troops attacked the Comandancía, the rebels were left with only one floor under their control. At that point, Noriega, who was unarmed, faced Giroldi down. Noriega walked over to Giroldi, who was armed, and said, "You are a dead man and I am a general."[7] Noriega took Giroldi's weapon, ending the coup.

U.S. Support

Despite the fact that Secretary of Defense Cheney refused to give a positive response about blocking the roads Giroldi requested, the United States did exactly that on Monday and Tuesday morning. Because advance notification of troop movements was given both days to the PDF liaison office, as routine procedures required, officers on the lookout for such a signal could easily have found it. The Bush administration may have assumed that Giroldi and his allies got the message that the U.S. forces planned to be at the very spots he had requested at the time he had specified. On Monday, October 2, the U.S. unit deployed for "physical training" along the road to Ft. Amador remained at that spot all day, despite the fact that their exercise was finished at 8:40 A.M. The Bush administration could have been confident that this deployment was noticed by officers planning the coup. That afternoon, after being told by Adela Giroldi that the coup was rescheduled for Tuesday morning, the U.S. officials again informed the PDF that exercises in securing U.S. installations were planned along the roads to Ft. Amador and Howard Air Force Base on Tuesday morning. Blocking those two roads would prevent the presumably loyal Fifth and Seventh Companies from counterattacking the Comandancía. During the coup on October 3, the former did not move, but the latter did and was blocked by U.S. forces. Another loyal unit, Battalion 2000 based at Ft. Cimmarrón, also came to Noriega's aid, using the airport highway to reach the Comandancía.

Controversy surrounds rebel requests to have the airport highway blocked and the Bush administration's failure to do so. According to Adela Giroldi, Battalion 2000, commanded by Maj. Francisco Olechea, was supposed to be part of the coup. She bitterly denounced Olechea as a traitor. The Bush administration later argued that Giroldi had not mentioned that route, and, moreover, that the United States did not have an obvious or plausibly deniable excuse for holding exercises along that third route.

Golden Opportunity or Fiasco?

Critics asserted that the United States passed up a golden opportunity by failing to use military force to prevent loyal troops from reaching the Comandancía. Two arguments supported this charge. One suggested that the Bush administration, having often called for a coup and having claimed to have no quarrel with the PDF, should have been ready and willing to use force to make sure a coup, once under way, succeeded. Whether Giroldi had mentioned the third road or not, once the administration saw that route in use, critics charged, it should have taken the initiative, blocked that road, and saved the coup. Sen. David Boren stressed the moral commitment inherent in calling for a coup: "Here you have the brave people of Panama . . . trying to rid themselves of a drug dealer and a thug who's taken over their country." Once the United States called for a coup, "it was . . . wrong for us with all our strength . . . to stand by . . . and allow these people to fail."[8] Sen. Sam Nunn made a stingingly brief assessment: "We have had a definite, longstanding policy in this country of encouraging a coup. . . . We should anticipate that our policy might succeed."[9] Where, Nunn asked, were the contingency plans? Why did administration officials treat the coup almost casually, failing to hold National Security Council meetings to integrate intelligence reports and devise a coordinated response?

A second argument about a golden opportunity suggested that, whatever its flaws, the Giroldi group was as good an alternative to Noriega as the United States was going to get. This argument faulted the Bush administration for complaining that Giroldi would not turn over Noriega for extradition, that he had not included calls for restoration of civilian rule in the coup announcement, and that he had been known as a Noriega loyalist. Instead, this argument suggested, if the United States wanted the PDF to reform itself, it would have to accept the leaders who emerged within the traditions of that institution. The Bush administration, defending its actions, said that it had never intended to offer carte blanche support for any conceivable coup. Rather, President Bush repeatedly said, he felt that he had to reserve the right to review a coup's credentials before committing U.S. resources. Georgie Anne Geyer provided an apt counter that typified criticism of the administration: when one is dealing with an institution like the PDF, one cannot expect a Charles de Gaulle to step forward to lead a coup.[10]

The substance of this second critique is that the United States changed its standards, without officially changing policy, once it was presented with a real coup. Moreover, the United States changed its standards without sending this signal to Panama; in fact, the movement of U.S. forces and the granting of asylum to Giroldi's family were clear signals of approval.

Previously, the idea of a coup and new leadership of a somewhat reformed PDF had seemed reasonable to U.S. officials. Over time, as Noriega changed the PDF, administration officials began to change their minds about prospects for reform from within the PDF and about the merits of a lasting relationship with a mildly reformed PDF. When the Bush administration confronted a choice between Noriega's regime and Giroldi's coup on October 3, the coup did not seem attractive enough to risk armed combat with Battalion 2000. The bottom line in Bush's advisers' thinking was this: If the United States were to risk a good number of casualties, the objective was going to have to be a lot more attractive than Noriega's retirement and mild reform of the PDF. At this point, U.S. objectives changed.

The Coup Fails

Meanwhile, the coup was in serious trouble and starting to look more like a fiasco than a golden opportunity. First, Noriega had arrived at the Comandancía, negating the entire premise of the plan. Second, when Noriega refused to give up, the rebel officers could not agree on how to proceed. Then, Giroldi would not kill Noriega. Some speculated that his past friendship with Noriega and loyalty to hierarchy inhibited Giroldi; others suggested that Giroldi feared losing U.S. support if he killed Noriega and thereby violated the U.S. ban on involvement in assassinations. To Giroldi's disadvantage, Noriega got two lucky breaks that he used to maximum advantage: Noriega talked his captors into letting him call his mistress, who then summoned troops to his rescue; then, in a direct confrontation, he intimidated and disarmed Giroldi.

Something also went wrong with the rebel's radio announcement. Most of their statement was aired on national radio, but the signal went dead during the broadcast, presumably cut by Noriega loyalists. Moments later, another commentator came on the air and denied what had just been announced. About an hour later, a unidentified PDF lieutenant colonel made an announcement on television: "Noriega's forces were ready to die on Noriega's behalf."[11] This was an audio announcement with only a clock on a wall shown by the camera. Thus, if the rebels had hoped that their announcement would swing regional commanders to their cause and, incidentally, instigate a popular uprising, their attempt was effectively neutralized.

Numerous communication problems prevented rapid, or even timely, exchange of information between the rebels and U.S. officials. Noriega was notorious for tapping phones, and a lack of secure lines may have deterred the rebels from calling SOUTHCOM. Alternatively, the Giroldi group may have been so intent on avoiding U.S. involvement that they waited until it was too late to seek additional support. Both sides later claimed to have had trouble contacting each other. At one point, two rebel officers actually left the Comandancía and went to Ft. Clayton to communicate, securely and directly, with General Cisneros.

Finally, the Bush administration did not achieve a consensus on additional steps it was willing to take until it was too late to act. Gen. Colin Powell, JCS chairman, relayed new instructions to General Thurman Tuesday afternoon. He could (1) accept Noriega if the rebels delivered him, or (2) "covertly remove Noriega to a U.S. base." The latter mission would have to be "carried out without a visible display of U.S. forces," the military personnel involved must be "operating undercover," and U.S. forces were to avoid the possibility of armed conflict with the PDF.[12] As a fallback position, Thurman was authorized to "develop a plan" using U.S. forces "to capture Noriega and bring him to a U.S. base in Panama," but that plan could be implemented only if President Bush gave his "specific approval."[13] By the time these options were relayed, the tide of the fighting at the Comandancía had shifted decisively in Noriega's favor. Noriega's supporters had regained control over most of the Comandancía and Giroldi had been killed. The new guidance came too late.

Postmortems

Washington experienced two weeks of recriminations, accusations, and lamentations. News analysts and members of Congress were particularly critical. National columnists wondered how a president and advisers with so much foreign policy experience could operate in so casual a fashion. Secretary Cheney and General Powell went to Capitol Hill for closed door committee sessions. There, Boren and Nunn faulted the administration for failing to be ready with contingency plans; they faulted top advisers in particular for poor decisionmaking; and they criticized Bush, Cheney, and others for maintaining their scheduled appointments instead of attending to the coup. The next day, Sen. Jesse Helms took a different approach: public criticism. Helms had a staff specialist with ready access to sources in Panama, so Helms quickly made a diagnosis of what had gone wrong with the coup and the administration's policy. He spoke at length on the floor, challenging the administration's version of events. All of this stung and embarrassed the administration.[14] White House Chief of Staff John Sununu ordered a review of procedures and performance. President Bush described this as fine-tuning; administration officials admitted privately that it was much more.

In Panama, the opposition was disheartened. Ricardo Arias Calderón, the first vice-presidential candidate, was angry. He warned, "A dog that barks better have a bite behind its bark, or otherwise it better shut up."[15] Noriega displayed two reactions to the coup: elation at having survived and suspicion that another attempt would follow. Noriega wasted little time in purging the PDF and cracking down on the opposition. His treatment of coup participants and others suspected of disloyalty was much tougher than in March 1988. Officers who participated in the first coup had been beaten and imprisoned; many were tortured, some severely, but none were killed. In October 1989, ten participants were killed and thirty-seven were taken prisoner. According to one account, Noriega shot Giroldi in a fit of rage.

Another, more credible, account asserted that the killings were all performed by a high-level aide. According to a U.S. report on these events, Giroldi was brutally interrogated for about twelve hours. Then he was taken out of his cell by the two interrogators and told that he was being transferred to another facility. Giroldi said, "No you're not. You're going to kill me." They shot him and sent his body to the morgue.[16] Giroldi's body bore broken bones and other signs of torture. Hundreds of PDF members were questioned. In the process, Noriega learned of other plots and consequently managed to purge the PDF of more dissenters than had been involved in Giroldi's coup.

As a result, the PDF came under tighter control and grew more loyal to Noriega than before October 1989. However, the PDF was also further transformed. The officer corps became increasingly less professional and more dependent on Noriega as the general promoted younger, less experienced, but more loyal men to positions on his staff. Although the PDF appeared more cohesive, one U.S. officer described that unity as a thin veneer, saying the PDF "also became more fragmented, demoralized and dispirited. There was no trust within the ranks."[17]

Noriega himself seemed to be changed by having survived a closer call than in March 1988. Physically, Noriega appeared exhilarated by the event. He often greeted crowds with his arms raised in a boxer's victory pose. He was portrayed, in a photo spread in the government-owned *La República*, as "A General with Nerves of Steel."[18] Noriega had experienced another victory; asserting his own will had terminated the coup, and he was responsible for his own survival. Noriega still had enemies, though, and he knew it.

On October 6, 1989, Noriega made a speech to government employees, some of whom had celebrated when news of the coup was first announced. He bluntly stated how he intended to operate: "Bullets for my enemies, beatings for the indecisive, and money for my friends."[19] This was his new "Three P's" policy: *plomo* (bullets), *palos* (truncheons), and *plata* (money). Noriega also announced sixteen new laws that would be promulgated to identify and punish dissenters. Finally, he called on government employees to expose traitors in their ranks.

The United States Reviews Its Options

The failure of the October coup narrowed the options available to the United States. Noriega's purge made the PDF less likely to attempt another coup in the near term. Nonetheless, the Bush administration soon authorized a covert operation (Panama 5) to encourage and support another coup, just in case. Negotiations seemed less auspicious now; Noriega was riding too high. Sanctions were continued, but little additional leverage on Noriega could be exerted with economic pressure. To widen its options, the administration modified the standing rules of engagement for coups. This step was designed to prepare for further action in Panama, as well as to respond to criticism of its handling of the October coup.

Reinterpreting the Assassination Ban

When the October coup occurred, the ban on assassinations initiated by President Gerald Ford was interpreted to mean that the United States could not encourage in any way, much less actively support, a coup that might result in the death of a foreign leader. President Reagan had renewed the ban in Executive Order 12333: "No person employed by or acting on behalf of the United States government may engage in, or conspire to engage in, assassination." After the coup failed, the administration and Congress reinterpreted the ban to clarify its limits and to expand the range of permissible U.S. roles. In particular, they wanted to let U.S. officials on the scene take a less inhibited approach to coup planners, including providing information about U.S. objectives and, by implication, likely U.S. responses. A senior official said, "We want them to get more details . . . more specific details."[20]

A new ruling was drafted in the office of the Army judge advocate general that "significantly" expanded the scope of legal military operations against terrorists, drug lords, or fugitives abroad. In drafting the ruling, complaints about the October coup were addressed in the broader context of calls for additional enforcement powers and military operations against terrorists and drug traffickers. An initial step reducing limits on enforcement activities had been instituted earlier, in June 1989, when the Department of Justice drafted a legal ruling on the use of U.S. military force to apprehend fugitives abroad. As described in leaks to the press, this ruling allowed the president to order a fugitive from a U.S. indictment to be picked up by U.S. officials in another country, even without that government's cooperation or consent.[21] In November, the *posse comitatus* statute was reinterpreted; thereafter, it did not apply on foreign soil if U.S. officials were apprehending fugitives. This new order would apply to Noriega because he was named in two federal indictments.

Military action aimed at Noriega's apprehension was now a legally available option. At this point, the use of force against Noriega was "ruled in" after having been ruled out since the beginning of the ouster crisis in 1987. Previously, SOUTHCOM had recommended against the use of force on the grounds that Panamanians has to solve their problem. General Woerner, SOUTHCOM's commander in chief from June 1987 through September 1989, felt that "the only chance that democracy really had in Panama was for the Panamanians to go through the catharsis of removing Noriega. If they succeeded in doing that they would have had an experience that contributed to the emergence of a democracy. But if we would go in and do it for them, it would be one more episode of many in Panamanian history, and a year later we would have a Panama that looks very much like the Panama we have seen recently except the military leader will be more discreet. But the military will still exercise the power. That was my concern." Therefore General Woerner had advised against the use of force. The bottom line of his recommendation to President Bush was this: "I can tell you how to go in. What I cannot tell you is how to get out of it and leave behind something worthwhile."[22] Woerner made that recommendation in September. In October, after Giroldi's coup failed, military options were evaluated in a very different context.

Thus, a major result of the administration's postcoup policy review was a consensus that the United States must have military options ready and available. Administration officials told Washington columnists that the "word has gone out" that the United States was going to take much more aggressive action.[23] A Pentagon official said that the coup "created a philosophical turnaround" in which many minds concluded that the United States could not rely on the existing formula—a Panamanian coup plus U.S. assistance—to remove Noriega.[24] A U.S. officer at SOUTHCOM suggested that events had reached a point where a U.S. invasion might be the only way out. Col. Jack Pryor expressed his view:

> I felt it wasn't a matter of if, but when. I felt this because of what Noriega was doing. Read Noriega; he laid it all out, and he was doing exactly what he advocated in "Psychological Operations" [psy-ops]. In his book, Noriega talks about how you change the faith of a society through corruption and favors. What he had going on here was not by accident. This was on purpose. There was a plan to it all. He had become a master of psy-ops and he knew exactly how to terrorize the Panamanian people. And he was not afraid to take risks. Look at what he did when he killed Billy Ford's body guard and beat up on Billy Ford that day. He really bashed the opposition. That was high stakes poker on his part, taking great risks. He knew that he would confront the international media on that, but he knew exactly how to put the Panamanian people in their place and to terrorize them. . . . He had conditioned the society over time on how he would operate. So that [May 10, 1989] was a great move for him. Now, he got a break there. [The Chinese government's crackdown at] Tienanmin Square deflected all of the international media attention away from Panama. Noriega understands that world opinion is fleeting and he was willing to take risks. That was a gutsy thing to do on his part, but it worked. Read Noriega. You'll see that it is laid right out in his book; that is exactly what he did.[25]

Implied in Col. Pryor's analysis is the conclusion that as long as Noriega could control Panamanian society and hold on to the instruments of force, Panamanians alone could not remove him from power. Two new options were considered: U.S. support for another coup (Panama 5) and direct military intervention.

Panama 5

President Bush authorized Panama 5 soon after the October coup failed. Unlike Panama 3, this plan received a positive congressional reception. The operation was budgeted at $3 million, significantly larger than Panama 3, and with "no restrictions" except for the continuing ban on assassinations, which was now more narrowly defined.[26] The purpose of the operation was to "topple Noriega"; an unidentified source said "we're going into it with the understanding that there may be loss of life."[27]

Beyond these few details, little has been revealed about Panama 5. A reporter who spoke with White House officials in late October was told that they thought another coup would occur.[28] A military source confirmed that contingency plans for aiding another coup were rehearsed, but that personnel did not receive a "go" order because another coup attempt did not materialize.[29]

Panama 5 may have been related to a joint Federal Bureau of Investigation/Drug Enforcement Administration operation that occurred during Thanksgiving weekend. In this covert nighttime operation, U.S. agents were flown into Panama City, using their own equipment, to seize a suspected stockpile of explosives and terrorist devices. If U.S. agents had found this evidence against Noriega, a larger military operation would have immediately been launched against the general.[30] The U.S. agents found the warehouse to be empty, and they were covertly withdrawn.

Panama 5 may or may not have been related to another covert operation begun in early December. This operation placed U.S. Special Forces in Panama to "snatch" Noriega and return him to the United States for trial. Noriega successfully evaded their efforts.

Plans for Major Military Actions

After the October coup, military contingency plans were reviewed and developed for a "broad continuum of possible responses."[31] The existing multistage plan for an invasion, Operation *Blue Spoon*, which envisioned an invasion of several days' duration, followed by phased restoration of public order and return of control to Panamanian authorities. When President Bush called for a review, General Thurman "compacted" the contingency plan into an overnight operation.[32]

Col. Jack Pryor, who participated in drafting the invasion plan, explained the process. The team started with *Blue Spoon*, which was based on a general policy and lots of contingencies, and as the Bush administration's policy became more focused, the plan was narrowed toward concrete objectives and operational issues, such as size of force, force packaging, logistics, and deployment. Pryor explained, "We felt we had to make it happen fast. We wanted to minimize death, damage, and collateral damage. We wanted to make a real impact on a few symbolic places: the Comandancía, Río Hato, and the international airport."[33]

Detailed plans for component military operations were drafted and rehearsed during November and December. Some of these rehearsals were reported as readiness exercises, and they did serve both purposes. Some of these exercises involved moving additional units from U.S. bases to Panama. On December 8, for example, a battalion (600 soldiers) from the 82nd Airborne Division went to Panama for exercises. Later, during the invasion, men from this unit were available to liberate the prison in Gamboa and participate in operations near Madden Dam.[34] Press reports also placed units from the 7th Light Infantry in Panama for jungle training at the time the invasion was launched.[35]

Training for units that might be used in planned missions was stepped up and, in some cases, changed to fit circumstances in Panama. The 193rd Infantry Brigade (Light), for example, shifted from jungle training to urban operations. Said one commander, "Jungle warfare used to be our big emphasis, but that was before the situation in Panama changed." "After all," another said, "there's no jungle in downtown Panama City."[36] During the invasion, the 193rd served as the main element in the nighttime attack on the Comandancía and Ft. Amador. Another unit that had been training for quick strikes against isolated drug labs shifted its exercises to urban terrain. Some of this training was a thin disguise for stepped-up operations against the PDF. Previously, operations orders for U.S. forces in Panama were to threaten and intimidate, but to do nothing provocative. After the October coup attempt, the limit on provocation was rescinded. A unit was ordered in November to provoke the PDF while on patrol; they challenged PDF guards and walked through Panamanian facilities. A U.S. officer on the scene later explained why these operations were escalated. "We were setting the PDF up so they would not know if U.S. forces were mounting an exercise or the real thing. We exercised around the clock. We had better command and control than they did. We were trying to out-tempo them." In addition to their preparatory value, stepped up U.S. activity also had an effect on the PDF, temporarily reducing the incidence of harassment of U.S. personnel. Equipment that might be needed for military options was pre-positioned, including Apache attack helicopters, which were brought into Panama on November 17.[37] Tanks were also pre-positioned in late November or early December.

The Invasion

Thus, by early December, the United States was prepared to use military options if events in Panama provided a threat or opportunity to do so. As the month progressed, the situation in Panama was deceptively calm. Little news about Panama was reported in the United States during November and early December; stepped-up military operations were not covered. Noriega's postcoup crackdown appeared to have had its intended effect on the opposition.

A Power Play and a State of War

Noriega was intensifying his already vigorous security practices. Panama 5 had been mentioned in the press; Noriega knew he was still a target. In mid-December, when PDF promotions were announced, analysts commented that Noriega was "tightening his grip."[38] Those promotions were announced on the eve of a meeting of the National Assembly. (The Assembly had been renamed Popular Power Assembly, but usually was referred to by its former name.) Noriega seemed to be making a major power play. Reports predicted that he would recommend, and automatically receive, grants of additional authority.

When the National Assembly met on Friday, December 15, 1989, it named Noriega chief of government, with the title maximum leader. This had been Omar Torrijos's title while he held extraordinary powers, from 1972 to 1978. The Assembly also granted to Noriega powers greater than those of the provisional president: power to appoint government officials, direct foreign affairs, and convene the Council of State as well as the cabinet and the Assembly itself. Thus Noriega emerged from the session with legal authority, including the right to overrule the civilian president, for the powers he routinely exercised behind the scenes. Even more significant from the U.S. perspective was passage of a declaratory resolution on the subject of U.S.-Panamanian relations.

The National Assembly passed a declaration finding Panama to be "in a state of war so long as the United States continues its policy of aggression."[39] A slightly different version was reported over the radio: "A state of war exists in Panama as a result of the North American aggression."[40] Noriega elaborated on this theme, saying "The North American scheme, through constant psychological and military harassment, has created a state of war in Panama."[41]

Opposition leaders characterized these moves as another attempt by Noriega "to perpetuate his dictatorship." The Bush administration's first official comment downplayed the significance of these words; the Assembly's action was characterized as "another hollow step."[42] In fact, the Panamanian government had made a similar statement in March 1988, describing its relations with the United States as "an undeclared war."[43] In December 1989, however, the context was quite different. Noriega's power play followed a coup and an escalating war of nerves. The next day, after a U.S. soldier was shot and killed, the U.S. reaction was much stronger. U.S. officials and reporters referred to the resolution as Panama's declaration of war against the

United States. The State Department's official statement on December 19 referred to "General Noriega's irresponsible declaration of war" and "Panama's declaration of war on the United States."[44]

A U.S. Casualty

The real story surrounding the death of 1st Lt. Robert Paz is not yet fully known. Rumors, which normally abound in Panama, challenge the official version. Some have characterized the event as a CIA surveillance operation, due to the troops' proximity to the Comandancía when they took a "wrong turn." Others asserted that the four U.S. officers involved were set up, in an incident deliberately staged by the United States to create the opportunity it needed to launch the invasion. The following account is based on public sources available soon after the events occurred.

On Saturday night, December 16, 1989, four officers assigned to SOUTHCOM headquarters got lost in the maze of streets in the poor neighborhood of Chorrillo that abutted the Comandancía. The driver, Capt. Richard Haddad, was assigned to SOUTHCOM intelligence. The men were off duty, unarmed, and dressed in civilian clothes. They had driven across town for dinner at La Cascada, a restaurant popular with U.S. personnel. While returning to base at about 9:00 P.M. they took a wrong turn.

Wrong turns are easy to make in Chorrillo. The neighborhood is filled with narrow, one-way streets that intersect at odd angles; the multistoried wooden buildings are like tall, dark walls and make it impossible to see around corners. One street looks much like another. Captain Haddad may indeed have simply taken a wrong turn.

When he turned onto Avenida A, Haddad saw a PDF checkpoint ahead; he pulled up behind two Panamanian cars. The roadblock was manned by five members of the Macho de Monte, a unit that takes its name from the Panamanian equivalent of a wild razorback hog. The Machos wore long beards and blue jeans, and they were armed with AK-47 rifles. The Macho de Monte had a well-deserved reputation for toughness; they had recently been brought into Panama City to beef up security at the Comandancía. On Saturday night, the Machos manning the roadblock were edgy. Earlier in the day they had gotten into a fire fight with some Dignity Battalions.

The four U.S. officers discussed what to do while they waited in line. By this time the five Macho de Monte had been joined by forty Panamanians. The Panamanians surrounded Haddad's car, which looked unmistakenly like a car a U.S. soldier would drive, and shouted anti-U.S. slogans. Someone opened a door and tried to pull one of the officers out of the car. Haddad decided to run the roadblock. He pressed the gas pedal to the floor. The Macho de Monte fired as the car accelerated past the checkpoint, heading toward the Comandancía. Bullets hit the car, and one hit Lieutenant Paz, who was in the back seat. Paz died soon after arriving at Gorgas Hospital.[45] The twenty-four-year-old Marine lieutenant was the first casualty in a heightened state of war.

Back at the roadblock, a Navy officer and his wife had witnessed the events from a nearby corner. Both were taken by the Macho de Monte, blindfolded, and conveyed to a PDF facility. According to the Bush administration, a senior PDF officer entered the room and, without asking questions or making a statement, hit the lieutenant across the mouth and kicked him in the groin. Then, the Panamanian officer beat the U.S. officer, threatened to kill him, and "sexually threatened" his wife. She was shoved against a wall and forced to stand there, with her arms overhead; after about thirty minutes she collapsed. Both were later released. Their treatment by the PDF intensified the Bush administration's reaction to Paz's death.

President Bush characterized the roadblock incidents as an "enormous outrage."[46] Administration officials described the situation as deteriorating. A Pentagon spokesman said, "Things are very tense. People fear for their lives in Panama right now."[47] SOUTHCOM went on a Delta-level personnel movement alert late Saturday night, which restricted movement to essential business only. In the United States, mission orders were given to various units to ready their C-130 transport planes for action and to go to designated pick-up points.[48] The airflow began moving on December 18 and was reported by U.S media on December 19.

Meanwhile, in Panama another incident occurred on December 17, when an Army lieutenant was leaving a laundry not far from SOUTHCOM headquarters at Quarry Heights. The laundry was less than a mile from the Comandancía. The lieutenant was approached by a PDF policeman, César Tajada, who signaled him to stop. As Corporal Tajada approached, the U.S. officer felt threatened; he thought the Panamanian was reaching for a weapon. The lieutenant drew his weapon and fired two shots. Tajada went down, wounded in a leg and an arm, then got up and left the scene. He later denied that he had reached for his gun.[49]

Incidents on December 16 and 17 were part of an ongoing war of nerves. The week before, a Panamanian soldier had pointed a gun at a U.S. officer near a garbage dump. During the weekend the roadblock incident occurred, the PDF had detained several U.S. military at the airport and taken their weapons and radios.[50] Two other incidents involving confrontations with PDF policemen also occurred, including one arrest of a U.S. soldier at another PDF checkpoint.

These incidents were like hundreds that had occurred during the last two years; many of those were minor, but some had been just as serious, including several beatings and one rape. The events of the December 16–17 weekend, particularly Lt. Paz's death, were perceived differently. They were interpreted in Washington as part of an increasingly threatening pattern, and, significantly, in the context of the National Assembly's declaration and Noriega's statements. In an interview broadcast on WBAI in New York,

General Noriega said that U.S. soldiers at the checkpoint had shot first and wounded several Panamanians, "including a young girl, a night watchman and an elderly man."[51] Those people had, in fact, been killed and wounded, but not by U.S. personnel—they were victims of the firefight between Dignity Batallions and Macho de Monte that had occurred earlier in the day.

The Bush administration now perceived a threatening pattern of escalation: individual Panamanian soldiers were out of control and Noriega was egging them on. Paz's death and the PDF's firing on Haddad's car represented a new level of violence, a step beyond intimidation and rival psychological operations. The situation was spiraling out of control. Marlin Fitzwater, the White House spokesman, said, "When you put all of these together, you begin to discern a certain climate of aggression that is very disturbing."[52] A U.S. military analyst agreed, asserting that Noriega "was furious" when he learned about the roadblock incident "because he realized the potential implications. That killing was not meant to happen, not at all." This analyst concluded, "Things just got away from him. That was loss of Noriega's people's control."

An officer assigned to SOUTHCOM at the time gave his perspective on these events, confirming the assessment in Washington that a new pattern had emerged. First, this officer emphasized a new assertiveness displayed by the Dignity Battalions. "You started seeing an open defiance on the part of the Dignity Battalions." In November, "you started seeing these guys around, with arms; they held static positions—down here around the corner at Fourth of July Avenue they had a little bunker. They had weapons out and they became very visible on the streets." The significance of this development was that it produced "heightened open friction," which was further intensified by the National Assembly's actions, the firefight at the Comandancía, the roadblock incidents, and the incident at the laundromat. The officer concluded, "You put all that together and you have a situation that just finally reached a trigger point. Something needed to be done."[53]

What had happened? Some speculated that Noriega lost control or simply began making mistakes as he experienced an episode of megalomania. Several U.S. Army officers on the scene disagreed. Col. Jack Pryor's assessment was that Noriega "over-prepped his people; he got them too stirred up. That's where I would say he lost control. He did not lose control of the machine; he wound it a little too tight." Pryor asserted that "the absolute last thing Noriega wanted was to have an American killed. He was adamant that that not happen." Why? Pryor, who had studied Noriega, made this argument. "He knows us; he knew there was a certain place the Congress and the American people draw the line, and then that's it. He did not want that trigger event to occur, so he controlled that very tightly." But during the last days, "he just got everything sprung up a little bit too much" and the trigger event occurred.[54]

Additional evidence provided confirmation for these conclusions. The

PDF erected additional barricades along the streets near the Comandancía and Noriega's residence. They used buses and trucks to block key intersections. Then, on December 19, the barricades were removed and the heavily armed troops returned to barracks.[55]

Deliberations in Washington

On Sunday afternoon, December 17, the day after Lt. Paz was killed, President Bush met with his advisers at the White House. Present were Fitzwater; Gen. Colin Powell; the JCS director of operations, Gen. Thomas W. Kelly; Vice-President Dan Quayle; NSC Adviser Brent Scowcroft and his deputy, Robert M. Gates; White House Chief of Staff Sununu; Secretary of Defense Cheney; and Secretary of State James Baker. The group reached a consensus on the situation: "It will only get worse."[56] President Bush said, "Enough is enough." The president and his advisers discussed military options and plans in detail for one and a half hours. Three objectives were clearly expressed: get Noriega out, protect U.S. lives, and put the Endara government in power. Finally, Bush said, "Let's do it."[57] At this point, the order went out from the JCS to alert specified units for possible deployment. Within hours, cargo planes were landing at Pope Air Force Base near Ft. Bragg.

The president met with his advisers again on Tuesday, December 19, at 3:00 P.M. In addition to Sunday's group, CIA Director Webster and Attorney General Richard Thornburgh were included. Scowcroft gave everyone "time lines," with tasks to accomplish between 6:00 P.M. and 1:00 A.M., December 20, when the invasion was scheduled to begin.[58] During the evening, President Bush alternated between Christmas parties and making calls to congressional leaders; at 9:00 P.M. he began calling heads of state. From 12:30 P.M. until 4:20 A.M. he remained in the Oval Office, receiving reports from the situation room and watching CNN. After a brief rest, President Bush addressed the nation at 7:20 A.M.; Cheney and Powell began their briefings for the press at 7:45 A.M.

Operation *Just Cause*

The U.S. invasion was not entirely a surprise. On Tuesday, December 19, Panama accused the United States of violating its airspace with observation planes and helicopters, activities that culminated three days of frequent movements of U.S. forces. On Tuesday afternoon, C-141 Starlifter transport planes filled with combat-loaded soldiers were landing in Panama every ten minutes. At Howard Air Force Base, a reporter saw six to eight helicopters instead of the usual three to four. At Ft. Clayton, U.S. troops were busied around tanks and trucks in plain view. "NBC Evening News" included a brief segment showing shots of transport planes flying from Ft. Bragg, home of the 82nd Airborne Division. Although SOUTHCOM spokesmen stated that "no unusual military activity" was under way and explained the activity as readiness exercises, invasion preparations were thinly disguised.[59]

The Invasion

At 1:35 A.M. on December 20, 1989, Marlin Fitzwater announced that the United States had launched a military operation against Panama. He added that a civilian government had been installed and that President Endara had called on the PDF to surrender peacefully. To aid the new government, the United States immediately released some Panamanian assets from escrow and lifted economic sanctions.

Despite advance signals, the invasion caught Noriega by surprise. He even ignored a tip-off conveyed to him at 10:00 P.M. Tuesday by one of his bodyguards, who overheard two U.S. soldiers discussing their positions for H-hour. Instead, Noriega had gone to La Siesta Motel near Torrijos (Tocumen) airport for a rendezvous. Some of his advisers took the warnings more seriously; at 11:00 P.M. a call went out for the PDF to mobilize to defend against a U.S. invasion.

Operation *Just Cause* combined a snatch operation with a massive military invasion. The snatch, designed to apprehend Noriega and return him to the United States for prosecution, was scheduled to occur just before H-hour (1:00 A.M.). The next day, General Kelly confirmed that Delta Force personnel were in place and ready to go. He explained why the operation failed: "We thought we had a pretty good idea where he was last night. We went there, and he wasn't there."[60] Information later released by SOUTHCOM provided the evidence they used to reach the conclusion that they had just missed Noriega: cigarettes left burning at Noriega's "witch house," women's purses left behind, and an open back door. It was clear that someone had just departed, but no evidence placed Noriega at that scene. After failing to capture Noriega with the snatch, to prevent him from fleeing the country by air, U.S. forces "closed" Panamanian airspace by securing Patilla Airport and several private airfields that he could have used. Noriega's yachts were also secured, moments before action in the vicinity indicated that Noriega or one of his aides was about to escape by sea.

The other primary aspect of Operation *Just Cause* was the invasion, which involved some 26,000 forces in the biggest military operation since Vietnam and the largest parachute drop since World War II.[61] Most of the U.S. forces were Army; several small, specialized units, Navy SEALs, and Marines were also included. Some 13,000 troops were deployed to supplement the 13,000 already in Panama. The operation's initial phase involved about 22,500 U.S. forces, providing a comparative forces ratio of six to one, counting 4,000 PDF soldiers and excluding police and other noncombat elements of the PDF.

As soon as the invasion was under way, Provisional President Rodríguez urged Panamanians to resist; he then disappeared. Although PDF invasion contingency plans called for battalions to split into small units and wage a guerrilla war, none of the regional commanders did so. Radio Nacional called on the Dignity Battalions to fight the United States, and these forces, rather than the PDF, mounted stiff armed resistance.

The invasion was designed to achieve three objectives: (1) to strike down the Comandancía, decapitating the PDF's command and communications center and preventing both short- and long-term resumption of command functions; (2) to bottle up PDF units at their bases, preventing a counterattack, denying havens for the PDF to recoup and organize a resistance, and cutting off Panama City from reinforcements; and (3) to secure Torrijos (Tocumen) International Airport as a safe landing area for U.S. reinforcements. These objectives were also cited in the report President Bush sent to the Congress on December 21, 1989, in accordance with the War Powers Resolution. For legal justification, Bush cited Article 51 of the United Nations Charter, which allows the use of force for self-defense, and the president's responsibility to protect U.S. lives.

When President Bush addressed the nation, he stated four goals of the invasion: "to safeguard the lives of Americans, to defend democracy in Panama, to combat drug trafficking and to protect the integrity of the Panama Canal treaty." He recalled Noriega's "reckless threats" and evoked images of the May elections when civilian presidential candidates were bloodied by Dignity Battalions.[62]

President Guillermo Endara and the two vice-presidents, Ricardo Arias Calderón and Billy Ford, were taken to Ft. Clayton to be sworn into office by Osvalvo Velasquez, the head of the Panamanian Commission on Human Rights, just forty-five minutes before the invasion began. The civilians remained at Ft. Clayton for the next thirty-six hours. President Endara issued a taped radio address, which was broadcast via Costa Rican Radio Impacta because Noriega's forces still controlled Panamanian stations.[63] For the first time in its history, the Panama Canal was closed for security reasons—parts of the canal's route pass close by the Comandancía, and hostilities were also likely at other canal facilities and areas. The canal reopened at 2:00 A.M. (Central Standard Time) on Thursday, December 21.

The worst of the fighting initially appeared to be over within eighteen hours after the invasion began. Although Noriega remained at large, he was not trying to orchestrate resistance. A taped message of Noriega calling on people to resist was broadcast occasionally, but there were no signs that Noriega was trying to contact the regional commanders. The officer most likely to mount a counterattack was Lt. Col. Luis del Cid, who commanded the Fifth Military Zone headquartered at David in the province of Chiriquí.

This was the zone where Noriega had once served and where he continued to have strong ties. Chiriquí was where most experts expected Noriega to flee, whether he decided to orchestrate a resistance or an escape. Instead of fighting, however, Colonel del Cid surrendered on December 22. Del Cid and other commanders were contacted by General Cisneros and a former PDF captain; Cisneros and the captain were credited with convincing the key commanders not to resist, thereby averting considerable loss of life. By December 24, four of the top PDF commanders had surrendered. Many of the 4,500 troops under del Cid's command also surrendered, reducing the prospects for a guerrilla initiative.[64] Del Cid, who had been indicted in February 1988 along with Noriega, was turned over to DEA agents and conveyed to Miami.

On the second day of the invasion, it became clear that the fighting would continue longer than expected, due to Dignity Battalion resistance combined with general chaos on city streets. Reportedly, military planners had estimated that the fighting would last three days; instead, it took seven.[65] The United States sent an additional 2,000 fresh troops from Ft. Ord on Saturday, December 23. The amount of looting and street violence that occurred exceeded the expectations of the operation's planners. By the third day, U.S. forces shifted from an invasion mode to operations in a low intensity conflict environment, combating street fighting, hit-and-run tactics, and sniper attacks.

To encourage PDF and Dignity Battalion members to surrender, and to quickly reduce the number of weapons on the streets, the United States offered a reward averaging $150 per firearm. The program worked; when "cash for weapons" began, the street fighting diminished and soon ceased. Some 50,000 weapons were eventually turned in or discovered.

But the idea of using a financial reward to gain information about Noriega did not work. The United States offered a reward of $1,000,000 for information that led to his apprehension. Many tips flowed in, but it was Noriega's own decision to seek asylum at the Nunciature, the embassy and residence of the Papal Nuncio, that ended the suspense over his whereabouts.

Casualty figures for Operation *Just Cause* were lower than expected on the U.S. side. Instead of the projected seventy casualties, twenty-three military personnel and three civilians died, and 323 military personnel were wounded. Figures announced for Panama generated considerable controversy, initially because a count was not being made or announced, and later because of challenges to the figures themselves. For Panama, the United States counted 314 soldiers killed and 124 wounded. Some 5,600 PDF members were detained. Civilian casualties among Panamanians were high, with most estimates ranging from 500 to 1000. Other sources reported mass graves with uncounted numbers of bodies. Some of these were later investigated and about one hundred bodies were exhumed for identification and proper burial.

Panamanian reaction to the invasion was one of mixed relief and resentment. Roberto Eisenmann characterized the way Panamanians felt about the invasion as a "national wound, a wound inflicted by Noriega on the country."[66] He added that many Panamanians wished that they could have accomplished Noriega's removal themselves. Nonetheless, in a public opinion poll taken during the first week of January, 92 percent approved of the invasion; a large majority also agreed with the statement that the U.S. military should stay for at least six months.[67] Observers cautioned that the United States probably would not be welcome much beyond that time.

Noriega's Surrender

For five days, Noriega and a group that included his bodyguards, aides, and others moved furtively from place to place. Noriega had been on the run since the invasion began, traveling in a small, yellow Hyundai instead of his well-known, dark, bullet-proof Mercedes. The administration and various commentators expected him to seek refuge in a foreign embassy—that of Cuba, Nicaragua, or Spain—in the hope that he could seek exile in a third country. To prevent such an outcome, U.S. forces surrounded these sites.[68] Noriega, however, developed a different plan, and surrendered at his own initiative on December 24, 1989. He went to a Dairy Queen store in a commercial neighborhood of Panama City, where he telephoned the Papal Nuncio, Monsignor José Sebastían Laboa, and asked for sanctuary. Laboa asked him on what grounds he was seeking sanctuary. Noriega replied by asking how he could be denied on Christmas Eve, reminding Laboa of Joseph and Mary seeking room at an inn. Laboa decided he could not turn Noriega away on Christmas Eve.

At 2:30 P.M., Noriega and ten others arrived at the Nunciature.[69] This began an occasionally tense ten-day diplomatic standoff between U.S. officials and the Papal Nuncio, punctuated with face-to-face conversations at the Nunciature gate. The Bush administration wanted Noriega and exerted considerable, and sometimes heavy-handed, pressure on Catholic authorities and the Nunciature.[70] For his part, Monsignor Laboa tried to accomplish three tasks: to facilitate Noriega's decision to give up; to fend off U.S. pressure, demands, and rock music; and to reconcile his embassy's responsibilities to the Vatican and the Panamanian government.

Initially, President Endara asserted that his government would not allow Noriega to be handed over to the United States by the Nuncio. His attorney general, Rogelio Cruz, strongly favored having Noriega tried in Panama; he filed charges against Noriega for killing and torturing officers involved in the October coup and for electoral fraud. Over the next several days, practical considerations swayed Endara's decision. Who, for example, would Noriega's jailers be? Endara, himself a lawyer, doubted that the current condition of Panama's legal and judicial systems could guarantee due process rights for Noriega. The Ministry of Justice had been sacked during the looting, and its records and facilities were a shambles. Evidence from Noriega's many offices and hideaways had been seized and taken by U.S. personnel. Cruz countered that Noriega could be held in a form of preventive detention in the United States.[71] Endara's final consideration was probably political: Panama needed to get on with its reconstruction and to look to the future, not the past.

The Nuncio was also in a tough spot. Diplomatically, the Nuncio and the Vatican were bound to uphold the centuries-old tradition of granting asylum. At the same time, the Nuncio did not want to obstruct justice if the government wanted to bring Noriega to trial. The Church had vocally and publicly criticized the Noriega regime; it was already committed to bringing Noriega and the PDF to justice. Technically, the Nuncio was accredited to deal only with the government of Panama, but much of his negotiating involved General Thurman, General Cisneros, and Deputy Assistant Secretary of State Michael Kozak.[72]

The Nuncio's most important task was to deal with Noriega. This eased somewhat when two of Noriega's aides decided to surrender on December 28, which set a precedent and deprived Noriega of some psychological support. Then a trusted senior adviser, Lt. Col. Nivaldo Madriñan, head of the secret police, surrendered and was taken into custody by U.S. troops. Noriega was increasingly isolated. Finally, the Nuncio made a significant inquiry: if tried in the United States as charged, could Noriega be sentenced to the death penalty? The United States responded that Noriega, who had been indicted before the drug law providing for that punishment was passed, would not face the death penalty in U.S. courts. This question was central to the Vatican's willingness to drop its insistence that Noriega could not be turned over to the United States.

A turning point came when Panama's twelve Catholic bishops called on the Vatican to turn Noriega over for trial in Panama or the United States. The central argument in their letter to Pope John Paul II was that Noriega must stand trial; exile was not the option they wanted for Noriega.

Noriega reportedly decided to give himself up at about 5:00 P.M. on January 4. Numerous news stories alleged that Laboa gave Noriega an ultimatum that he must leave at noon. A spokesman for the Nunciature said, however, that the Nuncio "told Noriega it would lift its diplomatic immunity and invite Panamanian forces inside to arrest him if he didn't leave . . . no specific deadline was set."[73] At that point, a trial in the United States probably looked like the better alternative. Noriega's decision was probably reinforced by massive demonstrations, staged the day he finally left the Nunciature, in which some 20,000 Panamanians gathered outside, chanting "Justice, justice," and demanding that he leave. One large sign held by a demonstrator read (in reference to Noriega's "Three P's" policy), "*Para Noriega: Las 3 "P" del Pueblo: Puño, Palo y Patadas!*" ("For Noriega: Three 'P's' of the People: Hit with a fist, strike with a stick, kick with a foot"). Some people chopped and smashed pineapples, actions Noriega could not see but ones that indicated the disposition of some in the crowd.[74]

Noriega walked out of the Nunciature at 8:48 P.M., accompanied by Monsignor Laboa. He had asked to wear his uniform, which U.S. officials obtained and provided. This was not a courtesy; they did not want to give Noriega any excuse to delay or renege. Noriega also asked for General Thurman to be present; Thurman was there, but he stood silently by, deliberately refusing to allow Noriega to make a military surrender. Instead, Noriega was taken across the field beside the Nunciature, placed aboard a Black Hawk helicopter and flown to Howard Air Force Base. There, he was transferred to DEA custody, searched, given a medical examination, dressed in a drab flight suit, and handcuffed. Noriega was transferred to a C-130 transport plane at 9:31 P.M.; once the plane entered U.S. jurisdiction, DEA agents read him his rights in Spanish and arrested him.[75]

A videotape of Noriega's surrender was shown repeatedly on U.S. television. Although General Thurman said Noriega looked "fine, vigorous and confident,"[76] the man who soon stood aboard the transport plane looked dazed. A U.S. official described Noriega as a "whipped and beaten little man."[77]

As news of the surrender spread through Panama City, demonstrations of joy and relief began. Prior to Noriega's departure, the invasion lacked a proper ending or closure. With Noriega finally en route to Homestead Air Force Base in south Florida, the Noriega years in Panama were officially over. Jubilant *pailas* took place as thousands filled the streets to cheer. President Endara said, "We are relieved to be rid of this criminal. . . . The people are happy to know that this monster has left our ground." A journalist reported from the scene: "Horns began to honk and fireworks went off around the Vatican mission. People yelled and laughed, and groups of youngsters raced up and down the streets waving Panamanian and U.S. flags."[78]

Criticism of the Invasion

The invasion was criticized in the United States and at international organizations as a violation of international law and the principle of nonintervention. One of the earliest moves was made by the Organization of American States. After debating throughout the night of December 21, 1989, the OAS passed a resolution criticizing the U.S. invasion. The United States tried to avert strong censure, but was only successful in gaining a slightly less stinging rebuke in English than in Spanish. The English version used the words "deeply regret"; the Spanish version was stronger, using "deeply deplore" to characterize the OAS position view of the invasion. The resolution also called on the United States to withdraw. Similar OAS initiatives had been attempted after the U.S. invasion of the Dominican Republic in 1965 and after Operation *Urgent Fury* in Grenada in 1983; both of those had been averted by the United States. In 1989, the United States stood alone: the vote on the resolution was twenty in favor, one against (the

United States), with six abstentions. This marked the first time in forty-two years—the entire history of the OAS—that the United States had been formally criticized in this way.[79]

To support the OAS resolution and indicate its opposition to U.S. policy, Peru broke diplomatic relations with the United States. Peru also refused, temporarily, to participate in an upcoming inter-American drug summit or joint drug enforcement activities.

The UN Security Council met on December 23 to consider a resolution sponsored by the Union of Soviet Socialist Republics and the People's Republic of China that strongly deplored U.S. actions and called for troop withdrawals. This was vetoed by the United States, France, and Great Britain. The invasion was then debated in the UN General Assembly on December 29. A resolution condemning the invasion as a "flagrant violation" of international law and calling for the swift removal of U.S. troops passed by a vote of seventy-five to twenty, with forty abstentions.[80] In addition to debating the invasion itself, the UN also faced a problem in deciding which Panamanian government—Provisional President Rodríguez's or President Endara's—to recognize as Panama's legitimate representative. Panama's UN ambassador had remained loyal to Noriega, unlike many in the diplomatic corps who had declared for Delvalle in 1988, and the General Assembly had given Panama's seat to the Rodríguez government in September.[81]

Other criticism, often made in the press, focused on the invasion itself, particularly on the destruction of El Chorrillo and the loss of life there when several blocks of wooden structures burned down. High numbers of Panamanian casualties, particularly civilian deaths, also drew criticism and were the subject of investigative reports. Several expert commentators on U.S. television broadcasts tried to question the legality of the U.S. invasion and to criticize the operation as an intervention contrary to international law.[82] By and large, however, criticism was muted and deflected by the Bush administration and by the generally enthusiastic tone of the media's coverage of the invasion.[83]

In Panama, criticism of the invasion was also muted. President Endara spoke forcefully against the OAS resolution, criticizing what he termed their "outmoded view" of nonintervention. He asserted that self-determination was a more important legal principle, and that self-determination must be based on the will of the people. "Everybody knew what the will of the Panamanian people was," he said.[84] To Endara, the results of the May 1989 election legitimated his presidency and should have overridden Latin American sensitivity on the issue of military intervention.

Endara, Arias Calderón, and Ford soon faced the challenge of trying to govern after coming to power through an invasion. The Bush administration had managed the December crisis and successfully executed a major military operation, but it, too, faced a new and more intractable challenge: establishing civilian government after twenty-one years of military rule.

Notes

1. Controversy still surrounds this point. Adela Giroldi later claimed that she emphatically stressed blocking *all* ("*todos*") the roads and that she conveyed a request for air support to prevent loyal troops from coming to Noriega's rescue by air. The Defense Department's version is that she referred to *two* ("*dos*") roads only and did not mention air support. The Department of State also disagreed with Mrs. Giroldi's account, asserting that her version changed after she went to Miami and was influenced by the exile community.

2. AP wire services, "Newswatch," October 3, 1989, 13:33 Central Time.

3. From 1987–1989, SOUTHCOM was commanded by General Woerner; his deputy CINC was Major General Fischer; the chief of staff was Rear Adm. Dick Ustick; J-2 was Brig. Gen. John Stewart; J-3 was Brig. Gen. Marc Cisneros; J-5 was Brig. Gen. Jim Le Cleir. Component commanders were: Army (USARSO), Maj. Gen. Bernard Loeffke; Air Force (USSOUTHAF), Lt. Gen. Peter Kempf; and Navy (USNAVSO), Rear Adm. Greckow. By October 3, these personnel changes were in effect: Thurman replaced Woerner, James replaced Fischer, Chandler replaced Ustick, Schneider replaced Steward, Hartzog replaced Cisneros, Fann replaced Le Cleir, and Cisneros replaced Loeffke.

4. Quoted in David E. Pitt, "Widow of Panamanian Coup Leader Says Fellow Plotter Betrayed Him," *The New York Times*, October 12, 1989.

5. David E. Pitt, "Panamanian Tells of Goal of Rebels," *The New York Times*, October 13, 1989, p. 6.

6. According to one report received in Washington, the rebels said they "want" to give up Noriega; a conflicting report said that they "won't" give up Noriega.

7. Quoted by Georgie Anne Geyer, "Washington Week in Review," PBS, October 6, 1989.

8. Pat Towell, "Failed Coup Against Noriega Stirs Hill Frustrations," *Congressional Quarterly Weekly Report*, October 7, 1989, p. 2660.

9. AP report, "Nunn: Bush Blew Coup Response," *Arkansas Democrat*, October 7, 1989, p. 5A.

10. Statement made on "Washington Week in Review," PBS, October 6, 1989.

11. AP report, October 3, 1989.

12. Bob Woodward and Joe Pichirallo, "Noriega Was to be Taken to U.S. Base, Sources Say," *The Washington Post*, October 8, 1989.

13. Ibid.

14. White House Chief of Staff John Sununu went so far as to summon two members of Helms's staff, including his Latin America specialist, Deborah DeMoss, to the White House and charge them with leaking classified information. DeMoss responded that she had her own, direct sources in Panama; Sununu was not satisfied. When DeMoss called the Comandancía to illustrate her access, Sununu desisted. This account is based on an interview with a Senate staff member, October 1990.

15. Statement made on "ABC News," ABC, October 4, 1989.

16. Interview with General Woerner, Washington, D.C., April 1990.

17. Personal interview, Panama City, August 1990.

18. AP report, "Noriega Courts Popularity, Lauds Support," *Arkansas Democrat*, October 9, 1989, 5A.

19. Quoted by Georgie Anne Geyer, "Washington Week in Review," PBS, October 6, 1989.

20. Andrew Rosenthal, "White House Aims to Sharpen Role in Panama Plots," *The New York Times*, October 13, 1989, p. 1.

21. The order was described by Jack Nelson on "Washington Week in Review," PBS, October 13, 1989. This order was also used as the legal basis for U.S. marshals to apprehend M. Ballesteros, an indicted drug trafficker, in Honduras.

22. Interview with General Woerner, Washington, D.C., April 1990.

23. Gordon, "U.S. Drafted Invasion Plan Weeks Ago," *The New York Times*, December 24, 1989, p. 5.

24. Ibid.

25. Interview with Col. Jack Pryor, Panama City, August 1990.

26. AP report, "CIA Plan to Oust Noriega Reported," November 17, 1989, p. 2.

27. Ibid.

28. Jack Nelson, "Washington Week in Review," PBS, October 27, 1989.

29. Personal interview, Panama City, August 1990.

30. NBC News, "Today," December 21, 1989. No other source, as yet, has confirmed this report.

31. Gordon, "U. S. Drafted Invasion Plan," p. 1.

32. Ibid.

33. Interview with Col. Jack Pryor, Panama City, August 1990.

34. Comments by Col. George Crocker, chief of staff of the 82nd Airborne Division, reported by Claude R. Marx, "Native Arkansan in Panama Defends Action," *Arkansas Democrat*, January 5, 1990, p. 9A.

35. Gordon, "U.S. Drafted Invasion . . . ," p. 5. This report also noted that the Pentagon, when asked whether the deployment of these units was related to the invasion, replied that their presence in Panama was "coincidental."

36. Miles, "Panama: Training to Fight," p. 39.

37. Statement by David Jones, National Public Radio reporter, Washington, D.C., April 1990.

38. AP report, *Arkansas Democrat*, December 14, 1989; this reported the promotion of forty-nine officers, including four new lieutenant colonels.

39. Reuters report, "Opposition Leader Rejects a Peace Offer by Noriega," December 17, 1989, p. 8.

40. This language was confirmed by several sources I interviewed in Panama City, August 1990. Each one considered the language to be a threat and a decisive departure from previous rhetoric.

41. "Opposition Leader Rejects," p. 8.

42. Ibid.

43. U.S. Department of State, Secret State 085518.

44. Cited in Michael R. Gordon, "U.S. Increases Panama Forces, Hinting Action," *The New York Times*, December 20, 1989, p. 1.

45. This account is a based on CNN and other news accounts and on Eloy O. Aguilar, "Crowd in Panama Slays U.S. Soldier," *Arkansas Democrat*, December 17, 1989, p. 1A.

46. Andrew Rosenthal, "President Calls Panama Slaying a Great Outrage," *The New York Times*, December 19, 1989, p. 1.

47. Gordon, "U.S. Increases," p. 11.

48. Sandy Davis, "Bullets Greeted Moves, C-130 Crewmen Recall," *Arkansas Democrat*, January 5, 1990, p. 1A. Lt. Col. Richard Mentemeyer, who was interviewed in this report, said he received these orders on October 17 but was not told about plans for the invasion until several days later.

49. Rosenthal, "President Calls Panama Slaying," p. 11; Eloy O. Aguilar, "U.S. officer shoots, injures Panamanian," *Arkansas Democrat*, December 19, 1989, p. 5A.

50. Rosenthal, "President Calls Panama Slaying," p. 11.

51. Ibid.

52. Ibid.

53. Interview with Col. Jack Pryor, Panama City, August 1990.

54. Ibid.

55. Lindsey Gruson, "Holiday Shopping for Panamanians," *The New York Times*, December 20, 1989, p. 11.

56. Quoted by Maureen Dowd, "Doing the Inevitable," *The New York Times*, December 24, 1989, p. 5.

57. Ibid.

58. Ibid.

59. "U.S. Troops Mobilize in Panama," *Arkansas Gazette*, December 20, 1989, p. 1; Michael R. Gordon, "U.S. Increases Panama Forces, Hinting Action," *The New York Times*, December 20, 1989, p. 1, 11.

60. CNN, "Pentagon Daily Briefing," December 21, 1989. General Woerner later commented that to catch Noriega, "it does not help to know where he was, nor very helpful to know where he is; what you must know is where he is going to be, if you want to be there at the same time." Paper presented at the annual meeting of the International Studies Association, Washington, D.C., April 1990.

61. An edited volume analyzing the operation, with contributions by military analysts, has just been published; this provides detailed assessments of *Just Cause* as an operation and its components, and contains comparisons to operations in Grenada and Saudi Arabia; Watson and Tsouras, *Operation Just Cause*.

62. "Transcript of the President's Speech," *The New York Times*, December 22, 1989.

63. "Panama's Would-Be President," *Time*, January 1, 1990, p. 30.

64. John McClintock, "3,500 Soldiers at Key Post Agree to Surrender," *Arkansas Democrat*, December 23, 1989, p. 10A.

65. "Passing the Manhood Test," *Time*, January 8, 1990, p. 43.

66. Interview on CNN, December 22, 1989.

67. "Noriega Surrenders," *Newsweek*, January 15, 1990, pp. 17–18.

68. Rodolfo Garcia, "Nicaraguan Demands Hearing on Search of Diplomat's Home," AP report, *Arkansas Democrat*, January 1, 1990, 11A.

69. An AP report ("Noriega's Fate in Hands of Vatican," *Arkansas Democrat*, December 29, 1989, p. 2A) said that this group included two top aides, Lt. Col. Carlos Velardes and Lt. Col. Arnulfo Castrejon. This report also stated that another aide, Lt. Col. Roberto Cedeno, was arrested elsewhere.

70. U.S. troops surrounded the Nunciature. One day they blared rock music at the building; selections included "No Place to Run," "Voodoo Chile," and "You're No Good." One report suggested that the troops were just frustrated and trying to pressure Noriega; another suggested that the loud noise was a necessary cover to block surveillance of conversations at the gate.

71. Eloy O. Aguilar, "Panama Brands Noriega Killer, Drafts Charges," *Arkansas Democrat*, January 1, 1990, p. 1A.

72. Andrew Rosenthal, "Vatican Issues an Ultimatum and a General Takes a Walk," *The New York Times*, January 5, 1990, p. 7.

73. AP report, "Week at a Glance," *Arkansas Democrat*, January 5, 1990, p. 9A.

74. Peter Copeland and Ann McFeatters, "Noriega Spent Embassy Time Alone," *Arkansas Democrat*, January 5, 1990, p. 9A.

75. "'Maximum Leader' Loses His Uniform," *Arkansas Gazette*, January 5, 1990, p. 8A.

76. AP report, "Noriega Flown to U.S. for Arraignment," *Arkansas Democrat*, January 4, 1990, p. 2A.

77. "Noriega's Surrender," p. 14.

78. AP report, Eloy O. Aguilar, "Noriega Walks into U.S. Arms, Ends Standoff," *Arkansas Democrat*, January 4, 1990, p. 1A.

79. John M. Goshko and Michael Isikoff, "OAS Passes Resolution of Censure," *The Washington Post*, reprinted in *Arkansas Democrat*, December 23, 1989, p. 10A.

80. AP report, *Arkansas Democrat*, December 24, 1989, p. 13A; AP report, *Arkansas Democrat*, December 30, 1989, p. 10A.

81. Paul Lewis, "Third World Likely to Seek Condemnation of U.S.," *The New York Times*, December 24, 1989, p. 4.

82. Charles Maechling, Jr., "Washington's Illegal Invasion."

83. For a critical analysis of news coverage of *Just Cause*, see Mark Hertsgaard, "How the News Media Let Us Down in Panama," *Rolling Stone*, March 8, 1990, pp. 77–78.

84. Guillermo Endara, "Address at the National Press Club," May 1, 1990, televised on C-SPAN.

8

After the Invasion:
Civilians In, But for How Long?

A new chapter in Panamanian politics and U.S.-Panamanian relations began
in January 1990. Ten years earlier, the United States had begun the decade
hoping that Gen. Omar Torrijos's plans for civilianization could be fulfilled.
Those plans were derailed during the Noriega years. In 1990 the dual process
of democratization and demilitarization resumed in rather different
circumstances than Torrijos had imagined. Given the enormity of the task and
the fragile base on which to build democratic institutions, many observers
gave odds that the new government would last less than a year. The civilians
were in power, but how long could they last?

In 1990 President George Bush and the civilian coalition—President
Guillermo Endara, First Vice-President Ricardo Arias Calderón, and Second
Vice-President Billy Ford—were committed to the goals of democratization
and demilitarization. Each had a clear and present vested interest in success.
The fate of the three Panamanian leaders, in the short term and in the 1994
election, will depend on their ability to deliver economic and political
progress and to reach a satisfactory and durable accommodation with the
military. For President Bush, the long-term evaluation of his decision to
launch Operation *Just Cause* will depend upon the performance of Panama's
civilian government. Moreover, during 1990–1991, U.S. policy toward the
region was also focused on democratization; Panama and Nicaragua are the
exemplars for Central America. According to the Department of State, U.S.
Panama policy had four objectives during 1990–1991: (1) to assist in
economic reconstruction and development, with a particular emphasis on
privatization as a strategy to decrease the size of the public sector, (2) to
assist the Panamanian government "toward achieving its goal of an apolitical
police force," (3) to continue implementation of the Panama Canal treaty and
needed maintenance of the canal, and (4) to gain Panamanian cooperation on
narcotics enforcement issues, particularly the as yet unsigned MLAT.[1]
Reinforcement for Panama policy from consistent objectives at the regional
level was expected to contribute to the provision of resources and attention to

Panama during the next few years while presidential attention necessarily shifted to other priorities. As the decade progresses, implementation of the 1978 Panama Canal treaty and U.S. concern about gaining base rights after the year 2000 should keep U.S. attention and resources focused on Panama. At the outset of the 1990s, prospects for U.S.-Panamian relations appeared to be favorable.

Aftermath of the Invasion

In Panama, 1990 began with democratization objectives taking a back seat to the immediate imperatives of restoring order, assuming office, and beginning a new administration without a transition. Normally, candidates have several months to prepare to take office, and although Endara, Arias Calderón, and Ford had hoped to take office eventually, their hasty installation deprived them of an orderly transition. Moreover, they were assuming command of institutions that had been looted and ravaged during Noriega's last year in power. The Treasury was almost empty, down to $70 million. Basic resources such as garbage trucks and insecticide were missing and unaccounted for, financial accounts were inaccessible, and government buildings had been sacked and looted. Before the philosophical and practical aspects of civilianization could be considered, the Endara "government" had to manage some immediate problems, including Noriega's legal case. The Endara government was operating in a disaster-filled environment. Politically, as they tried to make a new beginning, their task was complicated by old grudges crowding onto the agenda.

People denounced symbols of the old regime. At its opening session, the National Assembly debated whether a large mural of Torrijos, just outside the Legislative Palace, should be taken down. The outcry against Torrijos and "twenty-one years of dictatorship" was so great that authorities feared someone might desecrate Torrijos's burial site. The urn containing Torrijos's ashes was moved from his monument to a church down the street, supposedly a safer location; however, the urn was stolen from the church. Individuals associated with the military regime were castigated, in person and in the press.

Roberto Eisenmann returned from exile to publish *La Prensa*; the acerbic political commentator Guillermo Sánchez-Borbon was back at work, directing the barbs of "En Pocas Palabras" at Endara and his government instead of Noriega and the PDF. *La Prensa*, along with other newspapers and radio stations, took maximum advantage of the freedom of the press the media expected to enjoy under the new regime. Existing laws restraining the press, however, had not been changed, nor had the expectations or habits of politicians. The new government was no more comfortable being satirized and criticized than Noriega had been; the civilians' response was much milder, but its first inclination was to counterattack its critics. When Arias Calderón's decisions on a new military were vigorously debated in the press, the vice president called his critics "bad Panamanians," in an attempt to discredit their motives and intimidate them into silence. When Professor Miguel Bernal said, without naming names, that the government was guilty of nepotism, Endara's response was to suggest that he could be jailed. Two days later, Bernal was invited to meet Endara at the president's office; but he was neither jailed nor silenced. Instead, the meeting was covered on the nightly news, and a picture of the men talking cordially appeared on the front page of *La Prensa*.[2] The new government was different from the military regime, but it, too, exhibited a predisposition toward intolerance.

The new government tried to harness the public outcry against the old regime. The Comandancía—the headquarters of the PDF and the most visible symbol of Noriega's regime—had been badly damaged during the invasion. In January 1990, it was being leveled. President Endara and Vice-President Arias Calderón participated in a ceremony smashing the building with sledgehammers. Endara proclaimed, "On the ashes of militarism we will build a better Panama."[3] The imagery was similar to the destruction of the Berlin Wall: a symbol of the old regime was being torn down. In a few weeks, only rubble remained on the huge, vacant block where the massive military headquarters once stood. Plans were announced to build in its place a housing project, to be called *La Plaza de la Democracia* (Democracy Plaza), with sixty new buildings. Eight months later, a large billboard still asked residents to have patience: "*¡Tengan Paciencia . . . Reconstruiremos El Chorrillo!*" ("Be Patient . . . We Are Reconstructing El Chorrillo!") By the end of the year, however, the rubble still remained and only one pair of new apartments, named December 20 to commemorate the destruction of Chorrillo, had been built. By mid-1991, Democracy Plaza was still only a plan. A memorial marker had been placed at the former site of the Comandancía by activist Mayín Correa. The inscription on the small stone read: "*Monumento a los Martires Caidos Tras La Invasion Norteamericana a Panama 20 de Dic. de '89*" ("Monument to the Martyrs Killed in the North American Invasion of Panama 20 December 1989").

Ten blocks of Chorrillo were destroyed by the attack on the Comandancía and by fires, which quickly gutted the old wooden buildings. Between 10,000 and 18,000 people were left homeles, and hundreds were killed during the attack and fires. Human rights organizations spent the better part of the year trying to verify reports of deaths and missing persons who might have died during the invasion. Controversy continued over conflicting casualty counts; exhumations of mass graves of Chorrillo victims were particularly anguishing.[4]

Displaced residents of Chorrillo either moved in with relatives and friends or were temporarily housed at Balboa Junior High School and then settled into a camp in a massive hangar at Albrook Field. Those at the camp lived in tiny roofless cubicles measuring about twelve feet square. By mid-1991, thousands of families were still living at the camp. Young children attended classes at a preschool in a room at the back of the hangar; some of the older children were placed at schools, but many were not. Many of the men went to work or looked for work. To obtain the $6,500 per family available in U.S. assistance, applicants had to provide documentation of residence in Chorrillo and of financing or construction for replacement housing. This involved a lengthy process that was frustrating for applicants and administrators.

Residents of other areas, particularly in Panama City, experienced different problems: lack of water, electricity, and other services, and fear of crime. By June 1990, Panama was experiencing one murder per day, along with increasing numbers of thefts and robberies. At the same time that people were increasingly worried about personal security, they were also suspicious of the police and the former PDF personnel who joined the new force. Disgruntled citizens protested in the streets, blocking intersections and demanding better services. People used the new political climate to demand results from the government. At first the tactic worked, and street protests for services received emergency treatment. But the government quickly realized that crisis management triggered by street closings could not become the norm. After a few weeks, protests were disbursed by the new police force.

Economically, Panama had suffered not just the effects of the invasion but also the more devastating impact of two years of external economic sanctions and the pillaging of government facilities and the national treasury as Noriega struggled to survive. Even six months after the invasion, Panama's unemployment rate ranged from 30 to 40 percent. Panamanian Vice-President Ford estimated that 150,000 people were unemployed. President Endara identified unemployment as the biggest problem facing the country, but acknowledged that the government could do little. "We are bankrupt," he said.[5]

The Bush administration also faced political challenges in its dealings with postinvasion issues. Immediate assistance—in the form of food and blankets; medical supplies; civil affairs, other technical advisers, and U.S. MPs on patrol—was easily provided. Economic aid, however, faced severe competition between traditional recipients' claims and new claims arising from dramatic changes in Eastern Europe. Congress was slow to act on aid for Panama—so slow that in May, President Endara visited Capitol Hill to lobby. By the end of the year, although most of the U.S. aid package had been allocated, many of the dollars had not reached Panama.

The Endara government faced the enormous challenge of economic reconstruction and political reconciliation. As the year progressed, several thorny issues arose and remained on the rebuilding agenda. The most significant of these were civilian-military relations, aid for reconstruction and plans for national development, and constitutional reform. Before these long-term issues could be addressed, however, the new government had to deal with more immediate problems: Noriega's status and legal disposition and the form a new military force would take. As it considered these problems and issues, the new government seemed to bog down in intercoalition bickering, occasionally over issues, but more often over how to divide the spoils of office.

Noriega's Trial

Noriega began the year as U.S. Prisoner #41586 at the Metropolitan Correctional Center outside Miami, Florida. Early on January 5, 1990, a motorcade with tight security brought Noriega to the federal district courthouse in Miami. In the courtroom, Noriega's attorney, Frank Rubino, told Judge William Hoeveler that Noriega refused to submit to the jurisdiction of the court. Hoeveler rejected his claim that Noriega had immunity as a head of state. Next, Rubino argued that Noriega was a "political prisoner," brought to the United States "illegally."[6] Judge Hoeveler entered an innocent plea for Noriega. Then he asked Noriega, through an interpreter, if he was in good health ("Yes, sir."), had taken any medication in the last twelve hours ("No, sir."), or had seen a psychiatrist during the last year ("Absolutely not.").[7] The entire proceeding lasted only twenty minutes.

Preparations for Noriega's trial, however, lasted much longer. On the prosecution side, the case was considered to be long on testimony by Noriega's associates, most of whom were already indicted or convicted, but weak on physical evidence. The defense was expected to pursue an Oliver North–graymail strategy: using sensitive government documents to prove that the defendant was not guilty because he was acting with the knowledge of the U.S. government. On April 30, 1991, for example, Rubino claimed to have "documents showing attempts to assassinate General Noriega and Mr. Torrijos by agencies of the United States."[8]

Although the Endara government stripped him of his rank and dismissed him from the military in January, Noriega continued wearing his uniform. He made several court appearances during the year; most of these concerned defense motions to acquire funds for legal fees and access to evidence, estimated to amount to 50 tons of documents, seized during the invasion. The trial was originally scheduled to begin in April 1991. Noriega's lawyers asked for several delays, many on the grounds that they could not prepare an adequate defense because the Bush administration had frozen twenty-seven of Noriega's bank accounts, in the United States and abroad, depriving him of $20 million. In June 1990, Judge Hoeveler ordered government prosecutors to unfreeze $6 million for Noriega's defense, but by mid-November Noriega's attorneys still had not gained access to those funds.[9]

In January 1991, the government of Austria agreed to release $1.6

million from one of Noriega's accounts, and Noriega's defense team agreed to develop a reduced fee arrangement. The case was further complicated when the government of Panama filed a $5 million suit against Noriega in Miami federal district court. Nonetheless, in late January, Judge Hoeveler said, "This case is set to go to trial on June 24, and I will expect it will go to trial on that day."[10]

Demilitarization

After twenty-one years of military rule, the process of establishing civilian government was bound to be difficult, for officers as well as politicians. Those who forecast a short tenure for Panama's civilian leaders cited a military coup as one possible means of their demise. As of December 31, 1990, President Endara was still in office, but the government had been pressured to fire two top military commanders, in fairly rapid succession, and to replace the commander with a civilian official. Disgruntled officers staged an action in December 1990, widely described as an attempted coup, to protest government policies and lack of respect for the military. Although the civilians remained in power in mid-1991, expert observers continued to assert that their status was tenuous. The civilians spent much of their first year trying to reduce the power and status of the military, causing some analysts to wonder how long they could last.

The relationship between civilians and police was the most controversial issue in Panama and in U.S.-Panamanian relations during 1990. Changing that relationship involved two related struggles: one between the civilian government and the military, and one within the civilian government over who would not only control parts of the PF but also thereby gain a military power base. Several Panamanian leaders argued that the Costa Rican model—having a national police but no army—would be best. This view was advocated by prominent journalists, several legislators, and, not surprisingly, the president of Costa Rica, Oscar Arias. The United States initially appeared to advocate, with some Panamanian support, a dual force structure: national police plus specialized anti-guerrilla, anti-terrorist, and canal defense units. The police and security force structure that evolved during 1990 was clearly closer to the Costa Rican model than the PDF had been; however, a new anti-terrorist/anti-crime, fast reaction unit was trained and deployed in August 1990 in response to a series of major bank robberies. The power of the new National Police and the relationship between civilians and former military continue to evolve.

To promote both demilitarization and democratization, the legal basis of civilian authority over the military was strengthened. Although a new organic law has not yet been passed to replace Law 20, two cabinet decrees, #38 and #42, redefined the legal parameters within which police and security forces operate. Cabinet Decree #38, issued in mid-February 1990, formally created the *Fuerza Pública*, the Public Force (PF). The president was named commander in chief, and all PF members *must* swear loyalty to him and the constitution; moreover, police units *should* "act as agents of civilian authorities at the municipal and regional levels."

To further reduce the power of the PF, components of the military, enforcement, and investigative power were separated and assigned to different branches. The PF was described as subordinate to the executive branch, a relationship entirely different from the former legal provision, which required harmonious collaboration of the executive with the PDF. As checks on the president and minister of justice, Decree #38 specified that PF finances shall be the responsibility of the comptroller and that the size of the PF shall be determined by the legislative branch. This decree also prohibited PF members from engaging in any political activity, a provision which, if actually followed, would depart from approximately forty years of political tradition.[11] After only a little more than a year, and no severe test cases, it is too soon to judge the extent to which these formal provisions will affect the behavior of officers and politicians.

What was well established by mid-1991, however, was a clear sense of direction in the Ministry of Government and Justice. Arias Calderón's deputy in charge of the PF, Ebrahim Asvat, explained the policy. "We want a civilian police force. We must change the military mentality into a police mentality." He also addressed the functions of the specialized forces: "We are not going to have anything that is a national guard, but called a police, or an army called police. That is not our policy." To achieve and solidify the transformation from a military to a civilian mentality, the ministry sought to separate administrative responsibility from operations. Asvat explained, "Every policeman should be doing operational matters and leaving to civilians all the administrative aspects." A related change involved institutionalizing procedures and rules, "administrative rationality," into the operation of the police.

Through structural changes, separating specialized security forces from the National Police, and subordinating them to different civilian authorities, the ministry planned to create checks and balances to strengthen civilian administrative control. Different elements of the police and security forces were placed under the control of different branches. The Ministry of Government and Justice would administer the National Police, which was expected to number 8,000 police personnel; the Air Service, with about 380 personnel; the Coast Guard; and Immigration and Customs. The attorney general, who operates separately from the Ministry of Government and Justice, would administer prisons and hold security personnel accountable. The Technical Judicial Police (TPJ), is the investigation unit that replaced the PDF's National Department of Investigations (DENI). The president also has a security force that initially was formed to guard his safety but recently was reported to have also gained an intelligence function.[12] It contains about 800 members, and was also likely to be placed under the attorney general's control.

The Bush administration initially seemed divided over how Panama's military should be restructured, with a variety of options being debated in Washington. The consensus reached, under pressure from looting and crime on the streets plus the president's desire to bring U.S. troops home quickly, endorsed a police-plus-specialized forces. These "should be sufficiently strong to maintain order but not so strong that it could turn back into . . . a 'Praetorian Guard.'"[13] Panama's Ministry of Government and Justice and U.S. advisers were particularly interested in developing routines of due process and manuals for police officers to follow. Consultants and advisers from the United States, provided under the Department of Justice's International Criminal Investigations and Training Assistance Program (ICITAP), were closely involved in deliberations over structural and procedural changes. Some strains were evident between ICITAP advisers and some U.S. military advisers. Asvat posed the issue diplomatically: "The process of demilitarization in Panama will also require demilitarization of the relationship between the United States and Panama." In the past, both SOUTHCOM and the Department of Defense had more access to Panamanian politics than the Department of State; for demilitarization to succeed, Asvat argued, the formers' access must be redirected through civilian leaders. The U.S. military must learn, just as Panamanians must learn, to take their concerns to the civilian authorities, not the police sergeants. Moreover, Asvat argued, for the new mentality to be set, officers leading the National Police simply cannot be on an equal footing with U.S. generals and colonels.

One example of the strains that emerged between the United States and Panama concerned the name of the PF. Cabinet Decree #38 used *Fuerza Pública*, but Panamanians soon began referring to that entire entity as the *Policía Nacional*, the National Police. The symbolism was important to Panamanian civilians, but many U.S. officials insisted on calling the organization Public Force. Some officers in the PF also resisted the name National Police, just as they resisted relinquishing their olive drab for the new tan police uniforms the United States provided. After months of sparring, the Bush administration accepted the name National Police; whether the United States also accepted the limited mission the name implied is not yet clear.

Leaders in Panama and Washington were united in their immediate concern with forming a police organization to replace U.S. MPs on the streets. As a result, steps to recruit and deploy Panamanian police were taken before the larger issues of mission and structure for the new institution were resolved. Immediate needs of the United States to exit as quickly as possible and of the Endara government to have Panamanians join U.S. MPs on patrol dictated a political decision that had lasting implications.[14] The need to act quickly led directly to personnel choices that marred the image the National Police was supposed to project.

These needs dictated an answer to the controversial question of whether former PDF members could serve. The answer had to be yes, but that the worst elements would be excluded. The immediate problem was how to distinguish between those who could join the police and those who must be either purged or rejected. Early in January, thirty-nine "die-hard Noriega loyalists" were forcibly retired without benefits; another forty-two former high-ranking officers with more than twenty-five years of service were retired with full benefits.[15]

The United States put the remaining members of the PDF through what officials described as an "elaborate screening process to determine if any charges should be brought against them"; afterward, only 600 remained in custody.[16] The process was well intended, and, in the postinvasion context, any former PDF officer was bound to attract somebody's criticism. Nonetheless, the screening process was hasty and controversial. Repeated and severe criticism was voiced over the decision by Arias Calderón and U.S. officials to rapidly reemploy those who declared loyalty to the new government. A columnist summarized the critique: "Now we are signing up many of the same Panamanians and giving them guns in the name of law and order. They march about, proclaiming their new devotion to democracy. Americans may believe them, but not Panamanian civilians who may be beaten again by these guardians of freedom."[17] An editorial writer for *The Nation* who visited Panama in January 1990 asked government officials "What security threats do you have in mind?" The two most mentioned were "drug trafficking or subversion sponsored by Nicaragua or Cuba." Other people interviewed expressed the fear that the new PF would be used against labor activitists, leftist intellectuals, or "people involved in popular organizing." The editorialist drew this conclusion: "The crucial question is not whether the Public Force is a police force or an army but how it acts."[18] The situation was not helped by comments made by police officers that were rumored and reported in the press, such as, "When the gringos go home, we'll take over again."[19]

To inaugurate the new force, the Endara government attended a special mass, celebrated by Archbishop Marcos McGrath, with the new force on January 6, 1990. Present as officers were some who had opposed Noriega, some who had appeared neutral, and a number who had remained loyal to Noriega.[20] They comprised an uneasy coalition whose loyalty to the new government was uncertain. By late 1990, personnel in the National Police, including police and various specialized units, numbered between 10,000 and 12,000. Asvat kept a running tally on numbers of former PDF officers who were no longer serving at all. As of August 1990, all of the former PDF colonels were out; also out were 83 percent of the lieutenant colonels, 40 percent of the majors, 33 percent of the captains, 20 percent of the lieutenants, and 10 percent of the second lieutenants.[21] These figures reflected significant personnel changes, particularly at the higher ranks. Nonetheless, some of the officers who took senior positions in the National Police attracted substantial public criticism. Aristides Valdonedo's case illustrates the quandary that faced former officers as a group, the ministry, and Panamanian oppositionists.

Valdonedo had participated in the abortive March 1988 coup; he was one of the majors who recognized that the PDF had to be changed.[22] After the coup, he faced the same harsh treatment as other plotters who did not escape; Valdonedo was tortured and imprisoned for twenty-one months. To Vice-President Arias Calderón and U.S. advisers, Valdonedo had "paid his dues"; if he were willing to work with the new system, which would entail more reform than he had initially intended, they had a place for him. He was promoted to lieutenant colonel and made second in command of the National Police. To oppositionists who had been harassed and beaten by Valdonedo prior to March 1988, however, his new job was a travesty of justice. Roberto Arosemena Jaen, for example, wrote a statement for *La Prensa* describing how Valdoneda had banged his head against the wall, spit in his face, and supervised the beatings of *civilistas* who were rounded up and jailed on October 20, 1987. Arosemena held Valdonedo responsible for cowing the National Civic Crusade's protest movement just at the moment when Noriega was vulnerable.[23] He accused the new government of throwing an "amnesia blanket" over officers' past human rights violations; Arosemena was then accused by Arias Calderón of making a suspicious "attack on the military men who are committed to democracy."[24] Valdonedo was eventually removed from office, as was Fernando Quezada, another participant in the March 1988 coup, who also held a senior position in the National Police.

This controversy was more than a feud between two men; it was a clash of political forces. In the debate over blame to be assigned for past wrongs and over future directions for Panama, the clash between Arosemena and Valdonedo symbolized those broader issues. During 1987 and 1988, civilian oppositionists had felt pressed to work with former enemies when those broke ranks with Noriega; in 1990 that lesson was still difficult to learn. Valdonedo's case illustrates the intricate political context in which the new government was operating. Accusations of past wrongdoing were also leveled against Col. Eduardo Herrera Hassan, Col. Díaz Herrera, and against politicians, including former presidents Nicolás Barletta and Eric Arturo Delvalle. Past grievances were inserted into current policy debates; political rivalries abounded—among supporters of one leader, among supporters of rival leaders, among the leaders themselves, and between leaders and the opposition press. An outsider might consider Quezada and Valdonedo as the best alternatives available, from within the Panamanian military, to hold senior positions in the National Police and serve as a bridge between the old institution and the new. Neither of these military men could survive the intricacies of Panamanian politics and the multiple, cross-cutting power struggles that were under way during 1990.

The problem of selecting a commander for the National Police proved to be just as difficult. The first appointee, Col. Roberto Armijo, resigned on January 3, 1990, after less than two weeks in office. Armijo had been loyal to Noriega up until the invasion, but he was the only member of Noriega's inner circle who was acceptable to the Endara government and the United States. Because he was scheduled to retire in a few months, Armijo's past ties were considered less important than his image as a senior professional who could provide continuity during the crucial first few months. But Armijo's past ties soon proved to be too tainted for him to continue in office.[25] Investigations by the new attorney general brought to light evidence of Armijo's corruption: "unexplained bank certificates totalling as much as $1.5 million had been found in his personal account under his name."[26]

Armijo's resignation was also interpreted as part of the still unresolved debate over the mission and structure of the police. The choice of a successor provided an indicator of the progress of that debate. Col. Eduardo Herrera Hassan, who had broken with Noriega in 1983 and had been involved in the covert operation named Panama 3, was promoted from being Armijo's assistant to the position of commander. Rumors had credited Herrera Hassan with operational control of the new force during Armijo's brief tenure; thus, his selection represented a "normal" promotion. Herrera Hassan's opposition to Noriega, however, represented a power shift in favor of rebel and exiled officers, particularly the Miami group, who advocated a professional military. Although their aims were not entirely clear, officers associated with this group chafed under civilian control, the limits of a police organization, and what they perceived as lack of respect for their institution.

By September, 142 officers at the highest ranks were "retired," including the commander, Col. Herrera Hassan.[27] Civilian-military tensions were responsible for Herrera Hassan's removal and the appointment of a civilian, Ebrahim Asvat, as head of the National Police. A U.S. official assessed the significance of this change: "By putting in a civilian chief of police, there's a message to all concerned that it was time to climb on board, and if you're not going to be part of the transition, you're gone."[28]

Two threats to the new government were mounted by discontented officers, one before and one after Asvat's appointment. Col. Eduardo Herrera Hassan, the second commander of the PF who was fired in August 1990 on suspicion of involvement in plots, was implicated in the first and involved in the second. The first incident occurred in October, when a plot to take over the government in conjunction with labor demonstrations on October 16, 1990, was discovered and thwarted.[29] Few observers considered this plot to be a serious threat to the government. Two months later, disgruntled officers staged a more serious operation, which the government described as an attempted coup, to protest government policies and lack of respect for the military. In December, rebel officers sprung Herrera Hassan from jail, possibly against his will. The colonel and some thirty officers, plus between twenty and forty men, then stormed the national police headquarters, took over the building, and issued political demands. Instead of using its own personnel, the Endara government requested U.S. military assistance to regain control of the building and subdue the rebel officers. Some analysts argued that Herrera Hassan's action was politically motivated: the colonel was reluctantly drafted to represent the grievances of some officers who were more intent upon mounting a labor "action" than a coup.

Scenes of the incident looked strangely disproportionate. The colonel walked freely as he left the building, talking amiably with his unarmed escorts. The men involved in the operation, in marked contrast, were forcibly subdued, their faces pressed to the ground, by heavily armed U.S. soldiers. These events reflect the problems former officers have had about their status, respect, and treatment in transforming themselves into police. The fact that the government had to call on U.S. troops to come to its aid, in full battle gear, also reflects an incomplete transition.

As of May 1991, Asvat had vacated the commander's job and returned to his law practice, a step he had planned before accepting that assignment. The status of the National Police, as a law enforcement organization and as a political force, continues to evolve.

Two problems are apparent. First, on the officers' side of the reform equation, significant elements of the PF are dissatisfied with the reforms, as Herrera Hassan's removal and the October and December "incidents" revealed. The expected period of officers' testing the government's determination to exert civilian authority is still under way. Second, on the politicians' side, is the problem of resisting the temptation to turn responsibility over a military or security force into a power base for influencing other politicians and one's own political future. Panama has a long tradition of presidential hopefuls and incumbents developing a military or paramilitary base to further their political ambitions. Part of the current struggle between Endara and Arias Calderón and other PDC ministers, all of whom were removed from the Cabinet on April 9, 1991, concerns this temptation.

Economic Aid and Development

Initially, President Endara and private experts said that at least $1.5 billion would be needed to reconstruct the areas of Panama City destroyed in the invasion. Economic assistance from the United States, however, was much less. In addition to U.S. budget and deficit constraints, Panama's needs competed with other salient claims on the foreign aid bill. Aid for Panama had to compete with assistance for the newly elected Chamorro government in Nicaragua and with aid for Eastern Europe, in addition to the claims of traditional aid recipients. The Bush administration eventually obtained passage of $200 million in emergency economic aid for public employment programs and $40 million to rebuild homes in Chorrillo. For fiscal years 1990 and 1991, U.S. assistance to Panama includes $452 million in economic aid and $500 million in loans and guarantees.[30]

Vice-President Billy Ford, as minister of planning, was responsible for the national development plan and coordinating Panamanian and U.S. objectives. The Bush administration set several objectives for and constraints on U.S. aid to Panama; these were explicitly written into the aid agreement. Chief among these were restoration of the country's credit worthiness and payments of arrears owed to banks, reduction of the size of the public sector and privatization of various services, and gaining Panama's consent to a Mutual Legal Affairs Treaty and tougher banking laws that would facilitate prosecution of drug trafficking and money laundering.[31] Economic performance measures for 1990 showed some progress toward recovery. Panama's rate of GNP growth was estimated to be 5 percent; bank deposits increased by over $2 billion; unemployment decreased from 35 percent to about 21 percent; and inflation remained low.[32]

Democratization

As 1990 progressed, Panama seemed poised at a turning point. Much of the military regime had been swept away by the invasion. The institutions and connections that Torrijos and Noriega had built appeared to be smashed.

The new government comprised an uneasy coalition of three men with different personalities and agendas representing three different political parties. President Endara, who was one of Arnulfo Arias's closest aides, proclaimed himself to be an Arnulfista during 1990 and tried to capture that constituency. Endara lacked a strong base in the Legislative Assembly, however. Arias Calderón's party held the greatest number of seats, twenty-seven out of sixty-seven. This legislative bloc gave the first vice-president strong connections to the legislature, but his most pressing problems arose from his ministerial responsibilities over the police and judicial systems. Billy Ford's party, MOLIRENA, held fifteen Assembly seats. Acclaimed as the best politician among the three, Ford faced the most obdurate challenges with the fewest resources. As minister of planning, Ford was responsible for economic reconstruction and development. The governing coalition faced two serious challenges more fundamental than the practical problems they were trying to solve: they needed to show solidarity in the face of mounting opposition, and to overcome Arnulfo Arias's legacy of ineffective opposition to the military and an inability to govern. Tension among the three was reported early in 1990; the situation worsened in 1991. Endara's relations with Arias Calderón were described as strained, and PDC ministers were removed from the cabinet on April 9, 1991. For democratic governance to be institutionalized after military rule, many civilians—those in government, former oppositionists and supporters of the military regime, plus people previously excluded, repressed, or disinterested—must learn political behaviors appropriate to a representative political system.[33]

During 1990 and 1991, as the democratization process began, Panamanians debated the extent to which they possessed the democratic foundations necessary to build a new regime. The government faced a series of difficult issues: dealing with challenges to its legitimacy, undertaking institutional reform, and overcoming racial and class divisions. By mid-1991, some observers argued that politics as usual would no longer suffice and that these issues, along with fundamental constitutional reform, should be addressed in an extraordinary way.

Reinterpreting the Past

During the U.S. invasion, President Bush proclaimed that democracy had been restored to Panama. The extent to which a democratic tradition had existed in Panama which could be restored—vs. being established for the first time—has been a matter of debate. While Noriega was still in power, pages of *La Prensa Digest* carried an exchange on this question. That debate continued after the invasion.

A blunt characterization once made by Sol Linowitz, a business executive and former U.S. ambassador, typified one perspective: "Panama has no history of democratic rule."[34] Opposing positions were articulated by Panamanian lawyer and historian, Julio Linares, and by *La Prensa* editor Bobby Eisenmann, who characterized Panama's pre-1968 condition as "an imperfect, evolving constitutional democracy." As the *Digest* editor, Elizabeth Brannan Jaen, correctly opined, the debate over Panama's past experiences and traditions was being clouded with myths. Those who opposed the traditional power structure, which was dominated by the oligarchy, asserted that Panama had no democracy from 1903–1968; they claimed that the idea that democracy had existed during those years was a myth; the reality they perceived was a system of elite domination with frequent turnovers among a narrow group, fraudulent elections, and indifference to the needs of the people. Critics of the military regime characterized as myth the claim by the military and PRD that the "revolution of 1968" had initiated a form of representation and democracy. Steve C. Ropp, a scholar and close observer of Panamanian politics, warned of the danger of reinterpreting the past:

> I take serious exception to the argument that those who claim that Panama has never had a true democracy under either civilian *or* military rule are merely apologists for the current [Noriega] regime.
> I would argue that the myth that Panama has experienced past periods of democratic rule is even more dangerous because it suggests

that merely removing the PDF from power will be *sufficient in and of itself* to reestablish democracy. This is clearly not the case.[35]

Fraud has marred recent elections. Not only does Panama's history reflect a weak electoral tradition, it also reveals repeated lack of continuance in office once installed, and lack of stable successions from one administration to another. As Panamanian sociologist Marco Gandásegui points out, Panama only has one experience, in 1960, in which the opposition won a presidential election *and* achieved a successful transfer of power.[36] Such a weak foundation is one reason that predictions about the Endara government's prospects have been so cautious and qualified.

Legitimacy

The new government faced a crisis of credibility and legitimacy. Although the Endara slate was widely credited with having achieved a three-to-one vote margin against the PRD slate in the 1989 election, the candidates were installed by a foreign military intervention.

The U.S. invasion did provide a "new slate" in some respects. Operation *Just Cause* went much further in decapitating the PDF and removing Noriega and his inner circle from power than a coup would have done; it created an opening for civilian-directed change far wider than a post-election coalition government would have managed. Nonetheless, the lack of a "normal transition" lasting several months, during which constitutional issues might have been debated, if not considered legislatively, meant that the new government was immediately thrust into a crisis-management mode.

The decision to use military personnel from the old regime as the foundation for a new national police tarnished the new government. Not only did familiar faces from the old military force appear in the new Public Force, but the government's personnel decisions and infighting among supporters and various groups also generated criticism about "old habits." In fact, when a U.S. adviser was asked to identify the biggest problem the new government was encountering, he quickly said "revenge due to resentment of the past and current infighting." Col. Jack Pryor gave his perspective from SOUTHCOM's Office of Civil Affairs:

> Some way you've got to draw a line of amnesty. Everybody's got a little bit of guilt in this thing, whether you go back forty years or twenty-one years. There is a lot of resentment, and rightfully so. For the ones that were outside the law, take the appropriate action within the law. But in conjunction with that you have to start rebuilding the fabric of the nation, and you've got to lay out a plan and a program that changes the ethos of the nation. You also cannot use that as a scapegoat. You've got to take responsibility for here and now and make the choices.[37]

As the months passed, reinterpretation and revenge issues receded from the agenda. They were replaced with a different issue: criticism over the government's close working relations with U.S. advisers and its dependence on the United States. The government's dependence on U.S. military power for its installation and during the December "incident," as well as its past reliance on U.S. aid during the May 1989 election campaign, occasioned criticism from foreign as well as domestic observers. Former U.S. Ambassador Robert White bluntly described the Endara government as being pro-U.S. to the extent that it is negating the wishes of the majority for truly independent government.[38] Miguel Bernal argued that while "most people" voted for Endara, "This does not necessarily mean that today he has the support of the Panamanian people. This is especially true given the policies his government has followed since his installation."[39] Bernal continued, "If you want something done, you talk to the Americans. Then they tell the government what it needs to do. That's a source of deep shame to the Panamanian people. Even if he doesn't like the present situation, Endara works under Washington's direction." A civilian political activist, who styled himself as a "moderate," said that as of mid-1991, the government was being perceived among numerous constituencies as too pro-U.S. for its own and Panama's good.[40]

Oppositionists who had criticized the military regime soon found reasons to criticize the civilian government. Some oppositionists went so far as to suggest that a new opposition movement needed to be formed to act as a check on the Endara government. They suggested that elections every five years would be inadequate means of accountability, and that additional political checks were needed.

Institutional Reforms

During 1990, Panama made halting steps to strengthen the democratic characteristics and procedures of its political institutions. The Legislative Assembly's 1990 session was short on substance, partly because legislators' efforts focused on reorganization and reforms to strengthen its powers, particularly through a new budget law. Constitutional reforms are scheduled for the 1991 session.

New judges were appointed early in 1990. Major cases heard by the Supreme Court during 1990 concerned money laundering, wire taps, and habeas corpus appeals. Ambassador White commented critically, however, that not one drug trafficking case has yet to be prosecuted.[41] During 1991, numerous commentators asserted that the drug trade had not only resumed but actually reached levels higher than before the invasion. Steps were taken to repair and reform the judicial system, provide training for judges, and to make judicial administration more efficient. This has been a priority in U.S.-Panama policy, and aid has been targeted on judicial reforms. As of late October, 1990, however, some 17,000 cases remained pending; fewer than 15 percent of the people in prison had been tried.[42] As of April 1991, pre-trial detention and the backlog of unheard cases were still significant problems.

Race and Politics

Panamanian politics has always reflected racial and class divisions. Civilian politicians and military leaders in the past resorted to racial and class appeals in order to broaden and strengthen their constituency base and to tar their opponents. Although the new government has not blatantly followed these practices, it has not attempted to bridge the racial gap that afflicted Panama's politics. As Ropp has often noted, the military regime and the PRD reached out to the "blacks and mulattoes who have operated at the margins of Panamanian society."[43] Ropp made this assessment:

> What Panamanian history clearly shows is that two mutually isolated and hostile political blocs have existed, one largely "populist" and the other centering around the economic power of the urban commercial elite. Because these blocs have been highly polarized, both have attempted to perpetuate themselves in power through the use of military force and electoral fraud. Until some sort of *entendimiento* can be reached between representatives of these two blocs, fraudulent elections will continue to be the rule rather than the exception.[44]

Unless the current government, which is associated with the white urban commercial elite, moves to appeal across class and racial lines, political instability will surely continue. This is the danger Ropp predicts: "If the Panamanian military returns to power, it will probably do so because of continued political turmoil and the attempts by civilian politicians to elicit military help to win the 1994 presidential elections."[45]

Two positive developments that may counteract this danger are the continued activism of members of the National Civic Crusade, particularly behind the scenes in counseling the government, and the formation of the *Centro Pro Democracia* (Center for Democracy), an organization devoted to promoting grass-roots participation, particularly among young Panamanians. Both organizations reflect deliberate initiatives to build bridges to link diverse constituencies into a body politic.

Creating Consensus Through a Constitutional Assembly

One way of reconciling tensions between the two major political blocs in Panama, of reaching an *entendimiento*, would be through a constitutional convention or extended legislative session devoted to constitutional reform. This could provide an arena where competing elites and group representatives can meet to forge an "elite settlement," an agreement on the political rules for a new regime.

Endara, Arias Calderón, and Ford did not begin their term by addressing issues like separation of powers, judicial reform, legislative oversight, and electoral reform. Instead, they first addressed the immediate problems caused by post-invasion looting and violence, economic disaster, and the minutiae of assuming office. Some civilian activists initially focused on past grievances and revenge; others interpreted new freedoms as entailing no restraints or obligations. Thus, to the average Panamanian, the new government seemed much like the old regime. Moreover, as a coalition of three political parties, the new government was particularly prone to bogging down as it sought to devise compromises that would satisfy its main constituencies.

Focusing immediately on constitutional reforms may never have been a realistic option, given the determination of both the United States and the new government to reduce U.S. military forces as soon as possible and the problem of violence on the streets. Nonetheless, the decision to proceed straightaway to solving immediate problems meant that the new government was operating under the old rules and with the institutions of the old regime. Bernal characterized the 1972 Constitution, as amended in 1983, as "an authoritarian, anti-democratic document superimposed upon an unwilling population, by and for the military, with the purpose of keeping themselves in power and legitimizing their control."[46] "The bottom line," asserts Bernal, "is that our current constitution permits authoritarian government, and this is intolerable."[47] Political scientist Richard Millett drew a similar conclusion: "Panama needs a new constitution. . . . There should be major revisions of certain provisions, such as the complex relationship between the president and his cabinet, the nature and authority of local government, and the composition and power of the Electoral Tribunal."[48]

These obstructions to legitimizing the new government *as a new regime* in January 1990 may have been unavoidable. Now that the new government is well past that stage and into its second year in power, some opposition leaders are calling for a constitutional assembly. Bernal endorses the idea:

> We need to do what other countries have done after emerging from military government: change the constitution. This was done in Spain, Portugal, Uruguay, Peru and many other places, even in Honduras.
>
> A constitutional assembly is the best way to have a national conversation. For 21 years, the Panamanian people have not been able to talk to each other and hold a real dialogue. We may have varying ideas, but we at least need the environment to discuss them without any foreign pressure.
>
> Now, we are able to talk, but the government doesn't listen.[49]

Millett, however, warns of the dangers of initiating such a dialogue, which "could upset the delicate balance existing within the current government. . . . While the need for overhauling the constitution is urgent, such factors may put the task off until late in President Endara's term of office, or even until his successor takes power."[50] Now that Endara has moved against the PDC, reflecting a breakdown in that delicate balance, he and other political leaders may decide that the long-term benefits of constitutional reform outweigh the short-term political risks. Despite its aversion to the PRD, the Endara government may well find that its best hope for institutionalizing democracy may be to renew a dialogue with supporters of the former regime. Such discussions were under way sporadically between June 1987 and August 1989, focused on forming a government of national reconciliation that would accommodate the military, the PRD, and opposition parties who now hold office. A dialogue could resume among these parties and the new voices of opposition in Panama.

Notes

1. "Fact Sheet: Panama After Operation Just Cause," *U.S. Dept. of State Dispatch*, pp. 78–79.

2. *La Prensa*, August 6, 1990, p. 1.

3. *La Prensa Digest*, January 12, 1991, Volume 1/90, p. 7.

4. For an early treatment of the casuality figures debate, with evidence based on telephone calls to sources in Panama, see Alexander Cockburn, "Beat the Devil," *The Nation*, January 29, 1990, pp. 114–115.

5. Endara and Ford were interviewed by Charles Jaco on "The Invasion: Six Months Later," CNN News, July 5, 1990.

6. "Noriega Protests Capture," *Arkansas Gazette*, January 5, 1990, p. 1A. Noriega's cocounsel was Steven Kollin, who, along with Rubino, had been working for Noriega for the last two years.

7. Richard Berke, "Coercion Alleged," *The New York Times*, January 5, 1990, p. 1.

8. AP report, "Noriega Says He Can Prove U.S. Murder Plot," *Arkansas Democrat*, May 1, 1991, p. 3A. Those documents are probably memoranda dated 1971 or 1972 from the Bureau of Narcotics and Dangerous Drugs that listed assassination as one of several options for enforcing drug policy in Panama; that option was neither selected nor implemented.

9. At that point, the case took a bizarre turn when tapes of Noriega's telephone calls from prison, including conversations relating to his defense, were obtained and aired by CNN.

10. "Noriega's Trial Is On Track," *Washington Post Weekly Edition*, February 4–10, 1991, p. 39.

11. Decree #38 was summarized on February 15, 1990, in *La Prensa Digest*, Volume 6/90, p. 1.

12. Lee Hockstader, "The U.S. Attempts a Tricky Balance of Power in Panama: The security role is outweighing the rebuilding effort," *Washington Post Weekly Edition*, December 24–30, 1990, p. 16. Hockstader reported the following: "The CIA, having opposed setting up an intelligence section in the police force, is busy creating one in the office of the presidency."

13. David E. Pitt, "New Talk, New Photos, New Army (Or, Adjusting to Life After Noriega)," *The New York Times*, January 7, 1990, p. 15.

14. Joint patrols ended on November 27, 1990.

15. Pitt, "New Talk," p. 15.

16. Ibid.

17. A. M. Rosenthal, "Truths of the Pariahs," *The New York Times*, January 5, 1990, p. 23.

18. Phillip Berryman, "Arms and Panama," *The Nation*, February 19, 1990, p. 241.

19. Cited by Guillermo Sánchez-Borbon, "En pocas palabras," *La Prensa Digest*, February 8, 1990, Volume 5/90, p. 4.

20. "New Army, Old Faces," *Newsweek*, January 8, 1990, p. 31. Lt. Col. Armando Palacios Gondola was named commander of joint defense and security; he had served under Noriega in Chiriquí and was cashiered after the October coup when he did not come to Noriega's aid fast enough. Lt. Col. Fernando Quezada participated in the March coup. Lt. Col. Moisés Correa, who had once headed the Modelo prison in Panama City, was given a command. The chief of the new presidential guard, Maj. Juan Antonio Guisado, was described as never having wavered in his support for Noriega.

21. Interview with Deputy Minister of Government and Justice Ebrahim Asvat, Panama City, August 1990.

22. Valdonedo was rumored to be the officer who was in contact with opposition political parties before the coup.

23. Roberto Arosemena Jaen, "The Chief of Security in 1987," *La Prensa Digest*, April 10, 1990, Volume 14/90, p. 2.

24. Cited by Guillermo Sánchez-Borbon, "En pocas palabras," *La Prensa Digest*, Thursday April 26, 1990, Volume 16/90, p. 2.

25. Larry Rohter, "Head of Panamanian Security Force Resigns," *The New York Times*, January 4, 1990, p. 4.

26. Pitt, "New Talk," p. 15.

27. Lee Hockstader, "Faster Than a Speeding Glacier," *Washington Post Weekly Edition*, October 15–21, 1990, p. 19.

28. Ibid.

29. Officers implicated in the plot were Capt. Francisco Herrera Hassan, Eduardo Herrera Hassan's brother; Capt. Carlos Ivan Moreno, the National Police executive officer for Chiriquí; and two former members of UESAT, Sgt. Anibal Martínez and Corp. Julio César. See "Endara Weathers Destabilization Plans," *Washington Report on the Hemisphere (COHA)*, November 14, 1990, p. 5.

30. "Fact Sheet: Panama After Operation Just Cause," p. 78. This aid, touted as "the largest assistance package in the hemisphere and the third largest in the world (after Israel and Egypt)" covers food, housing, job creation, aid for looted businesses, police training, administration of justice, protection of canal watershed areas, promoting investment, and servicing the debt.

31. As of February 1991, Panama had not signed MLAT; the Endara government did sign the Mutual Cooperation Agreement covering narcotics and ship-boarding procedures, the Essential Chemicals Agreement, and the Bilateral Narcotics Control Accord ("Fact Sheet: Panama After Operation Just Casue," p. 79).

32. "Fact Sheet: Panama After Operation Just Case," p. 78.

33. An earlier version of this section was presented as "Democratization in Latin America: Whither Panama?," a paper prepared for Explorations 1991: Building Democracy in One-Party States, University of Central Arkansas, April 13–15, 1991.

34. Citations are from "From the Editor," *La Prensa Digest*, October 5, 1989, pp. 9–12.

35. "To the Editor," *La Prensa Digest*, November 30, 1989, pp. 9–10. For detailed treatments see Steve C. Ropp, *Panamanian Politics: From Guarded Nation*

to *National Guard* (New York: Praeger, 1982) and Marco A. Gandásegui, H. *La Democracia en Panamá* (Mexico: Editorial Mestiza, 1989).

36. Gandásegui, p. 11.

37. Interview with Col. Jack Pryor, Panama City, August 1990.

38. Statement made on "Frontline: War and Peace in Panama," April 8, 1991.

39. "We need real neutrality," p. 2.

40. Interview with Daniel Atencio, Board Member of the Center for Democracy, Little Rock, April 1991.

41. "Frontline: War and Peace in Panama."

42. Lee Hockstader, "Faster Than a Speeding Glacier," *Washington Post Weekly Edition*, October 15–21, 1990, p. 19.

43. Steve C. Ropp, "Panama: The United States Invasion and Its Aftermath," *Current History* 90(March 1991), p. 130.

44. Ropp, "To the Editor," p. 9.

45. Ropp, "Panama: The United States Invasion . . .," p. 130.

46. "We need real neutrality," p. 2.

47. Ibid.

48. Richard L. Millett, "The Aftermath of Intervention: Panama 1990," *Journal of Interamerican Studies and World Affairs*, 33(Spring 1991), p. 12.

49. "We need real neutrality," p. 2.

50. Millett, p. 12.

Bibliography

Arias Calderón, Ricardo. "The Challenge to Democracy," in *Report on Panama: Findings of the Study Group on United States–Panamanian Relations*, Occasional Paper No. 13, Central American and Caribbean Program, School of Advanced International Studies, The Johns Hopkins University, April 1987.

———. "Panama: Disaster or Democracy?" *Foreign Affairs* 66 (Winter 1987–1988), 328–347.

Arkansas Democrat, various issues, 1984–1991.

Arkansas Gazette, various issues, 1984–1991.

Atlanta Journal and Constitution, various issues, 1989.

Austin American Statesman, various issues, 1988.

Bailey, Norman. "Charges and Counter-Charges: Money, Arms and Drugs," in *Report on Panama: Findings of the Study Group on United States–Panamanian Relations*, Occasional Paper No. 13, Central American and Caribbean Program, School of Advanced International Studies, The Johns Hopkins University, April 1987.

Bernal, Miguel A. "Panamanian Election Just a Farce," *Alternativa* (May 1989), p. 1.

———. "Panama: A Prescription for Progress," *Lehigh Alumni Bulletin* (Winter 1989); reprinted in Miguel Antonio Bernal, *The Fax Against Noriega: A Panamanian Warrior in the U.S.* Lehigh, Pa.: Bernal, 1990, p. 74.

———. *A Panamanian Warrior in the United States: The Fax Against Noriega*. Bethlehem, Pa.: Bernal, 1990.

Berryman, Phillip. "Arms and Panama," *The Nation*, February 19, 1990, pp. 225, 241.

Black, George. "T.R.'s Intervention," *The Nation*, June 5, 1989, pp. 760–761.

Burns, E. Bradford, "Panama's Struggle for Independence," *Current History* (January 1974), pp. 19–22, 38.

Changmarin, Carlos Francisco. "Panama: The Torrijos Process and the Military," *World Marxist Review* 28(September 1985), 92–100.

Chepesiuk, R. "Faxing the News into Panama," *The New Leader*, August 8–22, 1988, pp. 7–9.

Christian Science Monitor, various issues, 1988.

Cockburn, Alexander. "Beat the Devil," *The Nation*, January 29, 1990, pp. 114–115.

Collett, M. "Pineapple Face," *The Nation*, June 28, 1986, pp. 876–887.

Congressional Quarterly Almanac, 1980–1989. Washington, D.C.: Congressional Quarterly.

Congressional Quarterly Weekly Report, 1989–1990. Washington, D.C.: Congressional Quarterly.

Conte-Porras, Jorge. *Requiem por la Revolución*. San José, Costa Rica: Litografía e Imprenta LIL, 1990.

Correa, Mayín, comp. *La gran rebelión blanca por la justicia y la democracia en Panama (Iniciada en junio de 1987): Los papeles de la libertad*, Tomo I y Tomo II. Miami: SIBI, 1987.

Cottam, Richard W. *Foreign Policy Motivation*. Pittsburgh: University of Pittsburgh Press, 1977.

———. *Iran and the United States: A Cold War Case Study*. Pittsburgh: University of Pittsburgh Press, 1988.

Dinges, John. *Our Man in Panama: How General Noriega Used the United States—and Made Millions in Drugs and Arms*. New York: Random House, 1990.

Drew, Elizabeth, "Letter from Washington," *The New Yorker*, October 30, 1989, pp. 100–108.

Drucker, Linda. "Washington Cries Uncle," *Commonweal*, July 15, 1988, pp. 391–392.

Eisenmann, Roberto. "Unanswered Questions: The Media Queries," in *Report on Panama:*

Findings of the Study Group on United States–Panamanian Relations, Occasional Paper No. 13, Central American and Caribbean Program, School of Advanced International Studies, The Johns Hopkins University, April 1987.

Emerson, Steven. *Secret Warriors: Inside the Covert Military Operations of the Reagan Era.* New York: Putnam's, 1988.

Evans-Pritchard, Ambrose. "Pineapple in America's Side," *The Spectator*, June 4, 1988, pp. 14–15.

"Fact Sheet: Panama After Operation Just Cause," *U.S. Department of State Dispatch*, February 4, 1991, pp. 78–79.

Farrar, L. L., Jr. "The Limits of Choice: July 1914 Reconsidered," *Journal of Conflict Resolution*, 16 (March 1972), pp. 1–23.

Forbes, Malcolm S. "Panama: The Canal, the Dope General, the U.S.," *Forbes*, March 21, 1988, p. 18.

Foreign Broadcast Information Service—Latin America (FBIS-LAT), 1987–1990.

Foster, D. "Teaching the Bully a Lesson," *Mother Jones*, June 1988, p. 10.

"Fraud Finalized at My House, Díaz Herrera Confesses," *La Prensa*, June 7, 1987.

Furlong, William L., and Margaret E. Scranton. *Dynamics of Foreign Policymaking: The President, the Congress and the 1978 Panama Canal Treaties.* Boulder: Westview, 1984.

Gandásequi, H., Marco A. *La Democracia en Panamá.* Mexico: Editorial Mestiza, 1989.

Greene, Graham. *Getting to Know the General: The Story of an Involvement.* Toronto: Lester & Orpen Dennys, 1984.

Gunther, Graham. *Inside Latin America.* New York: Harper & Brothers, 1941.

Gutman, Roy. *Banana Diplomacy: The Making of American Policy in Nicaragua 1981–1987.* New York: Simon and Schuster, 1988.

Hersh, Seymour. "The Creation of a Thug: Our Man in Panama," *Life*, March 1990, pp. 81–93.

Hertsgaard, Mark. "How the News Media Let Us Down in Panama." *Rolling Stone*, March 8, 1990, pp. 77–78.

Hertzberg, Hendrick. "TRB from Washington: Mr. Ex-President," *The New Republic*, June 5, 1989, p. 4.

Hockstader, Lee. "Faster than a Speeding Glacier," *Washington Post Weekly Edition*, October 15–21, 1990, p. 19.

"Is Panama Run by a Military 'Mafia'?" *US News and World Report*, July 7, 1986, pp. 36–37.

Jones, Charles O., ed. *The Reagan Legacy: Promise and Performance.* Chatham, N.J.: Chatham House, 1988.

Jorden, William J. *Panama Odyssey.* Austin: University of Texas Press, 1984.

Kahn, E. H. "Letter from Panama," *The New Yorker*, August 16, 1976, pp. 64–74.

Kempe, Frederick. *Divorcing the Dictator: America's Bungled Affair with Noriega.* New York: Putnam's, 1990.

Koenig, Gunter. "Hard Choices: The Panamanian Economy," in *Report on Panama: Findings of the Study Group on United States–Panamanian Relations*, Occasional Paper No. 13, Central American and Caribbean Program, School of Advanced International Studies, The Johns Hopkins University, April 1987.

Kohn, Howard, and Vicki Monks. "The Dirty Secrets of George Bush," *Rolling Stone*, November 3, 1988, pp. 42–50, 120.

Kondracke, Morton. "Shoot or Get Off the Pot," *The New Republic*, May 2, 1988, pp. 12–13.

Koster, R. M., and Guillermo Sanchez. *In the Time of the Tyrants: Panama 1968–1990.* New York: Norton, 1991.

LaFeber, Walter. *The Panama Canal: The Crisis in Historical Perspective.* New York: Oxford University Press, 1978 (rev. ed., 1990).

Lake, Anthony. *Somoza Falling: The Nicaraguan Dilemma: A Portrait of Washington at Work.* Boston: Houghton Mifflin, 1989.

Lane, C. "Yankee Come Here," *The New Republic*, April 4, 1988, pp. 9–10.

La Prensa, various issues, 1990.

La Prensa Digest, 1986–1990, ed. Elizabeth Brannan Jaen, June 1990.

Linares, Julio E. *Enrique Linares en la Historia Política de Panamá, 1869–1949*. San José, Costa Rica: Litografía e Imprenta LIL, 1989.

Lowenthal, Abraham F., and Samuel J. Fitch, eds. *Armies and Politics in Latin America*. New York: Holmes & Meier, rev. ed., 1986.

Madison, Christopher. "Raising the U.S. Ante in Panama," *National Journal*, 20(April 16, 1988), 1014–1015.

———. "No Easy Way Out of Panama?" *National Journal*, 20(May 21, 1988), 1356ff.

———. "Passing the Torch," *National Journal* (July 2, 1988), 1855.

Maechling, Charles, Jr. "Washington's Illegal Invasion," *Foreign Policy*, 79(Summer 1990), 113–131.

Martínez, José de Jesús. *Mi General Torrijos*. Bogotá, Colombia: Editorial La Oveja Negra, 1987.

Massing, M. "The Intervention that Misfired," *The Nation*, May 21, 1988, pp. 708–710.

———. "New Trouble in Panama," *The New York Review of Books*, May 17, 1990, pp. 43–49.

Meditz, Sandra W., and Dennis M. Hanratty. *Panama: A Country Study*. Washington, D.C.: Government Printing Office (GPO), 4th ed., 1989.

The Miami Herald, various issues, 1986, 1987.

Miles, Dona. "Panama: Training to Fight," *Soldiers*, February 1990, p. 37–42.

Miller, David Norman, "Panama and U.S. Policy," *Global Affairs* (Summer 1989), 129–147.

Millett, Richard. "Looking Beyond Noriega," *Foreign Policy*, 71(Summer 1988), 46–63.

———. "Government and Politics," in Sandra W. Meditz and Dennis M. Hanratty, *Panama: A Country Study*. Washington, D.C.: Government Printing Office, 1989.

———. "The Aftermath of Intervention: Panama, 1990," *Journal of Interamerican Studies and World Affairs*, 33(Spring 1991), 1–15.

Moss, Ambler. "The U.S.-Panamanian Relationship: An American Perspective," in *Report on Panama: Findings of the Study Group on United States-Panamanian Relations*, Occasional Paper No. 13, Central American and Caribbean Program, School of Advanced International Studies, The Johns Hopkins University, April 1987.

Needler, Martin C. "Omar Torrijos: The Panamanian Enigma," *Intellect*, February 1977, pp. 242–243.

The New York Times, various issues, 1980–1990.

Noriega, Manuel Antonio. "Psychological Operations." Manual of the Defense Forces of the Republic of Panama, April 14, 1975. Translated and released by U.S. SOUTHCOM, 1989.

———. "National Dignity Is Not For Sale," *World Marxist Review*, 32(June 1989), 76–78.

"Noriega's Surrender," *Newsweek*, January 15, 1990.

"Notes and Comment," *The New Yorker*, July 21, 1986, pp. 21ff.

Nyrop, Richard F., et al. *Panama: A Country Study*. Washington, D.C.: American University, 3rd ed., 1980.

O'Rourke, P. J. *Holidays in Hell*. New York: Vintage, 1988.

"Panama Banal: The Revolution Turns into an All-Too-Civil War," *Rolling Stone*, October 8, 1987, pp. 50–52ff.

Peters, Joan, "Panama's Genial Despot," *Harper's*, April 1978, pp. 61–70.

Priestley, George. *Military Government and Popular Participation in Panama: The Torrijos Regime, 1968–1975*. Boulder: Westview, 1986.

Report on Panama: Findings of the Study Group on United States–Panamanian Relations. Occasional Paper No. 13. Central American and Caribbean Program, School of Advanced International Studies: The Johns Hopkins Universtiy, April 1987.

Robbins, Carla Anne. "Cracking Down on Panama's General," *US News & World Report*, August 10, 1987.

———. "Growing Pains in Panama," *The New Republic*, May 28, 1990, pp. 29ff.

———. "Taking Aim At Noriega," *U.S. News and World Report*, May 1, 1989, pp. 40–41.

Rockman, Bert A. "The Style and Organization of the Reagan Presidency," in Charles O. Jones, ed., *The Reagan Legacy" Promise and Performance*. Chatham, N.J.: Chatham House, 1988.

Rogers, William D. *The Twilight Struggle*, New York: Random House, 1967.

Ropp, Steve C. *Panamanian Politics: From Guarded Nation to National Guard*. New York: Praeger, 1982.

————. "Panama," in Robert Wesson, ed., *The Latin American Military Institution*. New York: Praeger, 1986.

————. "General Noriega's Panama," *Current History*, December 1986, pp. 421–424, 431, 432.

————. "Panama's Struggle for Democracy," *Current History*, December 1987, pp. 421–424, 434–435.

————. "Panama's Defiant Noriega," *Current History*, December 1988, pp. 417–420, 431.

————. "National Security," in Sandra W. Meditz and Dennis M. Hanratty, eds., *Panama: A Country Study*. Washington, D.C.: Government Printing Office, 1989 (4th ed.).

————. Military Retrenchment and Decay in Panama," *Current History*, January 1990, pp. 17–20, 37–40.

————. "Panama: The United States Invasion and Its Aftermath," *Current History* 90(March 1991), 113–116, 130.

Rosenberg, Tina, "The Panama Perplex," *The New Republic*, January 25, 1988, pp. 17ff.

Rouquie, Alain. "Demilitarization and the Institutionalization of Military-Dominated Politics in Latin America," in Abraham F. Lowenthal and J. Samuel Fitch, eds., *Armies and Politics in Latin America*. New York: Holmes & Meier, 1986 (rev. ed.).

Sánchez-Borbon, Guillermo. "Panama Fallen Among Thieves," *Harper's*, December 1987, pp. 57–67.

Scranton, Margaret E., "Ratification of the Panama Canal Treaties: Lessons for SALT." Paper prepared for delivery at the annual meeting of the International Studies Association, Toronto, March 1979.

————. "Changing United States Foreign Policy: Negotiating New Panama Canal Treaties, 1958–1978." Ph.D. Dissertation, University of Pittsburgh, 1980.

————. "Elections as a U.S. Policy Option: The Case of Panama," paper presented at the annual meeting of the American Political Science Association, San Francisco, August 31–September 3, 1990.

————. "Democratization in Latin America: Whither Panama?" Paper prepared for Explorations in 1991: Building Democracy in One-Party Systems, University of Central Arkansas, April 15–16, 1991.

"Serving TV Winners," *The Atlantic*, March 1985, pp. 24ff.

Simon, Jocl. "Noriega Opponent Assails U.S.," in Miguel A. Bernal, *Faxing the Revolution: A Panamanian Warrior in the United States*, Lehigh, Pa.: Bernal, 1990.

Springdale News, various issues, 1985, 1988–1989.

"Surrender, Manny," *The New Republic*, June 5, 1989, pp. 9–10.

"The Reality of the Political Crisis in Panama: Beyond Drug Traffic," *Alternativa*, April 4, 1988.

Tulsa World, various issues, 1985, 1988–1989.

USA Today, various issues, 1988.

U.S. Congress. *Congressional Record*, 1986–1990.

————. Committee on Foreign Affairs. *Review of Latin American Narcotics Control Issues*. Hearing, 100th Congress, 1st session, March 18, 1987. Washington, D.C., GPO, 1987.

————. Subcommittees on Human Rights and International Organizations and on Western Hemisphere Affairs. *Human Rights and Political Developments in Panama*. Hearings, 99th Congress, 2nd session, April 29 and July 23, 1986. Washington, D.C.: GPO, 1986.

————. House of Representatives, Committee on Foreign Affairs. Subcommittee on Western Hemisphere Affairs. *The Political Situation in Panama and Options for U.S. Policy*. Hearings, 100th Congress, 2nd session, April 20, May 4, and June 1, 1988. Washington, D.C.: GPO, 1988.

————. Subcommittees on Western Hemisphere Affairs and International Economic Policy and Trade. *United States Policy Toward Panama in the Aftermath of the May 1 [sic], 1989, Elections*. Hearings, 101st Congress, 1st session, July 25, 26, 27, 1989. Washington, D.C.: GPO, 1990.

————. Task Force on International Narcotics Control. *Issues in U.S.-Panamanian Anti-Narcotics Control*. Hearing, 99th Congress, 2nd session, June 19, 1986. Washington, D.C.: GPO, 1986.

———. *Review of the Section 2013 Report and the State Department Mid-Year Update Report.* Hearing, 100th Congress, 2nd session, September 28, 1988. Washington, D.C.: GPO, 1988.

———. House of Representatives. Select Committee on Narcotics Abuse and Control. *Panama.* Hearing, 99th Congress, 2nd session, June 19, 1986. Washington, D.C.: GPO, 1986.

———. House of Representatives. Committee on Foreign Affairs, and Senate, Committee on Foreign Relations. *Country Reports on Human Rights Practices,* 1980–1990. Reports of the Department of State. Joint Committee Prints, 97th Congress, 1st session - 102nd Congress, 1st session. Washington, D.C.: GPO, 1980–1990.

———. Senate. Committee on Foreign Relations. *Drugs, Law Enforcement and Foreign Policy,* Part 1, Hearings before the Subcommittee on Terrorism, Narcotics and International Communications and International Economic Policy, Trade, Oceans and Environment, 100th Congress, 1st session, May 27, July 15, and October 30, 1987. Washington, D.C.: GPO, 1988.

———. Subcommittee on Terrorism, Narcotics and International Communications. *Drugs, Law Enforcement and Foreign Policy: Panama,* Part 2, Hearings, 100th Congress, 2nd session, February 8, 9, 10, and 11, 1988. Washington, D.C.: GPO, 1988.

———. Subcommittee on Terrorism, Narcotics and International Communications. *Drugs, Law Enforcement and Foreign Policy: The Cartel, Haiti and Central America,* Part 3, Hearings, 100th Congress, 2nd session, April 4, 5, 6, and 7, 1988. Washington, D.C.: GPO, 1988.

———. Subcommittee on Terrorism, Narcotics and International Communications. *Drugs, Law Enforcement and Foreign Policy: The Cartel, Haiti and Central America,* Part 4, Hearings, 100th Congress, 2nd session, July 11, 12, and 14, 1988. Washington, D.C.: GPO, 1988.

———. *Drugs, Law Enforcement and Foreign Policy.* Senate Report 100–165, 100th Congress, 2nd session, December 1988. Washington, D.C.: GPO, 1988.

———. *Report of the Senatorial Delegation to the Republic of Panama.* November 9–12, 1977, 95th Congress, 2nd session. Washington, D.C.: GPO, 1978.

———. Committee on Governmental Affairs. Permanent Subcommittee on Investigations. *Drugs and Money Laundering in Panama.* Hearing, 100th Congress, 2nd session, January 28, 1988. Washington, D.C.: GPA, 1988.

U.S. Department of Defense. Intelligence Information Report. "Biographic Information on LTC Manuel Antonio NORIEGA Morena, G-2, PANAMA, National Guard," November 7, 1974, p. 2.

———. Panama 10110. "Panama/Colombia M–19: The Panama Connection," November 9, 1981.

U.S. Department of State. Confidential Airgram 002005. "The 1984 Panamanian Election: The Question of Fraud and Voting Irregularities," September 20, 1984.

———. Confidential Caracas 02673, "Venezuela's Carlos Andrés Pérez (CAP) Refines His Approach to Panama," March 15, 1988.

———. Confidential Panama 00739. "Election 1984: Arnulfo Arias Hurls His Beret into the Ring," January 23, 1984.

———. Confidential Panama 00816. "Panamanian Election 1984: The Pieces Falling into Place," January 25, 1984.

———. Confidential Panama 01722. "Recommended Letter from the President to President Jorge Illueca," February 16, 1984.

———. Confidential Panama 02635. "Panamanian SitRep," March 8, 1988.

———. Confidential Panama 03578. "Panama Strike Loses Steam, While Organizers Vow to Continue 'Indefinitely'; Other Economic Developments," April 5, 1988.

———. Confidential Panama 07509. "Col. Díaz Summons Press, Claims Life Threatened," June 7, 1987.

———. Confidential Panama 07932. "Noriega Takes Command," August 17, 1983.

———. Confidential Panama 08855. "GOP Response to U.S. Protest Note on Embassy Attack," July 4, 1987.

———. Confidential Panama 08978. "Diplomatic Reaction to U.S. Press Attacks on Noriega Remains Subdued," June 17, 1986.

————. Confidential Panama 09899. "Díaz Herrera Captured," July 28, 1987.
————. Confidential Panama 10412. "Royo, Paredes Engage in Political Maneuvering," November 10, 1981.
————. Confidential Panama 10680. "Spadafora Remains Arrive in Panama," September 19, 1985.
————. Confidential Panama 10752. "Funeral Ceremonies Highlight Anguish Over Spadafora," September 20, 1985.
————. Confidential Panama 10803. "Barletta Recommends that Attorney General Name Commission to Investigate Spadafora Murder," September 23, 1985.
————. Confidential Panama 98658. "Paredes Steps Aside," September 7, 1983.
————. Confidential San José 08180. "Body Found in Costa Rica Believed to be Revolutionary Spadafora," September 17, 1985.
————. Confidential State 088690. "Panama Task Force Situation Report No. 12, March 22, 1988.
————. "Fact Sheet: Torrijos' Government and Human Rights—Pluses and Minuses," mimeo., September 1977.
————. Panama 11058. "Barletta's Resignation: Contingency Press Guidance," September 28, 1985.
————. Panama City 08671. "Embassy Bracing for Large Pro-government Demonstration," June 30, 1987.
————. Panama City 08672. "Midday Sitrep U.S. Embassy PM," June 30, 1987.
————. Secret Panama 10515. "Presumed Murder of Dr. Hugo Spadafora," September 17, 1985.
————. Secret Panama 10986. "Political Tensions Heighten Over Spadafora Case," September 26, 1985.
————. Secret Panama 11589. "The Coup d'Etat and Other Issues," October 16, 1985.
————. Secret State 058889. "Panama: Demarches to Host Country Presidents," February 27, 1988.
————. Secret State 082820, "Panama Task Force Situation Report No. 1, Situation as of 1700 EST 03/16/88," March 17, 1988.
————. Secret State 083949, "Panama Task Force Situation Report No. 2: Situation as of 0500 EST 3/17/88," March 17, 1988.
————. Secret State 085518. "Panama Task Force Situation Report No. 6," March 19, 1988.
————. Secret State 087336. "Panamanian Task Force Situation Report No. 7," March 20, 1988.
————. Secret State 094269. "Official—Informal," March 26, 1988.
————. Secret State 096142, "Situation Report No. 19, March 28, 1988," March 29, 1988.
————. Secret State 097764, "Panama Situation Report, March 29, 1700 hrs.," March 30, 1988.
————. Secret State 099809, "Panama Situation Report No. 21, 1700 Hrs. 3/30/88," March 31, 1988.
————. Secret State 402455. "Talking Points for Use in Call on President Delvalle," December 30, 1987.
————. Unclassified Panama 03001, "Panama Sitrep: March 16, 1600," March 16, 1988.
————. Unclassified Panama 07645. "Díaz Herrera Abandons the Field and Pleads 'Mea Culpa,'" June 9, 1987.
Vásquez, Juan Materno. *Omar Torrijos*. San José, Costa Rica: Litografía e Imprenta LIL, 1987.
The Washington Post, various issues, 1980–1990.
The Washington Post Weekly Edition, various issues, 1986–1991.
Washington Report on the Hemisphere, (COHA) 1990.
Watson, Bruce W., and Peter G. Tsouras, eds. *Operation Just Cause: The U.S. Intervention in Panama*. Boulder: Westview, 1991.
Wesson, Robert, ed. *The Latin American Military Institution*. New York: Praeger Special Studies, 1986.
Zhu Manting. "Panama: President Resigns Amid Controversy," *Beijing Review*, October 14, 1985, p. 14.

Index

About the Book and the Author

In December 1989, the United States launched an invasion of Panama designed to decapitate the Panama Defense Force (PDF), install a civilian government, and apprehend General Manuel Noriega. A masterful bargainer, Noriega had managed to endure and outwit each attempt, short of the use of military force, that the United States had made to remove him from power. Once the bedrock of his power base, the PDF was immobilized by the invasion. He turned himself in and began a new power game, this time in the U.S. federal courts.

Against this backrop, Margaret Scranton analyzes the evolution of U.S.-Panamanian relations during the past decade in terms of international dynamics, development within Panama, and decisionmaking players and processes. She explains why the United States for so long adopted a "live and let live" policy toward Panama—why it overlooked increasing military repression and corruption, electoral fraud, and a thriving international narcotics network—and also explores the development of a viable opposition movement in Panama, its strategies and objectives, and the 1989 election that it "won" but could not parlay into a longer term victory.

Scranton addresses the reasons for the repeated failure of U.S. attempts to remove Noriega from power, as well as the changes that led finally to a decision in Washington to place the military option on the table. The book closes with a look at prospects for U.S.-Panamanian relations.

Margaret E. Scranton is associate professor of political science at the University of Arkansas at Little Rock.